The
God-Idea
of the Ancients

(or Sex in Religion)
By
Eliza Burt Gamble

Preface

Much of the material for this volume was collected during the time that I was preparing for the press the Evolution of Woman, or while searching for data bearing on the subject of sex-specialization. While preparing that book for publication, it was my intention to include within it this branch of my investigation, but wishing to obtain certain facts relative to the foundations of religious belief and worship which were not accessible at that time, and knowing that considerable labor and patience would be required in securing these facts, I decided to publish the first part of the work, withholding for the time being that portion of it pertaining especially to the development of the God-idea.

As mankind construct their own gods, or as the prevailing ideas of the unknowable reflect the inner consciousness of human beings, a trustworthy history of the growth of religions must correspond to the processes involved in the mental, moral, and social development of the individual and the nation.

By means of data brought forward in these later times relative to the growth of the God-idea, it is observed that an independent chain of evidence has been produced in support of the facts recently set forth bearing upon the development of the two diverging lines of sexual demarcation. In other words, it has been found that sex is the fundamental fact not only in the operations of Nature but in the construction of a god.

In the Evolution of Woman it has been shown that the peculiar inheritance of the two sexes, female and male, is the result of the bias given to these separate lines of development during the earliest periods of sex-differentiation; and, as this division of labor was a necessary step in the evolutionary processes, the rate of progress depended largely on the subsequent adjustment of these two primary elements or forces. A comprehensive study of prehistoric records shows that in an earlier age of existence upon the earth, at a time when woman's influence was in the ascendancy over that of man, human energy was directed by the altruistic characters which originated in and have been transmitted through the female; but after the decline of woman's power, all human institutions, customs, forms, and habits of thought are seen to reflect the egoistic qualities acquired by the male.

Nowhere is the influence of sex more plainly manifested than in the formulation of religious conceptions and creeds. With the rise of male power and dominion, and the corresponding repression of the natural female instincts, the principles which originally constituted the God-idea gradually gave place to a Deity better suited to the peculiar bias which had been given to the male organism. An anthropomorphic god like that of the Jews–a god whose chief attributes are power and virile might–could have had its origin only under a system of masculine rule.

Religion is especially liable to reflect the vagaries and weaknesses of human nature; and, as the forms and habits of thought connected with worship take a firmer hold on the mental constitution than do those belonging to any other department of human experience, religious conceptions should be subjected to frequent and careful examination in order to perceive, if possible, the extent to which we are holding on to ideas which are unsuited to existing conditions.

In an age when every branch of inquiry is being subjected to reasonable criticism, it would seem that the origin and growth of religion should be investigated from beneath the surface, and that all the facts bearing upon it should be brought forward as a contribution to our fund of general information. As well might we hope to gain a complete knowledge of human history by studying only the present aspect of society, as to expect to reach reasonable conclusions respecting the prevailing God-idea by investigating the various creeds and dogmas of existing faiths.

The object of this volume is not only to furnish a brief outline of religious growth, but to show the effect which each of the two forces, female and male, has had on the development of our present God- idea, which investigation serves to accentuate the conclusions arrived at in the Evolution of Woman relative to the inheritance of each of the two lines of sexual demarcation.

E.B.G.

Introduction

Through a study of the primitive god-idea as manifested in monumental records in various parts of the world; through scientific investigation into the early religious conceptions of mankind as expressed by symbols which appear in the architecture and decorations of sacred edifices and shrines; by means of a careful examination of ancient holy objects and places still extant in every quarter of the globe, and through the study of antique art, it is not unlikely that a line of investigation has been marked out whereby a tolerably correct knowledge of the processes involved in our present religious systems may be obtained. The numberless figures and sacred emblems which appear carved in imperishable stone in the earliest cave temples; the huge towers, monoliths, and rocking stones found in nearly every country of the globe, and which are known to be closely connected with primitive belief and worship, and the records found on tablets which are being unearthed in various parts of the world, are, with the unravelling of extinct tongues, proving an almost inexhaustible source for obtaining information bearing upon the early history of the human race, and, together, furnish indisputable evidence of the origin, development, and unity of religious faiths.

By comparing the languages used by the earlier races to express their religious conceptions; by observing the similarity in the mythoses and sacred appellations among all tribe and nations, an through the discovery of the fact that the legends extant in the various countries of the globe are identical, or have the same foundation, it is probable that a clue has already been obtained whereby an outline of the religious history of the human family from a period even as remote as the "first dispersion," or from a time when one race comprehended the entire population of the globe, maybe traced. Humboldt in his Researches observes: "In every part of the globe, on the ridge of the Cordilleras as well as in the Isle of Samothrace, in the Aegean Sea, fragments of primitive languages are preserved in religious rites."

Regarding the identity of the fundamental ideas contained in the various systems of religion, both past and present, Hargrave Jennings, in referring to a parallel drawn by Sir William Jones, between the deities of Meru and Olympus, observes:

"All our speculations tend to the same conclusions. One day it is a discovery of cinerary vases, the next, it is etymological research; yet again it is ethnological investigation, and the day after, it is the publication of unsuspected tales from the Norse; but all go to heap up proof of our consanguinity with the peoples of history–and of an original general belief, we might add."

That the religious systems of India and Egypt were originally the same, there can be at the present time no reasonable doubt. The fact noted by various writers, of the British Sepoys, who, on their overland route from India, upon beholding the ruins of Dendera, prostrated themselves before the remains of the ancient temples and offered adoration to them, proves the identity of Indian and Egyptian deities. These foreign devotees, being asked to explain the reason of their strange conduct declared that they "saw sculptured before them the gods of their country."

Upon the subject of the identity of Eastern religions, Wilford remarks that one and the same code both of theology and of fabulous history, has been received through a range or belt about forty degrees broad across the old continent, in a southeast and northwest direction from the eastern shores of the Malaga peninsula to the western extremity of the British Isles, that, through this immense range the same religious notions reappear in various places under various modifications, as might be expected; and that there is not a greater difference between the tenets and worship of the Hindoos and the Greeks than exists between the churches of Home and Geneva.

Concerning the universality of certain religious beliefs and opinions, Faber, commenting upon the above statement of Wilford, observes that, immense as is this territorial range, it is by far too limited to include the entire phenomenon, that the observation

"applies with equal propriety to the entire habitable globe; for the arbitrary rites and opinions of every pagan nation bear so close a resemblance to each other, that such a coincidence can only have been produced by their having had a common origin. Barbarism itself has not been able to efface the strong primeval impression. Vestiges of the ancient general system may be traced in the recently discovered islands in the Pacific Ocean; and, when the American world was first opened to the hardy adventurers of Europe, its inhabitants from north to south venerated, with kindred ceremonies and kindred notions, the gods of Egypt and Hindostan, of Greece and Italy, of Phoenicia and Britain."[1]

"Though each religion has its own peculiar growth, the seed from which they spring is everywhere the same."[2]

The question as to whether the identity of conception and the similarity in detail observed in religious rites, ceremonies, and symbols in the various countries of the globe are due to the universal law of unity which governs human development, or whether, through the dispersion of one original people, the early conceptions of a Deity were spread broadcast over the entire earth, is perhaps not settled; yet, from the facts which have been brought forward during

---

[1] Pagan Idolatry, book i., ch. i.
[2] Max Muller, Origin and Growth of Religion, p. 48.

the last century, the latter theory seems altogether probable, such divergence in religious ideas as is observed among the various peoples of the earth being attributable to variations in temperament caused by changed conditions of life. In other words, the divergence in the course of religious development has doubtless been due to environment.

In an attempt to understand the history of the growth of the god-idea, the fact should be borne in mind that, from the earliest conception of a creative force in the animal and vegetable world to the latest development in theological speculation, there has never been what might consistently be termed a new religion. On the contrary, religion like everything else is subject to the law of growth; therefore the faiths of to-day are the legitimate result, or outcome, of the primary idea of a Deity developed in accordance with the laws governing the peculiar instincts which have been in the ascendancy during the life of mankind on the earth.

The erroneous impression which under a belief in the unknown has come to prevail, namely, that the moral law is the result of religion; or, in other words, that the human conscience is in some manner dependent on supernaturalism for its origin and maintenance, is, with a better and clearer understanding of the past history of the development of the human race, being gradually dispelled. On one point we may reasonably rest assured that the knowledge of right and wrong and our sense of justice and right-living have been developed quite independently of all religious beliefs. The moral law embodied in the golden rule is not an outgrowth of mysticism, or of man's notions of the unknowable; but, on the contrary, is the result of experience, and was formulated in response to a recognized law of human necessity,–a law which involves the fundamental principle of progress. The history of human development shows conclusively that mankind GREW into the recognition of the moral law, that through sympathy, or a desire for the welfare of others,–a character which had its root in maternal affection,–conscience and the moral sense were evolved.

While the moral law and the conscience may not be accounted as in any sense the result of man's ideas concerning the unknowable, neither can the errors and weaknesses developed in human nature be regarded as the result of religion. Although the sexual excesses which during three or four thousand years were practiced as sacred rites, and treated as part and parcel of religion in various parts of the world, have had the effect to stimulate and strengthen the animal nature in man, yet these rites may not be accounted as the primary cause of the supremacy of the lower nature over the higher faculties. On the contrary, the impulse which has been termed religion, with all the vagaries which its history presents, is to be regarded more as an effect than as a cause. The stage of a nation's development regulates its religion. Man creates his own gods; they are powerless to change him.

As written history records only those events in human experience which belong to a comparatively recent period of man's existence, and as the primitive conceptions of a Deity lie buried beneath ages of corruption, glimpses of the earlier faiths of mankind, as has already been stated, must be looked for in the traditions, monuments, and languages of extinct races.

In reviewing this matter we shall doubtless observe the fact that if the stage of a nation's growth is indicated by its religious conceptions, and if remnants of religious beliefs are everywhere present in the languages, traditions, and monuments of the past through a careful study of these subjects we may expect to gain a tolerably correct understanding not alone of the growth of the god-idea but of the stage of development reached by the nations which existed prior to the beginning of the historic age. We shall be enabled also to perceive whether or not the course of human development during the intervening ages has been continuous, or whether, for some cause hitherto unexplained, true progress throughout a portion of this time has been arrested, thus producing a backward movement, or degeneracy.

If we would unravel the mysteries involved in present religious faiths, we should begin not by attempting to analyze or explain any existing system or systems of belief and worship. Such a course is likely to end not only in confusion and in a subsequent denial of the existence of the religious nature in mankind, but is liable, also, to create an aversion for and a distrust of the entire subject of religious experience. In view of this fact it would appear to be not only useless but exceedingly unwise to spend one's time in attempting to gain a knowledge of this subject simply by studying the later developments in its history.

If we are really desirous of obtaining information regarding present religious phenomena, it is plain that we should adopt the scientific method and turn our attention to the remote past, where, by careful and systematic investigation, we are enabled to perceive the earliest conception of a creative force and the fundamental basis of all religious systems, from which may be traced the gradual development of the god-idea.

Chapter I.
Sex the Foundation of the God-Idea

In the study of primitive religion, the analogy existing between the growth of the god-idea and the development of the human race, and especially of the two sex-principles, is everywhere clearly apparent.

"Religion is to be found alone with its justification and explanation in the relations of the sexes. There and therein only."[3]

As the conception of a deity originated in sex, or in the creative agencies female and male which animate Nature, we may reasonably expect to find, in the history of the development of the two sex-principles and in the notions entertained concerning them throughout past ages, a tolerably correct account of the growth of the god-idea. We shall perceive that during an earlier age of human existence, not only were the reproductive powers throughout Nature, and especially in human beings and in animals, venerated as the Creator, but we shall find also that the prevailing ideas relative to the importance of either sex in the office of reproduction decided the sex of this universal creative force. We shall observe also that the ideas of a god have always corresponded with the current opinions regarding the importance of either sex in human society. In other words, so long as female power and influence were in the

---

[3] Hargrave Jennings, Phallicism.

ascendency, the creative force was regarded as embodying the principles of the female nature; later, however, when woman's power waned, and the supremacy of man was gained, the god-idea began gradually to assume the male characters and attributes.

Through scientific research the fact has been observed that, for ages after life appeared on the earth, the male had no separate existence; that the two sex-principles, the sperm and the germ, were contained within one and the same individual. Through the processes of differentiation, however, these elements became detached, and with the separation of the male from the female, the reproductive functions were henceforth confided to two separate individuals.

As originally, throughout Nature, the female was the visible organic unit within whom was contained the exclusive creative power, and as throughout the earlier ages of life on the earth she comprehended the male, it is not perhaps singular that, even after the appearance of mankind on the earth, the greater importance of the mother element in human society should have been recognized; nor, as the power to bring forth coupled with perceptive wisdom originally constituted the Creator, that the god-idea should have been female instead of male.

From the facts to be observed in relation to this subject, it is altogether probable that for ages the generating principle throughout Nature was venerated as female; but with that increase of knowledge which was the result of observation and experience, juster or more correct ideas came to prevail, and subsequently the great fructifying energy throughout the universe came to be regarded as a dual indivisible force–female and male. This force, or agency, constituted one God, which, as woman's functions in those ages were accounted of more importance than those of man, was oftener worshipped under the form of a female figure.

Neith, Minerva, Athene, and Cybele, the most important deities of their respective countries, were adored as Perceptive Wisdom, or Light, while Ceres and others represented Fertility. With the incoming of male dominion and supremacy, however, we observe the desire to annul the importance of the female and to enthrone one all-powerful male god whose chief attributes were power and might.

Notwithstanding the efforts which during the historic period have been put forward to magnify the importance of the male both in human affairs and in the god-idea, still, no one, I think, can study the mythologies and traditions of the nations of antiquity without being impressed with the prominence given to the female element, and the deeper the study the stronger will this impression grow.

During a certain stage of human development, religion was but a recognition of and a reliance upon the vivifying or fructifying forces throughout Nature, and in the earlier ages of man's career, worship consisted for the most part in the celebration of festivals at stated seasons of the year, notably during seed-time and harvest, to commemorate the benefits derived from the grain field and vineyard.

Doubtless the first deified object was Gaia, the Earth. As within the bosom of the earth was supposed to reside the fructifying, life-giving power, and as from it were received all the bounties of life, it was female. It was the Universal Mother, and to her as to no other divinity worshipped by mankind, was offered a spontaneity of devotion and a willing acknowledgment of dependence. Thus far in the history of mankind no temples dedicated to an undefined and undefinable God had been raised. The children of Mother Earth met in the open air, without the precincts of any man-made shrine, and under the aerial canopy of heaven, acknowledged the bounties of the great Deity and their dependence upon her gifts. She was a beneficent and all-wise God, a tender and loving parent–a mother, who demanded no bleeding sacrifice to reconcile her to her children. The ceremonies observed at these festive seasons consisted for the most part in merry-making and in general thanksgiving, in which the gratitude of the worshippers found expression in song and dance, and in invocations to their Deity for a return or continuance of her gifts.

Subsequently, through the awe and reverence inspired by the mysteries involved in birth and life, the adoration of the creative principles in vegetable existence became supplemented by the worship of the creative functions in human beings and in animals. The earth, including the power inherent in it by which the continuity of existence is maintained, and by which new forms are continuously called into life, embodied the idea of God; and, as this inner force was regarded as inherent in matter, or as a manifestation of it, in process of time earth and the heavens, body and spirit, came to be worshipped under the form of a mother and her child, this figure being the highest expression of a Creator which the human mind was able to conceive. Not only did this emblem represent fertility, or the fecundating energies of Nature, but with the power to create were combined or correlated all the mental qualities and attributes of the two sexes. In fact the whole universe was contained in the Mother idea–the child, which was sometimes female, sometimes male, being a scion or offshoot from the eternal or universal unit.

Underlying all ancient mythologies may be observed the idea that the earth, from which all things proceed, is female. Even in the mythology of the Finns, Lapps, and Esths, Mother Earth is the divinity adored. Tylor calls attention to the same idea in the mythology of England,

"from the days when the Anglo-Saxon called upon the Earth, 'Hal wes thu folde fira modor' (Hail, thou Earth, men's mother), to the time when mediaeval Englishmen made a riddle of her asking 'Who is Adam's mother?' and poetry continued what mythology was letting fall, when Milton's Archangel promised Adam a life to last

'. . . till like ripe fruit thou drop
Into thy Mother's lap.' "[4]

In the old religion the sky was the husband of the earth and the earth was mother of all the gods.[5] In the traditions of past ages the fact is clearly perceived that there was a time when the mother was not only the one recognized parent on earth, but that the female principle was worshipped as the more important creative force throughout Nature.

Doubtless the worship of the female energy prevailed under the matriarchal system, and was practised at a time when women were the recognized heads of families and when they were regarded as the more important factors in human society. The fact has been shown in a previous work that after women began to leave their homes at marriage, and after property, especially land, had fallen under the supervision and control of men, the latter, as they manipulated all the necessaries of life and the means of supplying them, began to regard themselves as superior beings, and later, to claim that as a factor in reproduction, or creation, the male was the more important. With this change the ideas of a Deity also began to undergo a modification. The dual principle necessary to creation, and which had hitherto been worshipped as an indivisible unity, began gradually to separate into its individual elements, the male representing spirit, the moving or forming force in the generative processes, the female being matter–the instrument through which spirit works. Spirit which is eternal had produced matter which is destructible. The fact

---

[4] Primitive Culture, vol. i., p. 295.
[5] Max Muller, Origin and Growth of Religion, p. 279.

will be observed that this doctrine prevails to a greater or less extent in the theologies of the present time.

A little observation and reflection will show us that during this change in the ideas relative to a creative principle, or God, descent and the rights of succession which had hitherto been reckoned through the mother were changed from the female to the male line, the father having in the meantime become the only recognized parent. In the Eumenides of Aeschylus, the plea of Orestes in extenuation of his crime is that he is not of kin to his mother. Euripides, also, puts into the mouth of Apollo the same physiological notion, that she who bears the child is only its nurse. The Hindoo Code of Menu, which, however, since its earliest conception, has undergone numberless mutilations to suit the purposes of the priests, declares that "the mother is but the field which brings forth the plant according to whatsoever seed is sown."

Although, through the accumulation of property in masses and the capture of women for wives, men had succeeded in gaining the ascendancy, and although the doctrine had been propounded that the father is the only parent, thereby reversing the established manner of reckoning descent, still, as we shall hereafter observe, thousands of years were required to eliminate the female element from the god-idea.

We must not lose sight of the fact that human society was first organized and held together by means of the gens, at the head of which was a woman. The several members of this organization were but parts of one body cemented together by the pure principle of maternity, the chief duty of these members being to defend and protect each other if needs be with their life blood. The fact has been observed, in an earlier work, that only through the gens was the organization of society possible. Without it mankind could have accomplished nothing toward its own advancement.

Thus, throughout the earlier ages of human existence, at a time when mankind lived nearer to Nature and before individual wealth and the stimulation of evil passions had engendered superstition, selfishness, and distrust, the maternal element constituted not only the binding and preserving principle in human society, but, together with the power to bring forth, constituted also the god-idea, which idea, as has already been observed, at a certain stage in the history of the race was portrayed by a female figure with a child in her arms.

From all sources of information at hand are to be derived evidences of the fact that the earliest religion of which we have any account was pure Nature-worship, that whatever at any given time might have been the object adored, whether it were the earth, a tree, water, or the sun, it was simply as an emblem of the great energizing agency in Nature. The moving or forming force in the universe constituted the god-idea. The figure of a mother with her child signified not only the power to bring forth, but Perceptive Wisdom, or Light, as well.

As through a study of Comparative Ethnology, or through an investigation into the customs, traditions, and mythoses of extant races in the various stages of development, have been discovered the beginnings of the religious idea and the mental qualities which among primitive races prompted worship, so, also, through extinct tongues and the symbolism used in religious rites and ceremonies, many of the processes have been unearthed whereby the original and beautiful conceptions of the Deity, and the worship inspired by the operations of Nature, and especially the creative functions in human beings gradually became obscured by the grossest ideas and the vilest practices. The symbols which appear in connection with early religious rites and ceremonies, and under which are veiled the conceptions of a still earlier and purer age, when compared with subsequently developed notions relative to the same objects, indicate plainly the change which has been wrought in the original ideas relative to the creative functions, and furnish an index to the direction which human development, or growth, has taken.

As the human race constructs its own gods, and as by the conceptions involved in the deities worshipped at any given time in the history of mankind we are able to form a correct estimate of the character, temperament, and aspirations of the worshippers, so the history of the gods of the race, as revealed to us through the means of symbols, monumental records, and the investigation of extinct tongues, proves that from a stage of Nature worship and a pure and rational conception of the creative forces in the universe, mankind, in course of time, degenerated into mere devotees of sensual pleasure. With the corruption of human nature and the decline of mental power which followed the supremacy of the animal instincts, the earlier abstract idea of God was gradually lost sight of, and man himself in the form of a potentate or ruler, together with the various emblems of virility, came to be worshipped as the Creator. From adorers of an abstract creative principle, mankind had lapsed into worshippers of the symbols under which this principle had been veiled.

Although at certain stages in the history of the human race the evils, which as a result of the supremacy of the ruder elements developed in mankind had befallen the race were lamented and bewailed, they could not be suppressed. Man had become a lost and ruined creature. The golden age had passed away.

Chapter II.
Tree, Plant, and Fruit Worship

When mankind first began to perceive the fact of an all-pervading agency throughout Nature, by or through which everything is produced, and when they began to speculate on the origin of life and the final cause and destiny of things, it is not in the least remarkable that various objects and elements, such as fire, air, water, trees, etc., should in their turn have been venerated as in some special manner embodying the divine essence. Neither is it surprising although this universal agency was regarded as one, or as a dual entity, they should have recognized its manifold expressions or manifestations.

To primitive man, the visible sources whence proceeded his daily sustenance doubtless constituted the first objects of his regard and adoration. Hence, in addition to the homage paid to the earth, in due course of time would be added the worship of trees, upon which the early race was directly dependent for food. At a time when the art of agriculture had not been attained, all such trees as yielded their fruit for the support of the human race, and which afforded to mankind pleasant beverages or cooling shade, would come to be regarded as embodying the universal beneficent principle–the great creating and preserving agency of Nature, and therefore as proper objects of veneration.

According to the Phoenician theogony, "the first gods which were worshipped by oblations and sacrifices were the fruits of the earth, on which they and their descendants lived as their forefathers had done."

Although, after the art of agriculture had been developed, mankind was gradually relieved from its past dependence on the tree as a means of support, it nevertheless continued to be regarded with veneration as an emblem of creative power or of productive energy.

Among the traditions and monuments of nearly every country of the globe are to be found traces of a sacred tree– a Tree of Life. In various countries there appear two traditional trees, the one typical of the continuation of physical life, the other representing spiritual life, or the life of the soul. After the age of pure Nature-worship had passed, however, and serpent, fire, and phallic faiths had been introduced, the original signification of the tree, like that of all other religious emblems, became considerably changed. Through its energies, or life-giving properties, existence had long been maintained, and for this reason, as has already been observed, it became an object of veneration; but, after the reproductive power in man had risen to the dignity of a supreme God, the tree, to the masses of the people, became a symbol of the physical, life-giving energy in mortals and in animals. In other words, it became a phallic emblem representing the continuation of existence, or the power to reproduce or continue life on the earth. As a religious symbol it became the traditional Tree of Life.

The tree, like nearly every other object in nature, was and still is, in various parts of the world, either female or male, and all ideas connected with it are sacred and closely interwoven with sex.

The extent to which trees have been venerated in past ages seems to be little understood, and there are doubtless few persons, at the present time, who would willingly believe that all along the religious stream, from its source to its latest developed branches, are to be observed traces of this ancient worship, which, in its earliest stages, was simply a recognition of Nature's bounties.

Barlow, in his work on Symbolism, says that "the most generally received symbol of life is a tree–as also the most appropriate."

Again the same writer observes: "Besides the monumental evidence thus furnished of a sacred tree, or Tree of Life, there is an historical and traditional evidence of the same thing, found in the early literature of various nations, in the customs, and popular usages."[6] As tree- and sun-worship, or the adoration of Nature's processes, finally became interwoven with phallic faiths, its history can be understood only after these later developments in the religious stream have been examined, or after the true significance of the serpent as a religious emblem, and the various ideas connected with the traditional Tree of Life, have been exposed.

The palm, the pine, the oak, the banian, or bo, and many other species of trees, have, at different times, and by various nations, been invested with divine honors; but, in oriental countries, by far the most sacred among them is the Ficus Religiosa, or the holy bo tree of India. Something of the true significance of the traditional Tree of Life may be observed in the ideas connected with the worship of this emblem. The fig, when planted with the palm, as it frequently is in the East, near temples and holy shrines, is regarded as a peculiarly sacred object. When entwining the palm, which is male, it is always female; from their embrace Kalpia, or passion, is developed. This union causes the continuation of existence and the "revolutions of time." The whole constitutes the Tree of Life.

---

[6] Essays on Symbolism, p. 84.

In Ceylon, there stands at the present time a tree which we are told is still worshipped by every follower of Buddha. It is a sacred bo, or Ficus Religiosa, which stands adjacent to an ancient holy shrine known as the Brazen Monastery, now in ruins. Of this tree Forlong remarks:

"Though now amidst ruins and wild forests, and although having stood thus in solitary desolation for some 1500 years, yet there it still grows, and is worshipped and deeply revered by more millions of our race than any other god, prophet, or idol, which the world has ever seen."[7]

This tree is sacred to Sakyu Mooni, is 2200 years old, and is said to be a slip from a tree planted by Bood Gaya, one of the three former Buddhas who, like Sakyu Mooni, visited Ceylon. Under the parent of this tree the great prophet reposed after he had attained perfect rest, or after he had overcome the flesh and become Buddha. It was under a bo tree that Mai, Queen of Heaven, brought him forth, and, in fact, very many of the most important incidents of his life are closely connected with this sacred emblem.

In an allusion to the bo tree of Ceylon, a slip of which is said to have been carried from India to that island by a certain priestess in the year 307 B.C., Forlong observes:

"This wonderful idol has furnished shoots to half Asia, and every shoot is trained as much as possible like the parent, and like it, also, enclosed and tended. Men watch and listen for signs and sounds from this holy tree just as the priests of Dodona did beneath their rustling oaks, and, as many people, even of these somewhat sceptical days, still do, beneath the pulpits of their pope, priest, or other oracle."[8]

The sacred Ficus is worshipped in India and in many of the Polynesian islands.

---

[7] Rivers of Life, vol. i., p. 35.

[8] Rivers of Life, vol. i., p, 36.

Regarding the palm, Inman assures us that it is emblematical of the active male energy, or the continuation of existence.[9]

Within the legends underlying the Jewish religion, it will be remembered that the tree appears mysteriously connected with the beginning of life and is interwoven with the first ideas of human action and experience. The literal sense, however, of the allegory in Genesis concerning the woman, the tree, and the serpent, and its meaning as generally accepted by laymen and the uneducated among the priesthood, has little in common with its true significance as understood by the initiated.

In Vedic times, the home tree was worshipped as a god, and to the exhilarating properties in its juice was ascribed that subtle quality which was regarded as the life-giving, or creative, energy supposed to reside in heat, and which was closely connected with passion or procreative energy. This quality was their Bacchus, Dionysos, or god-idea–the creator not alone of physical existence, but of good and evil as well. It was the Destroyer, yet the Regenerator, of life.

Of the Zoroastrian home, or sacred tree, which by the Persians was worshipped for thousands of years, Layard remarks: "The plant or its product was called the mystical body of God, the living water or food of eternal life, when duly consecrated and administered according to Zoroastrian rites." It has been suggested, and not without reason, that to this idea of the ancients, respecting the sacred character of the properties of the home juice, may be traced the "origin of the celebration of Jewish holy or paschal suppers and other eucharistic rites."

Although by the ancients water was sometimes regarded as the original principle, later, wine, or the intoxicating quality within it, came to constitute the god-idea. It was spirit, while water was matter; hence, in the

---

[9] Ancient Faiths Embodied in Ancient Names, vol. ii., p. 448.

sacraments, water and wine were commingled, wine representing the essence or blood of God; water, at the same time, standing for the people. Cyprian, the bishop martyr, while contending for the use of wine in the Sacrament of the Lord's Supper, makes use of the following argument:

"The Holy Spirit also is not silent in the Psalms on the sacrament of this thing, when He makes mention of the Lord's Cup, and says 'Thy intoxicating cup how excellent it is!' Now the cup which intoxicates is assuredly mingled with wine, for water cannot intoxicate anybody. And the Cup of the Lord in such wise inebriates, as Noe also was intoxicated drinking wine in Genesis. . . . For because Christ bore us all, in that he also bore our sins, we see that in the water is understood the people, but in the wine is showed the blood of Christ. . . . Thus, therefore, in consecrating the Cup of the Lord, water alone cannot be offered, even as wine alone cannot be offered. For if anyone offer wine only, the blood of Christ is dissociated from us; but if the water be alone, the people are dissociated from Christ."[10]

The Sacrament of the Lord's Supper, at which wine is mysteriously converted into the essence of Deity, or into the blood of Christ, is without doubt a relic of the idea once entertained regarding the homa tree. Certain writers entertain the opinion that from the use of the sacred homa juice have arisen various religious practices and rites, such for instance as offering oblations to the gods, anointing holy stones, and pouring wine on sacred hills, also the custom of pledging oaths over glasses of wine.

The May pole, a decidedly phallic emblem, whose festivals until a very recent time were celebrated in England by the old as well as the young, was usually if not always sprinkled with wine. From the accounts which we

---

[10] Epistles of Cyprian, vol. i., pp. 215-217.

have of this sacred emblem and its festival, it seems that no royal edict nor priestly denunciation was sufficient to expel it from the country.

According to Dr. Stevenson, the festival of Holi or the worship of Holika Devata, in the island of Ceylon, "has a close resemblance to the English festival of the May-pole, which originated in a religious ceremony or festival of the Cushites (called Phoenicians) who anciently occupied Western Europe."[11]

The ash is the Scandinavian Tree of Life, and, like the sacred trees of all nations, is emblematical of the continuation of existence. This tree has a triple root, which peculiarity doubtless accounts for its sacred character. It is both female and male, and is said to be regarded as a "sort of Logos or Wisdom." It is the first emanation from the Deity, and yet a Trinity in Unity. To insult or injure this tree was sacrilege, to cut it down was an offense punishable with death.

In the old Egyptian and Zoroastrian story, appear the descriptions of two Trees of Life, also a Tree of Knowledge. In the accounts given of these trees, the Ficus, the female Tree of Life, represents the life of the soul, while the palm, the male Tree of Life, is that which gives physical life, which also is the true significance of the word "lord." When, however, either of these trees stood alone, or unaccompanied by its counterpart, by it both of the creative principles were understood. By these ideas is suggested the thought which among a certain school of psychologists of the present century seems to be gaining ground, namely: that man is a dual entity, or, in other words, that he has a subjective mind and an objective self, which so long as this life endures must co-operate or work together.

---

[11] Quoted by Baldwin, Prehistoric Nations, p. 223.

In the following descriptions of Egyptian emblems, will be perceived some of the changes which finally took place relative to the idea of sex in the god-idea.

In the museum of Egyptian antiquities in Berlin is a sepulchral tablet representing the Tree of Life. This emblem figures the trunk of a tree, from the top of which emerges the bust of a woman–Netpe. She is the goddess of heavenly existence, and is administering to the deceased the water and the bread of life, the latter of which is represented by a substance in the form of cakes or rolls. The time at which this tablet was found is not known, but it is supposed to belong to the period of the XIXth dynasty, or about the time of Rameses II., 1400 years B.C.

There is also in the Berlin museum another representation of the Egyptian Tree of Life, in which the trunk has given place to the entire body of a woman. This, also, is Netpe, who is still spiritual wisdom or the maternal principle. We are informed by Forlong that Diana was worshipped by the Amazons under a sacred tree.[12] From this symbol the tree, which grew first into the figure of a divine woman, and later assumed the form of a divine man, arose the emblem of the cross.

On the Nineveh tablets is pictured a Tree of Life which is surrounded by winged spirits, bearing in their hands the pine cone, a symbol indicating life, and which is said to have the same significance as the crux-ansata, or cross, among the Egyptians.

In later ages, the Tree of Life, i. e., the divine man, or cross, or both together, furnish immortal food to those who lay hold upon them, exactly in the same manner as did Netpe, the goddess of wisdom, or spiritual life, in former times. According to the testimony of Barlow, this is the subject "most frequently symbolized on early Christian

---

[12] Rivers of Life, vol. i., p. 70.

sepulchral tablets and monuments."[13] Christ's body was the "bread of life," and his blood was the "wine from the Tree of Life," of which to partake was life eternal. The cross, as in earlier religions, represented completeness of life. The jambu tree, the Buddhist god-tree, is in the shape of a cross.[14]

Among the Kelti a tall oak was not only a symbol of the Deity, but it was Jupiter himself, while the earth from which it sprang was the Great Mother. Throughout Europe, in all ages, the oak has received divine honors. The fact that under its branches Jew, Pagan, and Christian alike swore their most solemn oaths, shows that its veneration was not confined to any particular nation or locality.

The sacredness of the oak among the Druids is well attested by all writers who have dealt with this interesting people. In Rome its branches formed the badge of victory worn by conquering heroes, this emblem being the highest mark of distinction which could be conferred upon them.

Forlong assures us that the oak was even more worshipped at the West than was the sacred Ficus at the East. Like it, the wood of the oak must be used

"to call down the sacred fire from Heaven and gladden in the yule (Suiel or Seul) log of Christmas-tide even Christian fires, as well as annually renew with fire direct from Ba-al, on Beltine day, the sacred flame on every public and private hearth, and this from the temples of Meroe on the Nile, to the farthest icy forests and mountains of the Sklavonian."[15]

Among the Druids, the mistletoe was also sacred especially when entwining the oak. Together they represented the Tree of Life, or the two generating agencies throughout Nature. Of the species of it which grows on the oak, Borlaise says that they deified the mistletoe and were

---

[13] Essays on Symbolism, p. 74.
[14] Wilford, Asiatic Researches.
[15] Faiths of Man in All Lands, vol. i., p. 68.

not to look upon it but in the most devout and reverential manner: "When the end of the year approached, they marched with great solemnity to gather the mistletoe of the oak in order to present it to Jupiter, inviting all the world to assist in the ceremony."[16]

According to the Latin writer Pliny, the "Druids have nothing more sacred than the mistletoe and the tree on which it grows, provided it be an oak." This plant, which is called All Heal, although sought after with the greatest religious ardor, is seldom found, but should the people who go forth at Christmas time in large numbers succeed in finding it they immediately set about preparing feasts under the tree upon which it grows; at the same time, in the most solemn manner, two white bulls are brought forth to be sacrificed. After the feast has been prepared and the sacrifice made ready, the priest ascends the tree and with a golden pruning-knife cuts the sacred branches of the mistletoe, dropping them into a white cloth prepared for the occasion. The bulls are then sacrificed and a prayer offered that "God would render his own gift prosperous to those on whom he has bestowed it." They believed that administered in a potion it would impart fecundity to any barren animal, and that it was a remedy against all kinds of poison. The branches of the mistletoe were then distributed among the faithful, each cherishing the token as the most sacred emblem of his faith. It is thought that the Christmas tree is a remnant of this custom.

Although the Christbaum of the Germans, the Yggdrasill of the Scandinavians, and the Christmas tree of the English speaking nations are still regarded as belonging exclusively to Christianity, their birthplace was the far East, and their origin long anterior to our present era. This subject will be referred to later in these pages. The palm, which in course of time became the most sacred tree of

---

[16] Borlaise.

Egypt, is said to have put forth a shoot every month during the year. At Christmas tide, or at the winter solstice, a branch from this tree was used as a symbol of the renewal of time or of the birth of the New Year.

On the Zodiac of Dendera, preserved in the National Library at Paris, are two trees, the one representing the East, or India and China, the other, the West, or Egypt. The former of these trees is putting forth a pair of leaves and is topped by the emblems of Siva, emblems which indicate the fructifying powers of Nature, whilst the Egyptian sacred tree, which is surmounted by the ostrich plume, the emblem of truth, is indicative of Light, Intelligence, or the life of the soul. In a discourse delivered by Dr. Stukeley in 1760, attention was directed to the grove of Abraham as "that famous oak grove of Beersheba, planted by the illustrious prophet and first Druid–Abraham; and from whom our celebrated British Druids came, who were of the same patriarchal reformed religion, and brought the use of sacred groves to Britain."[17]

The fact has been ascertained that in Arabia, in very ancient times, there was a goddess named Azra who was worshipped under the form of a tree called Samurch, and that in Yemen tree-worship still prevails. To the date is ascribed divine honors. This tree is said to have its regular priests, services, rites, and festivals, and is as zealously worshipped as are the gods of any other country. We are not informed as to whether the Jewish Tree of Life was borrowed from the Chaldeans or the Egyptians, but, as the significance is the same in all countries, it is of little consequence which furnished a copy for the writer in Genesis.

In Dr. Inman's Ancient Faiths, is a drawing from the original, by Colonel Coombs, of the "Temptation," or of the ancient tree-and-serpent myth in Genesis. This drawing,

---

[17] Barlow, Symbolism, p. 98.

in which it is observed that the Jewish idea of woman as tempter is reversed, was copied from the inner walls of a cave in Southern India. The picture is said to be a faithful representation of the version of the story as accepted in the East.

Of the myrtle, Payne Knight says that it "was a symbol both of Venus and Neptune, the male and female personifications of the productive powers of the waters, which appear to have been occasionally employed in the same sense as the fig and fig leaf."

The same writer refers to the fact that instead of beads, wreaths of foliage, generally of laurel, olive, myrtle, ivy, or oak, appear upon coins; sometimes encircling the symbolical figures, and sometimes as chaplets on their heads. According to Strabo, each of these is sacred to some particular personification of the Deity, and "significant of some particular attribute, and in general, all evergreens were Dionysiac plants, that is, symbols of the generative power, signifying perpetuity of youth and vigor." The crowns of laurel, olive, etc., with which the victors in the Roman triumphs and Grecian games were honored, were emblems of immortality, and not merely transitory marks of occasional distinction.[18]

The tree and serpent, according to Ferguson, are symbolized in all religious systems which the world has ever known. The two together are typical of the processes of reproduction or generation. They also symbolize good and evil and the cause which underlies the decline of virtue.

Among the numberless fruits which from time to time have been regarded as divine emblems, the principal are perhaps the fig, the pomegranate, the mandrake, the almond, and the olive. The peculiarly sacred character which we

---

[18] Payne Knight, Symbolism of Ancient Art. We are informed that this book was never sold, but only given away. Although a copy of it was formerly in the British Museum, care was taken by the trustees to keep it out of the catalogues.

find attached to the fig ceases to be a mystery so soon as we remember that the organs of generation, male and female, had, in process of time, come to be objects of worship and that the fig was the emblem of the latter.

A basket of this fruit is said to have been the most acceptable offering to the god Bacchus, and therefore, by his devotees, was regarded as the most sacred symbol. The favorite material for phallic devices was the wood of the sacred fig, for it was by rubbing together pieces of it that holy fire was supposed to be drawn from heaven. By holy fire, however, was meant not so much the natural visible element which was kindled, as that subtle substance contained in fire or heat which was supposed to contain the life principle, and which was sent in response to the cravings of pious devotees for procreative energy, which blessing, among various peoples, notably the Jews, was indicative of special divine favor.

By pagans, Jews, and Christians, the pomegranate has long been regarded as a sacred emblem. It is a symbol of reproductive energy. Representations of it were embroidered on the Ephod, and Solomon's Temple is reported as having been literally covered with decorations, in which, among the devices noticed, this particular fruit appears the most conspicuous. Its significance, as revealed by Inman and other writers, is too gross to be set forth in these pages.

Among the most sacred plants or flowers were the lotus and the fleur de lis, both of which were venerated because of some real or fancied organic sexual peculiarity. The lotus is adored as the female principle throughout Nature, or as the "womb of all creation," and is sacred throughout oriental countries. It is said to be androgynous or hermaphrodite–hence its peculiarly sacred character.

It has long been thought that this lily is produced without the aid of the male pollen, hence it would seem to be an appropriate emblem for that ancient sect which worshipped the female as the more important creative energy.

Of the lotus, Inman remarks: "Amongst fourteen kinds of food and flowers presented to the Sanskrit God Anata, the lotus only is indispensable." This emblem, as we have seen, was the symbol of the Great Mother, and we are assured that it was "little less sacred than the Queen of Heaven herself."

Regarding the lotus and its universal significance as a religious emblem, Payne Knight says:

"The lotus is the Nelumbo of Linnaeus. This plant grows in the water, and amongst its broad leaves puts forth a flower, in the center of which is formed the seed vessel, shaped like a bell or inverted cone, and punctured on the top with little cavities or cells, in which the seeds grow. The orifices of these cells being too small to let the seeds drop out when ripe, they shoot forth into new plants, in the places where they were formed, the bulb of the vessel serving as a matrix to nourish them until they acquire such a degree of magnitude as to burst it open and release themselves, after which, like other aquatic weeds, they take root wherever the current deposits them. This plant, therefore, being thus productive of itself, and vegetating from its own matrix, without being fostered in the earth, was naturally adopted as the symbol of the productive power of the waters, upon which the creative spirit of the Creator operated in giving life and vegetation to matter. We accordingly find it employed in every part of the Northern hemisphere, where the symbolical religion improperly called idolatry does or did prevail. The sacred images of the Tartars, Japanese, and Indians are almost all placed upon it, of which numerous instances occur in the publication of Kaempfer, Sonnerat, etc: The Brama of India is represented sitting upon a lotus throne, and the figures upon the Isaic table hold the stem of this plant, surmounted by the seed vessel in one hand, and the cross representing the male organs in the other: thus signifying the universal power, both active and passive, attributed to that goddess."[19]

The lotus is the most sacred and the most significant symbol connected with the sacred mysteries of the East. Upon this subject, Maurice observes that there is no plant which has received such a degree of honor as has the lotus. It was the consecrated symbol of the Great Mother who had brought forth the fecundative energies, female and male. Not only throughout the Northern hemisphere was it everywhere held in profound veneration, but among the modern Egyptians it is still worshipped as symbolical of the Great First Cause. The lotus was the emblem venerated in the solemn celebration of the Mysteries of Eleusis in Greece and the Phiditia in Carthage.

In referring to the degree of homage paid to the lotus by the ancients, Higgins says: "And we shall find in the sequel that it still continues to receive the respect, if not the adoration, of a great part of the Christian world, unconscious, perhaps, of the original reason of their conduct." It is a significant fact that in nearly all the sacred paintings of the Christians in the galleries throughout Europe, especially those of the Annunciation, a lily is always to be observed. In later ages as the original significance of the lotus was lost, any lily came to be substituted. Godfrey Higgins is sure that although the priests of the Romish Church are at the present time ignorant of the true meaning of the lotus, or lily, "it is, like many other very odd things, probably understood at the Vatican, or the Crypt of St. Peter's."[20]

Of the lotus of the Hindoos Nimrod says:

"The lotus is a well-known allegory, of which the expanse calyx represents the ships of the gods floating on the surface of the water, and the erect flower arising out of

---

[19] Symbolism of Ancient Art.
[20] Anacalypsis, book vii., ch. xi.

it, the mast thereof . . . but as the ship was Isis or Magna Mater, the female principle, and the mast in it the male deity, these parts of the flower came to have certain other significations, which seem to have been as well known at Samosata as at Benares."[21]

In other words it was a phallic emblem and represented the creative processes throughout Nature. Susa, the name of the capital of the Cushites, or ancient Ethiopians, meant "the City of Lilies." In India the lotus frequently appears among phallic devices in place of the sacred Yoni. From the foregoing pages the fact will be observed that the God of the ancients embodied the two creative agencies throughout the universe, but as nothing could exist without a mother, the great Om who was the indivisible God and the Creator of the sun was the mother of these two principles, while the Tree of Life was the original life-giving energy upon the earth, represented in the creation myths of the first man Adam, and the first woman Eve or Adama.

Throughout the ages, this force, or creative agency has been symbolized in various ways, many of which have been noted in the foregoing pages. We have observed that notwithstanding the fact that the supremacy of the male had been established, the sacred Yoni and the lotus were still reverenced as symbols of the most exalted God. Finally, when the masculine energy began to be worshipped as the more important agency in reproduction, the female, although still necessary to complete the god-idea, was veiled.

Among the sect known as Lingaites, those who adored the male creative power, Man, Phallus, and Creator in religious symbolism signified one and the same thing in the minds of the people. Each represented a Tree of Life, the beginning and end of all things.

---

[21] Quoted in Anacalypsis.

Tree-worship was condemned by the councils of Tours, Nantes, and Auxerre, and in the XIth century it was forbidden in England by the laws of Canute, but these edicts seem to have had little effect. In referring to this subject, Barlow says: "In the XVIIIth century it existed in Livonia, and traces of it may still be found in the British Isles."[22] The vast area over which tree- and plant-worship once extended, and the tenacity with which it still clings to the human race, indicate the hold which, at an earlier age in the history of mankind, it had taken upon the religious feelings of mankind.

So closely has this worship become entwined with that of serpent and phallic faiths, that it is impossible to consider it, even in a brief manner, without anticipating these later developments; yet linked with earth- and sun-worship, it doubtless prevailed for many ages absolutely unconnected with the grosser ideas with which it subsequently became associated.

---

[22] Essays on Symbolism, p. 118.

Chapter III.
Sun-Worship--Female and Male Energies in the Sun"

When we inquire into the worship of nations in the earliest periods to which we have access by writing or tradition, we find that the adoration of one God, without temples or images, universally prevailed."[23]

Underlying all the ancient religions of which we have any account, may be observed the great energizing force throughout Nature recognized and reverenced as the Deity. This force embraces not only the creative energies in human beings, in animals, and in plants, but in the earlier ages of human history it included also Wisdom, or Law-- that "power by which all things are discriminated or defined and held in their proper places." The most renowned writers who have dealt with this subject agree in the conclusion that, during thousands of years among all the nations of the earth, only one God was worshipped. This God was Light and Life, both of which proceeded from the sun, or more properly speaking were symbolized by the sun.

In Egyptian hymns the Creator is invoked as the being who "dwells concealed in the sun"; and Greek writers speak of this luminary as the "generator and nourisher of all things, the ruler of the world." It is thought, however, that neither of these nations worshipped the corporeal sun. It

---

[23] Godfrey Higgins, Celtic Druids.

was the "centre or body from which the pervading spirit, the original producer of order, fertility, and organization, continued to emanate to preserve the mighty structure which it had formed."

It is evident that at an early age, both in Egypt and in India, spiritualized conceptions of sun-worship had already been formed.

We have seen that Netpe, the Goddess of Light, or Heavenly Wisdom, conferred spiritual life on all who would accept it. The Great Mother of the Gods in India was not only the source whence all blessings flow, but she was the Beginning and the End of all things.

Of "Aditi, the boundless, the yonder, the beyond all and everything," Max Muller says that in later times she "may have become identified with the sky, also with the earth, but originally she was far beyond the sky and the earth."[24] The same writer quotes the following, also from a hymn of the Rig-Veda:

"O Mitra and Varuna, you mount your chariot which, at the dawning of the dawn is golden-colored and has iron poles at the setting of the sun; from thence you see Aditi and Diti–that is, what is yonder and what is here, what is infinite and what is finite, what is mortal and what is immortal."[25]

Aditi is the Great She that Is, the Everlasting. Muller refers to the fact that another Hindoo poet "speaks of the dawn as the face of Aditi; thus indicating that Aditi is here not the dawn itself, but something beyond the dawn." This Goddess, who is designated as the "Oldest," is implored "not only to drive away darkness and enemies that lurk in the dark, but likewise to deliver man from any sin which he may have committed." "May Aditi by day protect our cattle, may she, who never deceives, protect us from evil."

---

[24] Origin and Growth of Religion, p. 221.
[25] Ibid.

In the Egyptian as in the Indian and Hebrew religions, the two generating principles throughout Nature represent the Infinite, the Holy of Holies, the Elohim or Aleim–the Ieue. Within the records of the earliest religions of Ethiopia or Arabia, Chaldea, Assyria, and Babylonia, is revealed the same monad principle in the Deity. This monad conception, or dual unity, this God of Light and Life, or of Wisdom and generative force, is the same source whence all mythologies have sprung, and, as has been stated, among all peoples the fact is observed that the religious idea has followed substantially the same course of development, or growth. Within the sacred writings of the Hindoos there is but one Almighty Power, usually denominated as Brahm or Brahme– Om or Aum. This word in India was regarded with the same degree of veneration as was the sacred Ieue of the Jews. In later ages, the fact is being proved that this God, into whom all the deities worshipped at a certain period in human history resolve themselves, is the sun, or if not the actual corporeal sun, then the supreme agency within it which was acknowledged as the great creative or life-force– that dual principle which by the early races was recognized as Elohim, Om, Ormuzd, etc., and from which the productive power in human beings, in plants, and in animals was thought to emanate.

Prior to the development of either tree or phallic worship, the sun as an emblem of the Deity had doubtless become the principal object of veneration. Ages would probably elapse before primitive man would observe that all life is dependent on the warmth of the sun's rays, or before from experience he would perceive the fact that to its agency as well as to that of the earth he was indebted both for food and the power of motion. However, as soon as this knowledge had been gained, the great orb of day would assume the most prominent place among the objects of his regard and adoration. That such has been the case, that the sun, either as the actual Creator, or as an emblem of the great energizing force in Nature, has been worshipped by every nation of the globe, there is no lack of evidence to prove; neither do we lack proof to establish the fact that, since the adoption of the sun as a divine object, or perhaps I should say as the emblem of Wisdom and creative power, it has never been wholly eliminated from the god-idea of mankind.

Bryant produces numberless etymological proofs to establish the fact that all the early names of the Deity were derived or compounded from some word which originally meant the sun.

Max Muller says that Surya was the sun as shining in the sky. Savitri was the sun as bringing light and life. Vishnu was the sun as striding with three steps across the sky, etc.

Inman, whose etymological researches have given him considerable prominence as a Sanskrit and Hebrew scholar, says that Ra, Ilos, Helos, Bil, Baal, Al, Allah, and Elohim were names given to the sun as representative of the Creator.

We are assured by Godfrey Higgins that Brahme is the sun the same as Surya. Brahma sprang from the navel of Brahme. Faber in his Pagan Idolatry says that all the gods of the ancients "melt insensibly into one, they are all equally the sun." The word Apollo signifies the author or generator of Light. In the Rig Veda, Surya, the sun, is called Aditya. "Truly, Surya, thou art great; truly Aditya, thou art great."

Selden observes that whether the gods be called Osiris, or Omphis, or Nilus, or any other name, they all center in the sun.

According to Diodorus Siculus, it was the belief of the ancients that Dionysos, Osiris, Serapis, Pan, Jupiter and Pluto were all one. They were, the sun.

Max Muller says that a very low race in India named the Santhals call the sun Chandro, which means "bright."

These people declared to the missionaries who settled among them, that Chandro had created the world; and when told that it would be absurd to say that the sun had created the world, they replied: "We do not mean the visible Chandro, but an invisible one."

Not only did Dionysos, and all the rest of the gods who in later ages came to be regarded as men, represent the sun, but after the separation of the male and female elements in the originally indivisible God, Maut or Minerva, Demeter, Ceres, Isis, Juno, and others less important in the pagan world were also the sun, or, in other words, they represented the female power throughout the universe which was supposed to reside in the sun.

In most groups of Babylonian and Assyrian divine emblems, there occur two distinct representations of the sun, "one being figured with four rays or divisions within the orb, and the other, with eight." According to George Rawlinson, these figures represent a distinction between the male and female powers residing within the sun, the quartered disk signifying the male energy, and the eight-rayed orb appearing as the emblem of the female![26]

During an earlier age of human history, prior to the dissensions which arose over the relative importance of the sexes in reproduction, and at a time when a mother and her child represented the Deity, the sun was worshiped as the female Jove. Everything in the universe was a part of this great God. At that time there had been no division in the god-idea. The Creator constituted a dual but indivisible unity. Dionysos formerly represented this God, as did also Om, Jove, Mithras, and others. Jove was the "Great Virgin" whence everything proceeds.

---

[26] Essay x.

"Jove first exists, whose thunders roll above,
   Jove last, Jove midmost, all proceeds from Jove;
   Female is Jove, Immortal Jove is male;
   Jove the broad Earth, the heavens irradiate pale.
   Jove is the boundless Spirit, Jove the Fire,

   That warms the world with feeling and desire." In a former work the fact has been mentioned that the first clue obtained by Herr Bachofen, author of Das Mutterrecht, to a former condition of society under which gynaecocracy, or the social and political pre-eminence of women, prevailed, was the importance attached to the female principle in the Deity in all ancient mythologies.

According to the testimony of various writers, Om, although comprehending both elements of the Deity, was nevertheless female in signification. Sir William Jones observes that Om means oracle–matrix or womb.[27] Upon this subject Godfrey Higgins, quoting from Drummond, remarks:

"The word Om or Am in the Hebrew not only signifies might, strength, power, firmness, solidity, truth, but it means also Mother, as in Genesis ii., 24, and Love, whence the Latin Amo, Mamma. If the word be taken to mean strength, then Amon will mean (the first syllable being in regimine) the temple of the strength of the generative or creative power, or the temple of the mighty procreative power. If the word Am means Mother, then a still more recondite idea will be implied, viz.: the mother generative power, or the maternal generative power: perhaps the Urania of Persia or the Venus Aphrodite of Crete and Greece, or the Jupiter Genetrix of the masculine and feminine gender, or the Brahme Mai of India, or the Alma Venus of Lucretius. And the City of On or Heliopolis

---

[27] See Anacalypsis, book iii., ch. ii.

will be the City of the sun, or City of the procreative powers of nature of which the sun was always an emblem."

According to Prof. W. R. Smith, Om means uniting or binding, a fact which is explained by the early significance of the mother element in early society. The name of the great Deity Om or Aum scarcely passes the lips of its worshippers, and when it is pronounced is always reverently whispered. Regarding the mystic word Om, we are told that it is the name given to Delphi, and that "Delphi has the meaning of the female organs of generation called in India the Os Minxoe."

Although the great God of India was female and male, yet we are assured by Forlong that the female energy Maya, Queen of Heaven, even at the present time is more heard of than the male principle.

According to Bryant, the worship of Ham is the most ancient as well as the most universal of any in the world. This writer remarks that Ham, instead of representing an individual, is but a Greek corruption of Om or Aum, the great androgynous God of India, a God which is identical in significance with Aleim, Vesta, and all the other representatives of the early dual, universal power. "In the old language God was called Al, Ale, Alue, and Aleim, more frequently Aleim than any other name." According to the testimony of Higgins, Aleim denotes the feminine plural. The heathen divinities Ashtaroth and Beelzebub were both called Aleim, Ashtaroth being simply Astarte adorned with the horns of a ram. Ishtar not unfrequently appears with the horns of a cow. We are informed by Inman that whenever a goddess is observed with horns–emblems which by the way always indicate masculine power–it is to denote the fact that she is androgynous, or that within her is embodied the complete Deity–the dual reproductive energy throughout Nature. The "figure becomes the emblem of divinity and power."[28]

Mithras–the Savior, the great Persian Deity which was worshipped as the "Preserver," was both female and male. Among the representations of this divinity which appear in the Townley collection in the British Museum, is one in which it is figured in its female character, in the act of killing the bull. The Divinity Baal was both female and male. The God of the Jews in an early stage of their career was called Baal. The oriental Ormuzd was also dual or androgynous.

Orpheus teaches that the divine nature is both female and male. According to Proclus, Jupiter was an immortal maid, "the Queen of Heaven, and Mother of the Gods." All things were contained within the womb of Jupiter. This Virgin within whom was embodied the male principle "gave light and life to Eve." She was the life-giving, energizing power in Nature, and was identical with Aleim, Om, Astarte, and others. The Goddess Esta, or Vesta, or Hestia, whom Plato calls the "soul of the body of the universe," is believed by Beverly and others to be the Self-Existent, the Great "She that Is" of the Hindoos, whose significance is identical with the Cushite or Phoenician Deity, Aleim.

According to Marco Polo, the Chinese had but one supreme God of whom they had no image, and to whom they prayed for only two things–"a sound mind in a sound body." They had, however, a lesser god–probably the same as the "Lord" (masculine) of the Jews, to whom they petitioned for rain, fair weather, and all the minor accessories of existence. Upon the walls of the houses of the Chinese is a tablet to which they pay their devotion. On this tablet is the name of the "high, celestial, and supreme God." The principal word which this tablet contains is

---

[28] Ancient Faiths Embodied in Ancient Names, vol. i., p. 311.

"Tien." Of this Chinese Deity Barlow says: "The Chinese recognize in Tienhow, the Queen of Heaven nursing her infant son. Connected with this figure is a lotus bud, symbol of the new birth.

Originally in Chaldea and in Egypt, only one supreme God was worshipped. This Deity was figured by a mother and her child, as was the great Chinese God. It comprehended the universe and all the attributes of the Deity. It was worshipped thousands of years prior to the birth of Mary, the Mother of Christ, and representations of it are still extant, not only in oriental lands, but in many countries of Europe. Within the oldest temples of Egypt are still to be observed sacred apartments which contain the "Holy of Holies," and to which, in past ages, none might gain access but priests and priestesses of the highest order. Within these apartments are pictured the mysteries of birth, together with the symbols of generation emblems of procreation.

On the banks of the river Nile are observed the ruins of the temple of Philae, which structure, it is said, represents the most ancient style of architecture. Within these ruins is to be seen an inner chamber in which are depicted the birth scenes of the child god Horus, and, indeed, everywhere among the monuments and ruins of Egypt, is plainly visible the fact that the creative power and functions in human beings, in animals, and in vegetable life, together with Wisdom, once constituted the god-idea.

Between the ruins of the palace of Amunoph III. and the Nile are two colossal statues, each hewn from a single block of stone. These figures, although in a sitting posture, are sixty feet high. It is thought that they once formed the entrance to an avenue of similar figures leading up to the palace. It has been supposed that the most northern statue represents Ammon, and that its companion piece is his Mother. It is now believed by many writers, however, that these figures do not represent two persons at all, but that in a remote age of the world's history they were worshipped as the two great principles, female and male, which animate Nature. The fact has been observed that Am or Om was originally a female Deity, within whom was contained the male principle; when, however, through the changes wrought in the relative positions of the sexes, the male element in the Divinity adored came to be represented as a man instead of as a child, he was Ammon. He was the sun, yet notwithstanding the fact that he had drawn to himself the powers of the sun, he was still, himself, only a production of or emanation from the female Deity Om, Mother of the Gods and Queen of Heaven. She it was who had created or brought forth the sun.

There is a tradition which asserts that every morning a melodious sound is emitted from the first named of these two colossal figures as he salutes his rosy-fingered Mother whom he acknowledges as the source of all Light and Wisdom. The bodies are described as being "without motion, the faces without expression, the eyes looking straight forward, yet a certain grand simplicity occasions them to be universally admired."

The Goddess Disa or Isa of the North, as delineated on the sacred drums of the Laplanders, was accompanied by a child similar to the Horus of the Egyptians.[29] It is observed also that the ancient Muscovites worshipped a sacred group composed of a mother and her children, probably a representation of the Egyptian Isis and her offspring, or at least of the once universal idea of the Deity.

The following is from Payne Knight:

"A female Pantheitic figure in silver, with the borders of the drapery plated with gold, and the whole finished in a manner surpassing almost anything extant, was among the things found at Macon on the Saone, in the year 1764, and published by Caylus. It represents Cybele, the universal

---

[29] Jennings, Phallicism.

mother, with the mural crown on her head, and the wings of pervasion growing from her shoulders, mixing the productive elements of heat and moisture by making a libation upon the flames of an altar. On each side of her head is one of the Discouri, signifying the alternate influence of the diurnal and nocturnal Sun; and, upon a crescent supported by the tips of her wings, are the seven planets, each signified by a bust of its presiding deity resting upon a globe, and placed in the order of the days of the week named after them.

In her left hand she holds two cornucopiae, to signify the result of her operation on the two hemispheres of the Earth; and upon them are the busts of Apollo and Diana, the presiding deities of these hemispheres, with a golden disk, intersected by two transverse lines, such as is observed on other pieces of ancient art, and such as the barbarians of the North employed to represent the solar year, divided into four parts, at the back of each."[30]

It was doubtless at a time when woman constituted the head of the gens, and when the feminine element in the sun, in human beings, and in Nature generally was regarded as the more important, that Latona and her son Apollo were worshipped together. Latona, Apollo, and Diana constituted the triune God. The last two were the female and male energies, the former being the source whence they sprang. As soon as one is divested of a belief in the popular but erroneous opinion that the gods of the early Egyptians and Greeks were deified heroes of former ages, he is prepared to perceive the fact that, although to the uninitiated these gods appear numberless, in reality they all represent the same idea, namely: the dual, moving force in Nature, together with Light or Wisdom.

We have seen that when among the nations of antiquity civilization had reached its height, the god-idea was

---

[30] Symbolism of Ancient Art.

represented by the figure of a woman with her child; subsequently, however, as these nations began to decline, the creative energy comprehended simply physical life, or the power to reproduce, and was represented by various emblems which will be noticed farther on in this work. In still later ages, after male reproductive power had become God, and when, through superstition and sensuality, the masses of the people had descended to the rank of slaves, monarchs, representing themselves to their ignorant subjects as the source of all blessings, even of life itself, appropriated the titles of the sun, and claimed for themselves the adoration which had formerly belonged to it. From this fact has doubtless arisen the opinion so tenaciously upheld in recent times, that the gods of the ancients were only deified heroes of former times.

If, during the earlier ages of human existence, all the gods resolved themselves into the sun, and if Light and Life, or Wisdom and the power to reproduce and sustain life, constituted the Deity, then of course God or the sun would be female or male, or both, according to the prevailing belief in the comparative creative and sustaining forces of the sexes.

From what appears in the foregoing pages the fact has doubtless been perceived that the worship of a Virgin and Child does not, as is usually supposed, belong exclusively to the Romish Christian Church, but, on the contrary, that it constitutes the most remote idea of a Creator extant. As has been hinted, there is little doubt that the earliest worship of the woman and child was much simpler than was that which came to prevail in later ages, at a time when every religious conception was closely veiled beneath a mixture of astrology and mythology. After the planets came to be regarded as active agencies in reproduction, and powerful in directing all mundane affairs, the Virgin of the Sphere while she represented Nature was also the constellation which appeared above the horizon at the winter solstice, or at the time when the sun had reached its lowest point and had begun to return. At this time, the 25th of December, and just as the days began to lengthen, this Virgin gave birth to the Sun-God. It is said that he issued forth from her side, hence the legend that Gotama Buddha was produced from the side of Maya, and also the story believed by the Gnostics and other Christian sects that Jesus was taken from the side of Mary.[31]

Within the churches and in the streets of many cities of Germany are to be observed figures of this traditional Virgin. She is standing, one foot upon a crescent and the other on a serpent's head, in the mouth of which is the sprig of an apple tree on which is an apple. The tail of the serpent is wound about a globe which is partially enveloped in clouds. On one arm of the Virgin is the Child, and in the hand of the other arm she carries the sacred lotus. Her head is encircled with a halo of light similar to the rays of the sun.

One is frequently disposed to query: Do the initiated in the Romish Church regard these images as legitimate representations of Mary, the wife of Joseph and Mother of Christ, or are they aware of their true significance? Certainly the various accessories attached to this figure betray its ancient origin and reveal its identity with the Egyptian, Chaldean, and Phoenician Virgin of the Sphere.

The fact has already been observed that in the original representation of the "Temptation" in the cave temple of India, it is not the woman but the man who is the tempter, and a singular peculiarity observed in connection with this ancient female Deity is that it is SHE and NOT HER SEED who is trampling on the serpent, thus proving that originally woman and not man was worshipped as the Savior. Another significant feature noticed in connection

---

[31] The fact will doubtless be remembered that a similar belief was entertained concerning the birth of Julius Caesar.

with this subject is that the oldest figures which represent this Goddess are black, thus proving that she must have belonged to a dark skinned race.

This image, although black, or dark skinned, had long hair, hence not a negress. The most ancient statue of Ceres was black, and Pausanias says that at a place called Melangea in Arcadia there was a black Venus. In the Netherlands only a few years ago, was a church dedicated to a black goddess. The Virgin of the Sphere who treads on the head of the serpent represents universal womanhood. She is the Virgin of the first book of Genesis and mother of all the Earth. She represents not only creative power but Perceptive Wisdom. Although this Goddess is usually seen with the lotus in her hand, she sometimes carries ripe corn or wheat.

The mother of Gotama Buddha was called Mai or Maya, after the month in which the Earth is arrayed in her most beautiful attire.

Maya is the parent of universal Nature. According to Davis, the mother of Mercury "is the universal genius of Nature which discriminated all things according to their various kinds of species," the same as was Muth of Egypt. Mai is said to mean "one who begins to illuminate." She was in fact the mother of the sun whence everything proceeds. She was matter, within which was concealed spirit.

In the representations of Montfaucon appears the Goddess Isis sitting on the lotus. Her head, upon which is a globe, is surrounded by a radiant circle which evidently represents the sun. On the reverse side is Ieu, the word "which is the usual way of the ecclesiastical authors reading the Hebrew word Jehovah." Referring to this from Montfaucon, Godfrey Higgins observes: "Here Isis, whose veil no mortal shall ever draw aside, the celestial Virgin of the Sphere, is seated on the self-generating sacred lotus and is called Ieu or Jove."[32] She has also the mystic number 608 which stands for the Deity. Her breasts show plainly that it is a female representation, although connected with the figure appears the male emblem to indicate that within her are contained both elements, or that the universe is embodied within the female.

Higgins thinks there is no subject on which more mistakes have been made than on that of the Goddess Isis, both by ancients and moderns. He calls attention to the inconsistency of calling her the moon when in many countries the moon is masculine. He is quite positive that if Isis is the moon, Ceres, Proserpine, Venus, and all the other female gods were the same, which in view of the facts everywhere at hand cannot be true. It is true, however, that "the planet called the moon was dedicated to her in judicial astrology, the same as a planet was dedicated to Venus or Mars. But Venus and Mars were not these planets themselves, though these planets were sacred to them."[33] Higgins then calls attention to her temple at Sais in Egypt, and to the inscription which declares that "she comprehends all that is and was and is to be," that she is "parent of the sun," and he justly concludes that Isis can not be the moon.

Apuleius makes Isis say:

"I am the parent of all things, the sovereign of the elements, the primary progeny of time, the most exalted of the deities, the first of the heavenly gods and goddesses, whose single deity the whole world venerates in many forms, with various rites and various names. The Egyptians worship me with proper ceremonies and call me by my true name, Queen Isis."

---

[32] Anacalypsis, book v., ch. iv.
[33] Anacalypsis, book vi., ch. ii.

Isis, we are told, is called Myrionymus, or goddess with 10,000 names. She is the Persian Mithra, which is the same as Buddha, Minerva, Venus, and all the rest.

Faber admits that the female principle was formerly regarded as the Soul of the World. He says:

"Isis was the same as Neith or Minerva; hence the inscription at Sais was likewise applied to that goddess. Athenagoras informs us that Neith or the Athene of the Greeks was supposed to be Wisdom passing and diffusing itself through all things. Hence it is manifest that she was thought to be the Soul of the World; for such is precisely the character sustained by that mythological personage."[34]

The same writer says further:

"Ovid gives a similar character to Venus. He represents her as moderating the whole world; as giving laws to Heaven, Earth, and Ocean, as the common parent both of gods and men, and as the productive cause both of corn and trees. She is celebrated in the same manner by Lucretius, who ascribes to her that identical attribute of universality which the Hindoos give to their Goddess Isi or Devi."[35]

It seems to be the general belief of all writers whose object is to disclose rather than conceal the ancient mysteries, that until a comparatively recent time the moon was never worshipped as Isis. Until the origin and meaning of the ancient religion had been forgotten, and the ideas underlying the worship of Nature had been lost, the moon was never regarded as representing the female principle.

When man began to regard himself as the only important factor in procreation, and when the sun became masculine and heat or passion constituted the god-idea, the moon was called Isis. The moon represented the absence of heat, it therefore contained little of the recognized god-

---

[34] Pagan Idolatry, book i., p. 170.
[35] Ibid.

element. It was, perhaps, under the circumstances, a fitting emblem for woman.

In the sacred writings of the Hindoos there is an account of the moon, Soma, having been changed into a female called Chandra, "the white or silvery one."

While speaking of the moon, Kalisch says: "The whole ritual of the Phoenician Goddess Astarte with whom that Queen of Heaven is identical, and who was the goddess of fertility seems to have been transferred to her."[36]

To such an extent, in the earlier ages of the world had the female been regarded as the Creator, that in many countries where her worship subsequently became identified with that of the moon, Luna was adored as the producer of the sun. According to the Babylonian creation tablets, the moon was the most important heavenly body. In later ages, the gender of the sun and the moon seems to be exceedingly variable. The Achts of Vancouver's Island worship sun and moon–the sun as female, the moon as male.[37] In some of the countries of Africa the moon is adored as female and sun-worship is unknown. Among various peoples the sun and the moon are regarded as husband and wife, and among others as brother and sister. In some countries, both are female. I can find no instance in which both are male. Hindoos and Aztecs alike, at one time, said that Luna was male and often that the sun was female.

The fact that among the Persians the moon as well as the sun was at a certain period regarded as a source of procreative energy and as influencing the generative processes, is shown by various passages in the Avestas. In the Khordah Avesta, praise is offered to "the Moon which contains the seed of cattle, to the only begotten Bull, to the Bull of many kinds."

---

[36] Historical and Critical Commentary of the Old Testament.
[37] Tylor, Primitive Culture, vol. ii., p. 272.

Perhaps the most widely diffused and universally adored representation of the ancient female Deity in Egypt was the Virgin Neit or Neith, the Athene of the Greeks and the Minerva of the Romans. Her name signifies "I came from myself." This Deity represents not only creative power, but abstract intelligence, Wisdom or Light. Her temple at Sais was the largest in Egypt. It was open at the top and bore the following inscription: "I am all that was and is and is to be; no mortal has lifted up my veil, and the fruit which I brought forth was the sun." She was called also Muth, the universal mother. Kings were especially honored in the title "Son of Neith."

To express the idea that the female energy in the Deity comprehended not alone the power to bring forth, but that it involved all the natural powers, attributes, and possibilities of human nature, it was portrayed by a pure Virgin who was also a mother. According to Herodotus, the worship of Minerva was indigenous in Lybia, whence it travelled to Egypt and was carried from thence to Greece. Among the remnants of Egyptian mythology, the figure of a mother and child is everywhere observed. It is thought by various writers that the worship of the black virgin and child found its way to Italy from Egypt.

The change noted in the growth of the religious idea by which the male principle assumes the more important position in the Deity may, by a close investigation of the facts at hand, be easily traced, and, as has before been expressed, this change will be found to correspond with that which in an earlier age of the world took place in the relative positions of the sexes. In all the earliest representations of the Deity, the fact is observed that within the mother element is contained the divinity adored, while the male appears as a child and dependent on the ministrations of the female for existence and support. Gradually, however, as the importance of man begins to be recognized in human affairs, we find that the male energy in the Deity, instead of appearing as a child in the arms of its mother, is represented as a man, and that he is of equal importance with the woman; later he is identical with the sun, the woman, although still a necessary factor in the god-idea, being concealed or absorbed within the male. It is no longer woman who is to bruise the serpent's head, but the seed of the woman, or the son. He is Bacchus in Greece, Adonis in Syria, Christna in India. He is indeed the new sun which is born on the 25th of December, or at the time when the solar orb has reached its lowest position and begins to ascend. It is not perhaps necessary to add that he is also the Christ of Bethlehem, the son of the Virgin.

Nowhere, perhaps, is the growing importance of the male in the god-idea more clearly traced than in the history of the Arabians. Among this people are still to be found certain remnants of the matriarchal age–an age in which women were the recognized heads of families and the eponymous leaders of the gentes or clans. Concerning the worship of a man and woman as god by the early Arabians, Prof. Robertson Smith remarks:

"Except the comparatively modern Isaf and Naila in the sanctuary at Mecca where there are traditions of Syrian influence, I am not aware that the Arabs had pairs of gods represented as man and wife. In the time of Mohammed the female deities, such as Al-lat, were regarded as daughters of the supreme male God. But the older conception as we see from a Nabataean inscription in De Vogue, page 119, is that Al-lat is mother of the gods. At Petra the mother-goddess and her son were worshipped together, and there are sufficient traces of the same thing elsewhere to lead us to regard this as having been the general rule when a god and goddess were worshipped in one sanctuary."[38]

As the worship of the black virgin and child is connected with the earliest religion of which we may catch

---

[38] Kinship and Marriage in Early Arabia, ch. vi., p. 179.

a glimpse, the exact locality in which it first appeared must be somewhat a matter of conjecture, but that this idea constituted the Deity among the Ethiopian or early Cushite race, the people who doubtless carried civilization to Egypt, India, and Chaldea, is quite probable.

If we bear in mind the fact that the gods of the ancients represented principles and powers, we shall not be surprised to find that Muth, Neith, or Isis, who was creator of the sun, was also the first emanation from the sun. Minerva is Wisdom–the Logos, the Word. She is Perception, Light, etc. At a later stage in the history of religion, all emanations from the Deity are males who are "Saviors."

That the office of the male as a creative agency is dependent on the female, is a fact so patent that for ages the mother principle could not be eliminated from the conception of a Deity, and the homage paid to Athene or Minerva, even after women had become only sexual slaves and household tools, shows the extent to which the idea of female supremacy in Nature and in the Deity had taken root.

Notwithstanding the efforts which during numberless ages were made to dethrone the female principle in the god-idea, the Great Mother, under some one of her various appellations, continued, down to a late period in the history of the human race, to claim the homage and adoration of a large portion of the inhabitants of the globe. And so difficult was it, even after the male element had declared itself supreme, to conceive of a creative force independently of the female principle, that oftentimes, during the earlier ages of their attempted separation, great confusion and obscurity are observed in determining the positions of male deities. Zeus who in later times came to be worshipped as male was formerly represented as "the great dyke, the terrible virgin who breathes out on crime, anger, and death." Grote refers to numerous writers as authority for the statement that Dionysos, who usually appears in Greece as masculine, and who was doubtless the Jehovah of the Jews, was indigenous in Thrace, Phrygia, and Lydia as the Great Mother Cybele. He was identical with Bacchus, who although represented on various coins as a "bearded venerable figure" appears with the limbs, features, and character of a beautiful young woman. Sometimes this Deity is portrayed with sprouting horns, and again with a crown of ivy. The Phrygian Attis and the Syrian Adonis, as represented in monuments of ancient art, are androgynous personifications of the same attributes. According to the testimony of the geographer Dionysius, the worship of Bacchus was formerly carried on in the British Islands in exactly the same manner as it had been in an earlier age in Thrace and on the banks of the Ganges.

In referring to the Idean Zeus in Crete, to Demeter at Eleusis, to the Cabairi in Samothrace, and Dionysos at Delphi and Thebes, Grote observes: "That they were all to a great degree analogous, is shown by the way in which they necessarily run together and become confused in the minds of various authors."

Concerning Sadi, Sadim, or Shaddai, Higgins remarks:

"Parkhurst tells us it means all-bountiful–the pourer forth of blessings; among the Heathen, the Dea Multimammia; in fact the Diana of Ephesus, the Urania of Persia, the Jove of Greece, called by Orpheus the Mother of the Gods, each male as well as female–the Venus Aphrodite; in short, the genial powers of Nature."

To which Higgins adds: "And I maintain that it means the figure which is often found in collections of ancient statues, most beautifully executed, and called the Hermaphrodite."

As in the old language there was no neuter gender, the gods must always appear either as female or male. For apparent reasons, in all the translations, through the pronouns and adjectives used, the more important ancient deities have all been made to appear as males.

By at least two ancient writers Jupiter is called the Mother of the Gods. In reference to a certain Greek appellation, Bryant observes that it is a masculine name for a feminine deity–a name which is said to be a corruption of Mai, the Hindoo Queen of Heaven.

In process of time, as the world became more and more masculinized, so important did it become that the male should occupy the more exalted place in the Deity, that even the Great Mother of the Gods, as we have seen, is represented as male.

The androgynous or plural form of the ancient Phoenician God Aleim, the Creator referred to in the opening chapter of Genesis, is clearly apparent. This God, speaking to his counterpart, Wisdom, the female energy, says: "Let us make man in our own image, in our own likeness," and accordingly males and females are produced. By those whose duty it has been in the past to prove that the Deity here represented is composed only of the masculine attributes, we are given to understand that God was really "speaking to himself," and that in his divine cogitations excessive modesty dictated the "polite form of speech"; he did not, therefore, say exactly what he meant, or at least did not mean precisely what he said. We have to bear in mind, however, that as man had not at that time been created, if there were no female element present, this excess of politeness on the part of the "Lord" was wholly lost. Surely, in a matter involving such an enormous stretch of power as the creation of man independently of the female energy, we would scarcely expect to find the high and mighty male potentate which was subsequently worshipped as the Lord of the Israelites laying aside his usual "I the Lord," simply out of deference to the animals.

In Christian countries, during the past eighteen hundred years, the greatest care has been exercised to conceal the fact that sun-worship underlies all forms of religion, and under Protestant Christianity no pains has been spared in eliminating the female element from the god-idea; hence the ignorance which prevails at the present time in relation to the fact that the Creator once comprehended the forces of Nature, which by an older race were worshipped as female.

Chapter IV.
The Dual God of the Ancients a Trinity Also

Although the God of the most ancient people was a dual Unity, in later ages it came to be worshipped as a Trinity. When mankind began to speculate on the origin of the life principle, they came to worship their Deity in its three capacities as Creator, Preserver, and Destroyer or Regenerator, each of which was female and male. We have observed that, according to Higgins, when this Trinity was spoken of collectively, it was called after the feminine plural.

By the various writers who have dealt with this subject during the last century, much surprise has been manifested over the fact that for untold ages the people of the earth have worshipped a Trinity. Forster, in his Sketches of Hindoo Mythology, says: "One circumstance which forcibly struck my attention was the Hindoo belief of a Trinity."

Maurice, in his Indian Antiquities, observes that the idea of three persons in the Deity was diffused amongst all the nations of the earth, in regions as distant as Japan and Peru, that it was memorially acknowledged throughout the whole extent of Egypt and India, "flourishing with equal vigor amidst the snowy mountains of Thibet, and the vast deserts of Siberia." The idea of a Trinity is supposed to have been first elaborated on the banks of the Indus, whence it was carried to the Greek and Latin nations. Astrologically the triune Deity of the ancients portrayed the processes of Nature.

This recondite doctrine as understood by the very ancient people which originated it, involved a knowledge of Nature far too deep to be appreciated or understood by their degenerate descendants, except perhaps by a few philosophers and scholars who imbibed it in a modified form from original sources in the far East.

After the establishment of the Trinity, the creative energy, which had formerly been represented by a mother and child, came to be figured by the mother, father, and the life derived therefrom. Sometimes the Trinity took the form of the two creative forces, female and male, and the Great Mother.

Whenever the two creative principles were considered separately, there always appeared stationed over or above them, as their Creator, an indivisible unity. This Creator was the "Beyond," the "most High God"–Om or Aleim. It was the Mother of the Gods in whom were contained all the elements of the Deity. Among the representations of the god-idea which are to be observed on the monuments and in the temples of Egypt appear triads, each of which is composed of a woman stationed between a male figure and that of a child. She is depicted as the Light of the sun, or Wisdom, while the male is manifested as the Heat of the orb of day. She is crowned and always bears the male symbol of life– the crux-ansata.

Later, it is observed that the worship of Light has in a measure given place to the adoration of Heat, in other words Light is no longer adored as essence of the Deity, Heat or Passion having become the most important element in creative power.

After the ancient worship of the Virgin and Child had become somewhat changed or modified so as to better accommodate itself to the growing importance of the male, the most exalted conception of the Deity in Egypt seems to have been that of a trinity composed of Mout the Mother, Ammon the Father, and Chons the Infant Life derived from the other two. Mout is identical with Neith, but she has become the wife as well as the mother of Ammon. Directly below this conception of the Deity is a triad representing less exalted attributes, or lower degrees of wisdom, under the appellations of Sate, Kneph, and the child Anouk; and thus downward, through the varying spheres of celestial light and life involved in their theogony are observed the divine creative energies represented under the figures of Mother, Father, and the Life proceeding therefrom, until, finally, when the earth is reached, Isis, Osiris, and Horus appear as the representation of the creative forces in human beings, and therefore as the embodiment of the divine in the human.

The Deity invoked in all the earlier inscriptions is a triad, and we are assured that in Babylonia, where Beltis is associated with Belus, "no god appears without a goddess."

The supreme Deity of Assyria was Asshur, who was worshipped sometimes as female, sometimes as male. This God doubtless represents the dual or triple creative principle observed in all the earlier forms of worship. Asshur had no distinct temple, but as her position was at the head of the Pantheon, all the shrines throughout Assyria were supposed to have been open to her worship.

According to Bunsen, in the Sidonian Tyrian district, there were originally three great gods, at the head of which appears Astarte–a woman who represents pure reason or intelligence; then follows Zeus, Demarius, and Adorus. Without doubt this triad represents a monad Deity similar in character to the one observed in Egypt and other countries.

In the minds of all well-informed persons, there is no longer any doubt that in Abraham's time the Canaanites worshipped the same gods as did the Persians and all the other nations about them– namely, Elohim, the dual or triune creative force in Nature. As the Sun was the source whence proceeded all light and life as well as reproductive or generative power, it had become the object of adoration, and as the emblem of the Deity, it was worshipped by all the nations of the earth in its three capacities as Creator, Preserver, and Destroyer or Regenerator each female and male.

Melchizedek, who was a priest of the most high God, blessed Abraham, who was a worshipper of the same Deity. On this subject Dr. Shuckford says:

"It is evident that Abraham and his descendants worshipped not only the true and living God, but they invoked him in the name of the Lord, and they worshipped the Lord whose name they invoked, so that two persons were the object of their worship, God and this Lord: and the Scriptures have distinguished these two persons from one another by this circumstance, that God no man hath seen at any time nor can see but the Lord whom Abraham and his descendants worshipped was the person who appeared to them."

We are told that when chap. xxi., verse 33, of Genesis is correctly translated, Abraham is represented as having invoked Jehovah, the everlasting God.

In the Hebrew name Yod-He-Vau (Jehovah), was set forth the triune character of the Creator; in other words, this name "comprehended the essential perfections of the great God," and was used in their Scriptures as a "kind of summary or revelation of the attributes of the Deity."

Although Abraham, while in Egypt, was the worshipper of idols, we are assured that "the peculiar privilege vouchsafed to him lay in the revelation of God's holy name, Yod-He-Vau. There is indeed much evidence going to prove that the people represented by Abraham understood the earlier conception of a Deity, and that while the great universal principle whose name it was sacrilege to pronounce was still acknowledged, there was another God (the Lord), the same as in China, whose worship they were beginning to adopt. "And Jacob vowed a vow, saying, If God will be with me, and will keep me in this way that I go, and will give me bread to eat, and raiment to put on,

So that I come again to my Father's house in peace; then shall the Lord be my God."

He then declared that the pillar or stone which he had set up, and which was the emblem of male procreative energy, should be God's house.

As at the time represented by Jacob there was evidently little or no spirituality among the Israelites, this Lord whom they worshipped was simply a life-giver in the most material or practical sense.

The reproductive energy in man had become deified. It had, in other words, come to possess all the attributes of a god, or of a powerful man, which in reality was the same thing. It is this god personified which is represented as appearing to Abraham and talking with him face to face. With this same god Jacob wrestled, while the real God–the dual or triune principle, the Jehovah or Iav, no man could behold and live.

To conceal the fact that the God of Abraham originally consisted of a dual or triple unity, and that the Deity was identical in significance with that of contemporary peoples, the priests have, as usual, had recourse to a trick to deceive the ignorant or uninitiated. In reference to this subject Godfrey Higgins says:

"In the second book of Genesis the creation is described not to have been made by Aleim, or the Aleim, but by a God of a double name Ieue Aleim; which the priests have translated Lord God. By using the word Lord, their object evidently is to conceal from their readers several difficulties which afterward arise respecting the names of God and this word, and which show clearly that the books of the Pentateuch are the writings of different persons."[39]

Upon this subject Bishop Colenso observes:

"And it is especially to be noted that when the Elohistic passages are all extracted and copied one after another, they form a complete, connected narrative; from which we infer that these must have composed the original story, and that the other passages were afterwards inserted by another writer, who wished to enlarge or supplement the primary record. And he seems to have used the compound Jehovah Aleim in the first portion of his work in order to impress upon the reader that Jehovah, of whom he goes on to speak in the later portions, is the same Great Being who is called simply Elohim by the older writer, and notably in the first account of the creation."[40]

We are informed by Bunsen that El, or Elohim, comprehends the true significance of the Deity among all the Aramaic or Canaanitish races, El representing the abstract principle taken collectively, Elohim pertaining to the separate elements as Creator, Preserver, and Regenerator. Each of these Canaanitish races had inherited these ideas from their fathers, and, although they had become grossly idolatrous, "Moses knew, and educated Israelites remained a long time conscious, that they used them not merely in their real but in their most ancient sense."[41] Maurice and other writers call attention to the fact that Moses himself uses this word Elohim with verbs and adjectives in the plural. That the God worshipped by the more ancient peoples, namely Aleim, or Elohim, the same who said, "Let us make man in our image," was not the Lord adored at a later age by the Jews, is a fact which at the present time seems to be clearly proven; that it constituted, however, the dual or triune unity venerated by all the

---

[39] Anacalypsis, book ii., ch, i.
[40] Lectures on the Pentateuch and the Moabite Stone, p. 7.
[41] Bunsen, History of Egypt, vol. iv., p. 421.

nations on the globe of which we have any record, appears to be well established.

We have seen that although the two sex-principles which underlie Nature constituted the Creator, the ancients thought of it only as one and indivisible. This indivisible aspect was the sacred Iav, the Holy of Holies. When it was contemplated in its individual aspect it was Creator, Preserver, and Destroyer, each of which was female and male.

The difficulty of the ancients in establishing a First Cause seems to have been exactly the same as is ours at the present time. When we say there must have been a God who created all things, the question at once arises, Who created God? According to their theories, nothing could be brought forth without the interaction of two creative principles, female and male; yet everything, even these principles, must proceed from an indivisible energy–an energy which, as the idea of the sex functions became more and more clearly defined, could not be contemplated except in its dual aspect. So soon, therefore, as the Great First Cause was separated into its elements, a still higher power was immediately stationed above it as its Creator. This Creator was designated as female. It was the Mother idea Even gods could not be produced without a mother.

In referring to the doctrines contained in the Geeta, one of the sacred writings of the Hindoos, Faber observes:

"In the single character of Brahm, all the three offices of Brahma, Vishnu, and Siva are united. He is at once the Creator, the Preserver, and the Destroyer. He is the primeval Hermaphrodite, or the Great Father and the Great Mother blended together in one person."

The fact that a trinity in unity, representing the female and male energies symbolized by the organs of generation, formerly constituted the Deity throughout Asia is acknowledged by all those who have examined either the literature or monumental records of oriental countries. The

Rev. Mr. Maurice bears testimony to the character of Eastern religious ideas in the following language:

"Whoever will read the Geeta with attention, will perceive in that small tract the outlines of all the various systems of theology in Asia. The curious and ancient doctrine of the Creator being both male and female, mentioned on a preceding page, to be designated in Indian temples by a very indecent exhibition of the masculine and feminine organs of generation in union, occurs in the following passage: 'I am the Father and Mother of this world; I plant myself upon my own nature and create again and again this assemblage of beings; I am generation and dissolution, the place where all things are deposited, and the inexhaustible seed of all Nature. I am the beginning, the middle, and the end of all things.'"[42]

According to Sir W. Jones, the Brahme, Vishnu, and Siva coalesce to form the mystic Om, which means the essence of life or divine fire. In the Bhagavat Geeta the supreme God speaks thus concerning itself: "I am the holy one worthy to be known"; and immediately adds: "I am the mystic [trilateral] figure Om; the Reig, the Yagush, and the Saman Vedas." It is a unity and still a trinity. This Om or Aum stands for the Creator, Preserver, and Destroyer or Regenerator, and represents the threefold aspect of the force within the sun. The doctrine maintained throughout the Geeta is not only that the great life-force represents a trinity in unity, but that it is both female and male. On this subject Maurice, in his Indian Antiquities, says:

"This notion of three persons in the Deity was diffused amongst all the nations of the earth, established at once in regions so distant as Japan and Peru, immemorially acknowledged throughout the whole extent of Egypt and India, and flourishing with equal vigor amidst the snowy mountains of Thibet, and the vast deserts of Siberia."

---

[42] Maurice, Indian Antiquities, vol. iv., p. 705.

We have observed that the idea of a trinity as conceived by the so-called ancients, although at all times founded on the same conception, viz., that of the reproductive powers of Nature and especially of mankind, differed in expression according to its application. Although in human beings this triune creative idea was expressed by the mother, father, and child, as set forth in the temples and on the monuments of Egypt, when applied directly to the sun and the planets, it appears as the Creator, Preserver, and Regenerator or Destroyer.

Destruction, or the absence of the sun's heat, represented by winter, was necessary to life, and therefore the Destroyer was also the Regenerator and equally with the Creator and Preserver constituted a beneficent factor in the god-idea. In fact as this third element really embodied the substance of the other two, it finally became the supreme God, little afterward being heard about the Creator and Preserver. The Regenerator or Destroyer was of course the sun, which in winter died away and rose again in the spring-time as a beneficent Savior or renewer of life. The principle involved in these processes represented Fertility, Life, reproductive energy. As applied to mortals, it comprehended the power to create combined with perceptive Wisdom or Knowledge.

This idea, portrayed as it was by a mother and her child, linked woman with the stars. It produced the "Virgin of the Sphere," Queen of Heaven, "Isiac Controller of the Zodiac," at the same time that it made her the mother of all mankind.

Every year this Virgin of the Sphere as she appeared above the horizon at the winter solstice gave birth to the sun. Astronomically this new sun was the Regenerator, by which all Nature was renewed. Mythologically, after the higher truths contained in these doctrines were lost, it came to be the Savior, the Son of the Virgin, the seed of the woman, which was to bruise the serpent's head.

That the religion of an ancient race comprehended a knowledge of the evolutionary processes of Nature may not be doubted. The myths still extant, and even the oldest Assyrian inscriptions which have been deciphered, reveal the fact that the seeds of the visible universe were hidden in the "great deep"–that animal creation sprang from the earth and the sea through the influence of the sun's rays.

It is now known that the philosophy of an older race involved a belief in the Eternity of Matter. The abstruse doctrine of Reincarnation and the Renewal of Worlds seems to have formed the basis of their philosophy. According to these speculations, a portion of the earth was destroyed or resolved into its primary elements every six hundred years, while at the end of each Kalpia, or great Cycle of several thousand years, the entire earth was renovated or absorbed into the two fecundating principles of the universe. These two indivisible forces represented by Vishnu rested in the water, or brooded on the face of the deep. When stirred by love for each other they again became active, and from the germs of a former world, which had been absorbed by themselves, created again the earth and everything upon it. In other words, "the earth sprang from the navel of Vishnu or Brahme." According to the Buddhists of Ceylon, the universe has perished ten different times, and each time has been renewed by the operations of Nature, or by the preservation of germs from a former world. In their mythology these germs are represented by a parent and a triplicated offspring. It is perhaps unnecessary to add that this monad trinity is the Creator, Preserver, and Destroyer with their great parent, the Mother of the Gods, which in process of time came to be regarded as male. According to Wilford, Hindoo chronology presents fourteen different periods, six of which have already elapsed; we are in the seventh, which began with the flood. Each of these periods is called a Manwantara, the presiding genius or Deity of which is a

Menu. At the close of each dynasty a total destruction of the world takes place, everything being destroyed except the ruler, or Menu, who "escapes in a boat." Each new world is an exact counterpart of the one destroyed, and each Menu is a representation of all preceding ones. Thus the history of one dynasty serves for all the rest. This doctrine of a triplicated Deity appearing at the beginning of a new creation may be traced in nearly every country of the globe. Among the Buddhists of China, Fo is mysteriously multiplied into three persons in the same manner as is Fo-hi, who is evidently Noah. Among the Hindoos is observed the triad Brahma, Vishnu, and Siva springing from the monad Brahm or Brahme. This triad appears on the earth at the beginning of each Manwantara in the human form of Menu and his three sons. We are assured that among the Tartars evident traces are found of a similar God, who is seated on the lotus. It is also figured on a Siberian medal in the imperial collection at St. Petersburg. The Jakuthi Tartars, who are said to be the most numerous people of Siberia, worship a triplicated Deity under the three denominations of Artugon and Schugo-tangon and Tangara. Faber tells us that this Tartar God is the same even in appellation with the Tanga-tanga of the Peruvians, who, like other tribes of America, seem plainly to have crossed over from the North-eastern extremity of Siberia. Upon this subject the same writer remarks thus:

"Agreeably to the mystical notion so familiar to the Hindoos, that the self-triplicated Great Father yet remained but one in essence, the Peruvians supposed their Tanga-tanga to be one in three, and three in one: and in consequence of the union of hero worship with the astronomical and material systems of idolatry they venerated the sun and the air, each under three images and three names. The same opinions equally prevailed throughout the nations which lie to the west of Hindostan. Thus the Persians had their Ormuzd, Mithras, and Ahriman:

or, as the matter was sometimes represented, their self-triplicating Mithras. The Syrians had their Monimus, Aziz, and Ares. The Egyptians had their Emeph, Eicton, and Phtha. The Greeks and Romans had their Jupiter, Neptune, and Pluto; three in number, though one in essence, and all springing from Cronus, a fourth, yet older God. The Canaanites had their Baal-Spalisha or self-triplicated Baal. The Goths had their Odin, Vile, and Ve, who are described as the three sons of Bura, the offspring of the mysterious cow, and the Celts had their three bulls, venerated as the living symbols of the triple Hu or Menu. To the same class we must ascribe the triads of the Orphic and Pythagorean and Platonic schools; each of which must again be identified with the imperial triad of the old Chaldaic or Babylonian philosophy."[43]

The history of the catastrophe known as the deluge, which, it is claimed, took place either in Armenia, at Cashgar, or at some other place in the East, is observed, in later ages, to furnish a covering beneath which have been veiled the mythical doctrines of the priests. Of the catastrophes which from time to time have visited our planet, and of the belief which has come to be entertained by ecclesiastics that the earth will be destroyed by fire, Celsus writes:

"The belief has spread among them, from a misunderstanding of the accounts of these occurrences, that after lengthened cycles of time, and the returns and conjunctions of planets, conflagrations, and floods are wont to happen, and because after the last flood, which took place in the time of Deucalion, the lapse of time, agreeably to the vicissitude of all things, requires a conflagration; and this made them give utterance to the erroneous opinion that God will descend, bringing fire like a torturer."[44]

---

[43] Faber, Pagan Idolatry, book vi., ch. ii., p. 470.
[44] Origen against Celsus, book iv., ch. xi.

The mythologies of all nations are largely founded upon the "religious history" of a flood. The doctrine of a triplicated God saved from destruction by a storm-tossed ark which rested on some local mountain answering to Ararat, and which was filled with the natural elements of reproduction, is found amongst the traditions of every country of the globe. In Egypt, the destructive agency drives the God into the ark–or into the fish's belly, where he is obliged to remain until the flood subsides. In other words, at the time of the destruction of the world, the creative agency is forced within the womb of Nature, there to remain until it again comes forth to recreate the world; nor does the symbolism end here, for this God–the sun, or the reproductive power within it, which every year is put to death by the cold of winter, must for a season remain lifeless, but, at the proper time, will come forth with healing in his wings. This God must issue forth to life through female Nature.

The god-man, Noah, who appears under one appellation or another in all extant mythologies, was slain, or shut up in a box, ark, or chest in which he or his seed was preserved from the ravages of a mighty flood, or from destruction by the calamity which had befallen the rest of mankind. In one sense he represents a Savior, in another sense he is the saved, for he is the seed of a former world and is born again from a boat, a symbol which always represents the female energy. Sometimes he is shut up in a wooden cow, from which he issues forth to new life. Again this storm tossed mariner is born from a cave, or the door of a rocky cavern, within which he had been preserved from some terrible catastrophe, caused either by water or fire.

Sir W. Jones, Faber, Higgins, and many others who have investigated this subject are confident that the Noah of Genesis is identical with Menu, the law-giver of India, and that both are Adam, a man who appears with his three sons at the end of each cycle, or six hundred years, to renovate the world. In the six hundred and first year of Noah's life, in the first month, on the first day of the month, the waters were dried up from the earth. The drying of the waters, and the beginning anew just at the close of the six hundred years, are thought to refer to the end of the cycle of the Neros. A year of Menu or Buddha had expired and a new dynasty or Mamwantara was to begin.

Regarding this trinity, Faber remarks:

"Brahm then at the head of the Indian triad is Menu at the head of his three sons. But that by the first Menu we are to understand Adam, is evident, both from the remarkable circumstance of himself and his consort bearing the titles of Adima and Iva, and from the no less remarkable tradition that one of his three sons was murdered by his brother at a sacrifice. Hence it will follow, that Brahm at the head of the Indian triad is Adam at the head of his three sons, Cain, Abel, and Seth. Each Menu with his triple offspring is only the reappearance of a former Menu with his triple offspring; for, in every such manifestation at the commencement of each Mamwantara, the Hindoo Trimurti, or triad, becomes incarnate, by transmigrating from the human bodies occupied during a former incarnation; Brahm or the Unity appearing as the paternal Menu of a new age, while the triad, Brahma, Vishnu, and Siva, is exhibited in the person of his three sons. . . . But the ark-preserved Menu–Satyavrata and his three sons are certainly Noah and his three sons, Shem, Ham, and Japhet."

Hesiod teaches that, after the flood, Chaos, Night, and black Erebus first appeared.[45] At this time, when there was no Earth, no Heaven, and no Air, an egg floated on the face of the deep, which, being parted, brought forth Love, or Cupid. Out of Chaos this God created or formed all things. Now Cupid is the same as the Greek Phanes, and Phanes is

---

[45] The Theogony.

Noah, the egg being the ark or female principle from which he was produced. The Greek God Phanes is the same as the Egyptian Osiris, who was driven into the ark by the "wind that blasts," or by the evil principle.

"As Cupid is indifferently said to have been produced from an egg at a time when the whole world was in disorder, and from the womb of the marine goddess Venus, the egg and the womb of that goddess must denote the same thing. Accordingly we shall find that, on the one hand, Venus is immediately connected with the symbolical egg; and, on the other hand, that she is identical with Derceto and Isis, and is declared to be that general receptacle out of which all the hero-gods were produced. Now there can be little doubt in what sense we are to understand this expression, when we are told that the peculiar symbol of Isis was a ship; and when we learn that the form assumed at the period of the deluge, by the Indian Isi or Bhavani, who is clearly the same as the Egyptian Isis, was the ship Argha, in which her consort Siva floated securely on the surface of the ocean. Venus, therefore, or the Great Mother, the parent of Cupid from whom all mankind descended, must be the Ark: consequently, the egg, with which she is connected, must be the Ark also. Aristophanes informs us that the egg out of which Love was born, was produced by Night in the bosom of Erebus. But the Goddess Night, as we learn from the Orphic poet, was the very same person as Venus; and he celebrates her as the parent of the Universe, and as the general mother both of the hero-gods and of man. The egg therefore produced by Night was produced by Venus: but Venus and the egg meant the same thing: even that vast floating machine, which was esteemed an epitome of the world, and from which was born that Deity who is also literally said to have been set afloat in an ark. Sometimes the order of production was inverted; and, instead of the egg being produced by Night or Venus, Venus herself was fabled to have been produced from the egg. There is a remarkable legend of this sort which ascribes Venus and her egg to the age of Typhon and Osiris, in other words, to the age in which Noah was compelled by the deluge to enter into the ark."[46]

The Preserver of the Persians, who is seated on a rainbow in front of their rock temples, is Mithras, who is identical with Noah. Sometimes this ancient mariner is represented as riding on the back of a fish, and again as floating in a boat. The God of Hindostan, like the classical Dionysos, was enclosed in an ark and driven into the sea. According to the Gothic traditions as recorded in the Eddas, there once existed a beautiful world, which was destroyed by fire. Another was created, which, with all its inhabitants save a giant and his three sons, who were saved in a ship, were destroyed by water. With this triad, which originally sprang from a mysterious cow, the new world began. This new world, which represents the present system, will in time be devoured by flames; but another earth will arise from the ocean,–an earth far more beautiful than this, upon which all kinds of grain and delicious fruits will grow without cultivation. Veda and Vile will be there, for the conflagration will have been powerless to destroy them. While the flames are devouring all things, two human beings, a female and a male, will be concealed under a hill, where they will feed upon dew, and will propagate so abundantly that the earth will soon be peopled with a new race of beings. During the catastrophe, the sun will be devoured by a wolf, but before her death she will give birth to a daughter as resplendent as herself, who will go in the same path formerly trodden by her mother.

The doctrines of the Gothic philosophers, as they appear in the Eddas, concerning the eternity of matter, the renewal or succession of worlds, and reincarnation are the

---

[46] Origin of Pagan Idolatry, book i., ch. iv.

same as those taught by Pythagoras, the Stoics, and other Greek schools of thought.

Brahme or Vishnu, resting on the bottom of the sea–a goddess who was symbolized by the self-generating lotus– was in later ages the mysterious Cow of the Goths.

After the natural truths concealed beneath their religious symbolism were wholly forgotten, and human nature through the over-stimulation of the animal instincts had become corrupted, Adam and Eve, names which doubtless for ages represented the two fecundating principles throughout Nature, with their sons, Cain, Abel, and Seth, comprehended the god-idea. The fact has been observed that just six hundred years from the creation of Adam, or at the close of the cycle, Noah appears with his three sons to save or perpetuate the race.

It is now believed that this account of Noah and his three sons is an allegory beneath which are concealed the religious doctrines, or perhaps I should say, the philosophical speculations of an older race. The God of the ancients was identified with the life of man individually and with that of mankind collectively. As men die each day, and as every day men are born, this Deity is said to die and to be renewed each day; and as he is the sun, or the incarnation of the sun, the rising and setting of this luminary depict the constantly dying and regenerating God of Nature, the same as do the changing seasons. A similar idea reappears in their system of the renewal of worlds and reincarnation.

Regarding the doctrine of the eternity of matter held by the ancients, Origen mentions a belief of the Egyptians that the

"world or its substance was never produced, but that it has existed from all eternity. Neither is there any such thing as death. Those who perish about us every day are simply changed, either they take on other forms or are removed to some other place. God cannot be destroyed, and as all things are parts of the Deity everything lives and has always lived, seeming death being simply change. Remnants of these doctrines are found in every portion of the globe; among the Mexicans of the west as well as among the rude mountaineers of the Burman Empire."

While contemplating the philosophical speculations of an ancient race Bailly gave expression to the belief, that a "profoundly learned race of people existed previous to the formation of any of our systems." The wiser among the Greek philosophers, those who, it is believed, borrowed their philosophical doctrines from the East, declare that "there is no production of anything which was not before; no new substance made which did not really pre-exist." Equally with matter was spirit indestructible. "Our soul," says Plato, "was somewhere, before it came to exist in this present form; whence it appears to be immortal. . . . Who knows whether that which is demonstrated living, be not indeed rather dying, and whether that which is styled dying be not rather living?"

To one who has given attention to the various legends relative to the destruction of the world by a flood, and a storm-tossed mariner saved in an ark or boat, it is plain that they all have the same significance, all are but different versions of the same myth, which in an early age was used to conceal the philosophical doctrines of an ancient people.

That the early historic nations understood little concerning the origin and true meaning of the legends which they had inherited from an older race is quite evident. The ignorance of the Greeks regarding the significance of these legends is shown by the following: When Solon, wishing to acquaint himself with the history of the oldest times, inquired of an Egyptian priest concerning the time of the flood, and the age of Deucalion or Phroneous or Noah, this functionary replied:

"O Solon, Solon, you Greeks are always children, nor is there an old man among you! Having no ancient traditions nor any acquaintance with chronology, you are as yet in a state of intellectual infancy. The true origin of such mutilated fables as you possess is this. There have been and shall again be in the course of many revolving ages, numerous destructions of the human race; the greatest of them by fire and water, but others in an almost endless succession of shorter intervals."[47]

We have observed that the symbol of the universe was an egg. The egg was also the symbol of the earth and of the ark, which meant universal womanhood. From the mundane egg the triplicated Deity sprang. There can be little doubt at the present time that Adam, Noah, Menu, Osiris, and Dionysos all represent the fructifying power of the sun. In process of time they each came to figure as male reproductive energy, and during certain periods of the earth's history they have each in turn been worshipped as the Deity. That not only the ark was female, but that the god element or reproductive principle within the ark was both female and male, is a fact which has been lost sight of during the historic period, or during those ages of the world in which the attempt has been made to prove Nature motherless.

All the germs and living creatures which were within the ark, and which were to reanimate the earth, were in pairs, females and males; and, besides, the Dove (female), the emblem of peace, was also present. Even Noah himself was produced from an egg, which, as we have seen, is the symbol of Venus, or universal womanhood. In after ages the female principle was not mentioned, but, on the contrary, was concealed beneath convenient symbols; and as the philosophical ideas underlying natural religion were lost or forgotten, and mankind had become too ignorant to perceive that a dual force, female and male which was also a Trinity, pervades Nature, the notion came gradually to

---

[47] Quoted by Plato; also by Clement of Alexandria.

prevail that the creative agency, which is spirit, is altogether male. Hence the formulation of the inconceivable doctrine of a Trinity composed of a Father, Son, and Holy Ghost.

Chapter V.
Separation of the Female and Male Elements in the Deity

Glimpses of antiquity as far back as human ken can reach reveal the fact that in early ages of human society the physiological question of sex was a theme of the utmost importance, while various proofs are at hand showing that throughout the past the question of the relative importance of the female and male elements in procreation has been a fruitful source of religious contention and strife. These struggles, which from time to time involved the entire habitable globe, were of long duration, subsiding only after the adherents of the one sex or the other had gained sufficient ascendancy over the opposite party to successfully erect its altars and compel the worship of its own peculiar gods, which worship usually included a large share of the temporal power. Only since the male sex has gained sufficient influence to control not only human action, but human thought as well, have these contentions subsided.[48]

That religious wars have not been confined to more modern times, and that among an early race the attempt to exalt the male principle met with obstinate resistance which involved mankind in a conflict, the violence of which has

---

[48] At the present time, through causes which are not difficult to understand, the question of the relative importance of the two sexes is again assuming a degree of importance indicative of the changes which are taking place in human thought, and for the reason that we are just witnessing the dawn of an intellectual age, the problems to be solved will admit of no answers other than those based upon a scientific foundation.

never been exceeded, are facts which seem altogether probable. Indeed, there is much evidence going to show that the cause of the original dispersion of a primitive race was the contention which arose respecting their religious faith or regarding the physiological question of the relative importance of the sexes in the function of reproduction; and that the general war indicated in the Puranas, which began in India and extended over the entire habitable globe, and which was celebrated by the poets as "the basis of Grecian mythology," originated in this conflict over the precedence of one or the other of the sex-principles contained in the Deity. Although there are no records of these wars in extant history, accounts of them are still preserved in the traditions and religious monuments of oriental countries. In Egypt, in India, and to a greater or less extent in other Eastern countries, these physiological contests have been disguised under a veil of allegory, the true significance of which it is no longer difficult to understand. With the light which more recent investigation has thrown upon the subject of the separation of the original sex-elements contained in the Deity, the significance of the following legend in the Servarasa is at once apparent.

When Parvati (Devi) was united in marriage to Mahadeva (Siva), the divine pair had once a dispute on the comparative influence of the sexes in producing animated beings, and each resolved by mutual agreement to create a new race of men. The race produced by Mahadeva were very numerous, and devoted themselves exclusively to the worship of the male Deity, but their intellects were dull, their bodies feeble, their limbs distorted, and their complexions of many different hues. Parvati had at the same time created a multitude of human beings, who adored the female power only, and were well shaped, with sweet aspects and fine complexions. A furious contest ensued between the two nations, and the Lingajas, or adorers of the male principle, were defeated in battle, but

Mahadeva, enraged against the Yonigas (the worshippers of the female element), would have destroyed them with the fire of his eye if Parvati had not interposed and appeased him, but he would spare them only on condition that they should instantly leave the country with a promise to see it no more, and from the Yoni, which they adored as the sole cause of their existence, they were named Yavanas.

The fact has been noticed in a previous work[49] that, according to Wilford, the Greeks were the descendants of the Yavanas of India, and that when the Ionians emigrated they adopted the name to distinguish themselves as adorers of the female, in opposition to a strong sect of male worshippers which had been driven from the mother country. We are taught by the Puranas that they settled partly on the borders of Varaha-Dwip, or Europe, where they became the progenitors of the Greeks; and partly in the two Dwipas of Cusha, Asiatic and African. In the Asiatic Cusha-Dwip they supported themselves by violence and rapine. Parvati, however, or their tutelary goddess, Yoni, always protected them; and at length, in the fine country which they occupied, they became a flourishing nation.[50] Wilford relates that there is a sect of Hindoos who, attempting to reconcile the two systems, declare in their allegorical style that "Parvati and Mahadeva found their concurrence essential to the perfection of their offspring, and that Vishnu, at the request of the goddess, effected a reconciliation between them."[51]

The people who were dominant in Asia long before the rise of the late Assyrian monarchy, are said to be those whom scriptural writers represent as Cushim, and the Hindoos as Cushas. They were the descendants of Cush, or Cuth, and were believed to have been the architects of the Tower of Babel. Epiphanius, Eusebius, and others assert

---

[49] See The Evolution of Women, p. 303.
[50] Asiatic Researches, vol. iii., pp. 125-132.
[51] Asiatic Researches, "Egypt and the Nile," vol. iii., pp. 361-363.

that at the time of the building of this tower there existed two rival beliefs, the one demonstrated as Scuthism, the other as Ionism, or Hellenism, the latter of which embodied the worship of the Great Mother, or the female element, which was worshipped in the shape of the mystic "Iona or Dove." The Scuths, on the other hand, believed in the pre-eminence of a Great Father, or, perhaps I should say, in a Deity composed of a triad containing the elements of a male parent. Upon this subject the learned Faber remarks: "I am much mistaken if some dissension on these points did not prevail at Babel itself; and I think there is reason for believing that the altercation between the rival sects aided the confusion of languages in producing the dispersion."[52]

Those who believed in the superiority of the male in the processes of reproduction, adored the male element in the Deity, while those who held that the female is the more important, worshipped the female energy throughout Nature under one or another of its symbols, sometimes as a woman with her child and sometimes as a dove, but oftener as an ark, box, or chest.

It is evident from the sacred writings of the Hindoos that in India, during a period of several thousand years, there existed various sects, those who worshipped the male as the only creative force, others who adored the female as the origin of life, and those who paid homage to both, as alike important in the office of reproduction.

It would seem that the fierce wars which had devastated the land had ceased prior to the beginning of the Tower of Babel. According to the testimony of Moses, the Lord himself declared "Behold the people is one." This unanimity of belief, as is plainly shown, was of short duration, for the Tower arose "upright and defiant," not, however, as an emblem of the primeval dual or triune God in which the female energy was predominant, but as a

---

[52] Pagan Idolatry, book vi., ch. ii.

symbol of male creative power. It was the type of virility which in the subsequent history of religion was to assume the position of the "one only and true God."

It is not improbable that idolatry began with the Tower of Babel.

Indeed it has been confidently asserted by certain writers that the earliest idols set up as emblems of the Deity, or as expressions of the peculiar worship of the Lingajas, were obelisks, columns, or towers, the first of which we have any account being the Tower of Babel, erected probably at Nipur in Chaldea. Until a comparatively recent time, the actual significance of this monument seems to have been little understood. Later research, however, points to the fact that it was a phallic device erected in opposition to a religion which recognized the female element throughout Nature as God. The length of time which the adherents of these two doctrines had contended for the mastery is not known, but through the deciphered monuments of ancient nations, by facts gathered from their sacred writings, and by the general voice of tradition, it has been ascertained with a considerable degree of certainty that this great upheaval of society was the culmination of a dispute which had long been waged between two contending powers, and which finally resulted in a separation of the people, and in the final success, for the time being, of the sect which refused longer to recognize the superior importance of the female in the god-idea.

At what time in the history of mankind the Tower of Babel was erected has not been ascertained, but the great antiquity of Chaldea is no longer questioned. Sir Henry Rawlinson, in the Royal Geographical Journal says:

"When Chaldea was first colonized, or at any rate when the seat of empire was first established there, the emporium of trade seems to have been at Ur of the Chaldees, which is now 150 miles from the sea, the Persian

Gulf having retired nearly that distance before the sediment brought down by the Euphrates and Tigris."

To which Baldwin adds:

"A little reflection on the vast period of time required to effect geological changes so great as this will enable us to see to what a remote age in the deeps of antiquity we must go to find the beginning of civilization in the Mesopotamian Valley."[53]

Although at the time of the building of the Tower of Babel the worship of a Deity in which the male principle was pre-eminent had not become universal, still the facts seem to indicate that the doctrine of male superiority which for ages had been steadily advancing had at length gained the ascendancy over the older religion. The new faith and worship had corrupted the old, and through the conditions which had been imposed upon women, and the consequent stimulation of the lower nature in man, even the adherents of the older faith were losing sight of those higher principles which in preceding ages they had adored as God.

We have seen that in every country upon the earth there is a tradition recounting the ravages of a flood. Whether or not this legend is to be traced to an actual calamity by which a large portion of Asia was inundated, is not for a certainty known; but the fact that there was a deluge of contention and strife, surpassing anything perhaps which the world has ever witnessed, seems altogether probable.

Not long after the catastrophe designated as the flood, emblems of the Deity, representations of the male and female elements, appear in profusion. Babylon, at which place was erected the Tower of Belus, and Memphis, which contained the Pyramids, were among the first cities which were built. As the tower typified the Deity worshipped by those who claimed superiority for the male, so the pyramids

---

[53] Prehistoric Nations, p. 191.

symbolized the creative agency and peculiar qualities of the female, or of the dual Deity which was worshipped as female.

Although the grosser elements in human nature were rapidly assuming a more intensely aggressive attitude, and although the higher principles involved in an earlier religion were in a measure forgotten, it is evident that at this time humanity had not become wholly sensualized, and that the lower propensities and appetites had not assumed dominion over the reasoning faculties.

The Great Mother Cybele, who is represented by the Sphinx, had doubtless been adored as a pure abstraction, her worship being that of the universal female principle in Nature. She is pictured as the "Eldest Daughter of the Mythologies," and as "The Great First Cause." She represented the past and the future. She was the source whence all that was and is had proceeded.

In its earliest representations, the Sphinx is figured with the head of a woman and the body of a lion. By various writers it is stated that the Sphinxes which were brought as spoils from Asia, the very cradle of religion, were thus represented. The lion, which symbolizes royal power and intellectual strength, is always attached to the chariot of Cybele. The Sphinx is supposed to typify not only Cybele, but the great androgynous God of Africa as well. However, as Cybele and Muth portrayed the same idea, namely, female power and wisdom, we are not surprised that they should have been worshipped under the same emblem. Neither is it remarkable, when we recall the fact that the female was supposed to comprehend both sexes, that in certain instances a beard appears as an accompanying feature of the Sphinx. We are told that the fourth avatar of Vishnu was a Sphinx, but a further search into the history of this Deity reveals the fact that her ninth avatar is Brahm (masculine). The female principle has at length succumbed to the predominance of male power, and Vishnu herself has become transformed into a male God.

Although the rites connected with the worship of Cybele were phallic they were absolutely pure. In an allusion to this worship, Hargrave Jennings admits that the "spirituality to which women in that age of the world were observed to be more liable than men was peculiarly adverse to all sensual indulgence, and especially that of the sexes."

Although the creative principle was adored under its representatives, the Yoni and the Lingham, still the principal object seems to have been, when administering the rites pertaining to the worship of Cybele, to ignore sex and the usual sex distinctions; hence we find that, in order to assume an androgynous appearance, the priestesses of this Goddess officiated in the costumes of males, while priests appeared in the dress peculiar to females. However, that the sensuous element was to a certain extent already assuming dominion over the higher nature, and that priests were regarded as being incapable of self-control, is observed in the fact that in the later ages of female worship one of the principal requirements of a priest of Cybele was castration.

It is the opinion of Grote that the story which appears in the Hesiodic Theogony, of the castration of Saturn and Uranus by their sons with sickles forged by the mother, was borrowed from the Phrygians, or from the worship of the Great Mother.

In India, the strictest chastity was prescribed to the priests of Siva, a God which was worshipped as the Destroyer or Regenerator, and which in its earlier conception was the same as the Great Mother Cybele. These priests were frequently obliged to officiate in a nude state, and during the ceremony should it appear that the symbols with which they came in contact had appealed to other than their highest emotions, they were immediately stoned by the people.[54]

The identity of the religions of India and Egypt has been noted in an earlier portion of this work. Wilford, in his dissertations upon Egypt and the Nile, says that in a conversation which he had with some learned Brahmins, upon describing to them the form and peculiarities of the Great Pyramid, they told him that "it was a temple appropriated to the worship of Padma Devi." The true Coptic name of these edifices is Pire Honc, which signifies a sunbeam. Padma Devi means the lotus, or the Deity of generation.

It is thought by many writers that these gigantic structures were erected by the Cushite conquerors of Egypt, who invaded and civilized the country, as emblems of the female Deity whom they worshipped. Certainly the magnitude of these monuments and the ingenuity displayed in their construction indicate the intelligence of their builders and the exalted character of the Deity adored. The Great Pyramid is in the form of a square, each side of whose base is seven hundred and fifty-five feet, and covers an area of nearly fourteen acres. An able writer in describing the pyramids says that the first thing which impresses one is the uniform precision and systematic design apparent in their architecture. They all have their sides accurately adapted to the four cardinal points.

"In six of them which have been opened, the principal passage preserves the same inclination of 26 degrees to the horizon, being directed toward the polar star. . . . Their obliquity being so adjusted as to make the north side coincide with the obliquity of the sun's rays at the summer's solstice, has, combined with the former particulars, led some to suppose they were solely intended for astronomical uses; and certainly, if not altogether true,

---

[54] Sonnerat, Voyage aux Indes, i., 311.

it bespeaks, at all events, an intimate acquaintance with astronomical rules, as well as a due regard to the principles of geometry. Others have fancied them intended for sepulchres; and as the Egyptians, taught by their ancient Chaldean victors, connected astronomy with their funereal and religious ceremonies, they seem in this to be not far astray, if we but extend the application to their sacred bulls and other animals, and not merely to their kings, as Herodotus would have us suppose."[55]

According to the testimony of Inman, the pyramid is an emblem of the Trinity–three in one. The triangle typifies the flame of sacred fire emerging from the holy lamp. With its base upwards it typifies the Delta, or the door through which all come into the world. With its apex uppermost, it is an emblem of the phallic triad. The union of these triangles typifies the male and female principles uniting with each other, thus producing a new figure, a star, while each retains its own identity.[56]

Thus the primary significance of the pyramid was religious, and in its peculiar architectural construction was manifested the prevailing conception of the Deity worshipped; namely, the fructifying energies in the sun. We are informed that "all nations have at one time or another passed through violent stages of pyrolatry, a word which reminds us that fire and phallic cult flourished around the pyramids. . . . Every town in Greece had a Pyrtano."[57]

As not alone the sun but the stars also had come to be venerated as agencies in reproduction, the worship of these objects was, as we have seen, closely interwoven with that of the generative processes throughout Nature. The attempt to solve the great problem of the origin of life on the earth led these people to contemplate with the profoundest reverence all the visible objects which were believed to

---

[55] The Round Towers of Ireland, p. 159.
[56] Ancient Faiths, vol. i., p. 145.
[57] Forlong, Rivers of Life, or Faiths of Man in All Lands, vol. i., p. 325.

affect human destiny. Hence both the pyramid and the tower served a double purpose, first, as emblems of the Deity worshipped, and, second, as monuments for the study of the heavenly bodies with which their religious ideas were so intimately connected.

While comparing the early emblems which prefigure the primitive elements in the god-idea, Hargrave Jennings observes:

"In the conveyance of certain ideas to those who contemplate it, the pyramid boasts of prouder significance, and impresses with a hint of still more impenetrable mystery. We seem to gather dim supernatural ideas of the mighty Mother of Nature . . . that almost two-sexed entity, without a name–She of the Veil which is never to be lifted, perhaps not even by the angels, for their knowledge is limited. In short, this tremendous abstraction, Cybele, Ideae, Mater, Isiac controller of the Zodiacs, whatever she may be, has her representative in the half-buried Sphinx even to our own day, watching the stars although nearly swallowed up in the engulphing sands."[58]

From the time when the two religious elements began to separate in the minds of the people, the prophets, seers, and priestesses of the old religion, those who continued to worship the Virgin and Child, had prophesied that a mortal woman, a virgin, would, independently of the male principle, bring forth a child, the fulfilment of which prophecy would vindicate the ancient faith and forever settle the dispute relative to the superiority of the female in the office of reproduction. Thus would the woman "bruise the serpent's head." In process of time not only Yonigas, but Lingajas as well, came to accept the doctrine of the incarnation of the sun in the bodies of earthly virgins. By Lingaites, however, it was the seed of the woman and not the woman herself who was to conquer evil. Finally, with

---

[58] Phallicism, p. 25.

the increasing importance of the male in human society, it is observed that a reconciliation has been effected between the female worshippers and those of the male. Athene herself has acquiesced in the doctrine of male superiority.

Thalat, the great Chaldean Deity, who presided over Chaos prior to the existence of organized matter, is finally transformed into a male God. The Hindoo Vishnu, who as she slept on the bottom of the sea brought forth all creation, has changed her sex. Brahm, the Creator, is male, and appears as a triplicated Deity in the form of three sons within whom is contained the essence of a Great Father, the female creative principle being closely veiled.

Hence we see that the God of the ancients, the universal dual force which resides in the sun and which creates all things, is no longer worshipped under the figure of a mother and her child. Although the female principle is still a necessary factor in the creative processes, and although it is capable of producing gods, the mother element possesses none of the essentials which constitute a Deity. In other words, woman is not a Creator. From the father is derived the soul of the child, while from the mother, or from matter, the body is formed. Hence the prevalence at a certain stage of human history of divine fathers and earthly mothers; for instance, Alexander of Macedon, Julius Caesar, and later the mythical Christ who superseded Jesus, the Judean philosopher and teacher of mankind.

Henceforth, caves, wells, cows, boxes and chests, arks, etc., stand for or symbolize the female power. We are given to understand, however, that for ages these symbols were as holy as the God himself, and among many peoples even more revered and worshipped.

We have seen that the ancients knew that matter and force were alike indestructible. According to their doctrine all Nature proceeded from the sun. Hence the power back of the sun, which they worshipped as the Destroyer or

Regenerator, or, in other words, as the mother of the sun, was the Great Aum or Om, the Aleim or Elohim, who was the indivisible God. The creative agency which proceeded from the sun was both male and female, yet one in essence. Later, the male appeared as spirit, the female as matter. Spirit was something above and independent of Nature.

It had indeed created matter from nothing. The fact will be remembered that man claimed supremacy over woman on the ground that the male is spirit, while the female is only matter; in other words, that she was simply a covering for the soul, which is divine.

Thus was the god-idea divorced from Nature, and a masculine principle, outside and independent of matter, set up as a personal potentate or ruler over the universe.

The logic by which the great female principle in the Deity has been eliminated, and the subterfuges which have been and still are employed to construct and sustain a Creator who of himself is powerless to create, is as amusing as it is suggestive, and forcibly recalls to mind la couvade, in which, among certain tribes, the father, assuming all the duties of procreation, goes to bed when a child is born.[59]

All mythologies prove conclusively that ages elapsed before human beings were rash enough, or sufficiently blinded by falsehood and superstition, to attempt to construct a creative force unaided by the female principle. Just here it may not be out of place to refer to the fact that in the attempt to divorce God from Nature have arisen all the superstitions and senseless religious theories with which, since the earliest ages of metaphysical speculation, the human mind has been crowded.

To this separation of the two original elements in the Deity, and the consequent exaltation of one of the factors in the creative processes, is to be traced the beginning of our

---

[59] The Evolution of Woman, p. 127.

present false, unnatural, and unphilosophical masculine system of religion–a system under which a father appears as the sole parent of the universe.

The fact is tolerably well understood that mysticism and the accumulation of superstitious ideas are the result of the over-stimulation of the lower animal instincts. When the agencies which had hitherto held the lower nature in check became inoperative–when man began to regard himself as a Creator and therefore as the superior of woman–he had reached a point at which he was largely controlled by supernatural or mystical influences.

The fact is observed that in course of time the governmental powers are no longer in the hands of the people; the masses have become enslaved. Their rulers are priests–deified tyrants who are unable to maintain their authority except through the ignorance and credulity of the masses. Hence one is not surprised to find that the change which took place at a certain stage of human growth in respect to the manner of reckoning descent was instigated and enforced by religion. Apollo had declared that woman is but the nurse to her own offspring. Neither is it remarkable at this stage in the human career, as women had lost their position as heads of families, and as they were no longer recognized as of kin to their children, that man should have attempted to lessen the importance of the female element in the god-idea.

Wherever in the history of the human race we observe a change in the relations of the sexes involving greater or more oppressive restrictions on the natural rights of women, such change, whether it assume a legal, social, or religious form, will, if traced to its source, always be found deeply rooted in the wiles of priestcraft. Since the decay of the earliest form of religion, namely, Nature-worship, the gods have never been found ranged on the side of women.

Later investigations are proving that the primitive idea of a Deity had its foundation in actual physical facts and experiences; and, as the maternal principle constituted the most important as well as the most obvious of the facts which entered into the conception of a Creator, and as it was the only natural bond capable of binding human society together, so long as reason was not wholly clouded by superstition and warped by sensuality, it could not be eliminated. In other words, a Creator in which the more essential element of creative force was wanting, was contrary to all human experience and observation. Indeed nothing could be plainer than that the deified male principle could of itself create nothing, and that it was dependent for its very existence on the female element.

By this attempt to construct a masculine Deity, absurdities were presented to the human judgment and understanding which for ages could not be overcome, and by it contradictions were necessitated which could not be reconciled with human reason and with the ideas of Nature which had hitherto been held by mankind. It was not, therefore, until reason had been suspended in all matters pertaining to religion, and blind faith in the machinations of priestcraft had been established, that a male God was set up as the sole Creator of the universe.

When women, who had become the legitimate plunder not only of individuals but of bands of warriors whose avowed object was the capture of women for wives, had degenerated into mere tools or instruments for the gratification and pleasure of men, Perceptive Wisdom or Light, and Maternal Affection the Preserver of the race, gradually became eliminated from the god-idea of mankind. Passion became God. It was the Creator in the narrowest and most restricted sense.

Although in an age of pure Nature-worship the ideas connected with reproduction, like those related to all other natural functions, were wholly unconnected with impurity either of thought or deed, still when an age arrived in which all checks to human passion had been withdrawn, and the lower propensities had gained dominion over the higher faculties, the influence of fertility or passion-worship on human development or growth may in a degree be imagined.

The fact must be borne in mind that curing the later ages of passion-worship the creative processes and the reproductive organs were deified, not as an expression or symbol of the operations of Nature, but as a means to the stimulation of the lower animal instincts in man.

With religion bestialized and its management regulated wholly with an idea to the gratification of man's sensuous desires, religious temples, under the supervision of the priesthood, became brothels, in which were openly practiced as part and parcel of religious rites and ceremonies the most wanton profligacy and the most shameless self-abandonment. The worship of Aphrodite or Venus, and also that of Bacchus, originally consisted in homage paid to the reproductive principles contained in the earth, water, and sun, but, as is well known, this pure and beautiful worship, in later times, and especially after it was carried to Greece, became synonymous with the grossest practices and the most lawless disregard of human decency.

With the light which in these later ages science and ethnological research are throwing upon the physiological and religious disputes of the ancients, the correctness of the primitive doctrines elaborated under purer conditions at an age when human beings lived nearer to Nature is being proved–namely, that matter like spirit is eternal and indestructible, and therefore that the one is as difficult of comprehension as the other, and that Nature, instead of being separated from spirit, is filled with it and can not be divorced from it; also that the female is the original organic unit of creation, without which nothing is or can be created.

Chapter VI.
Civilization of an Ancient Race

The profound doctrines of abstractions or emanations; of the absorption of the individual soul into the divine ether or essence; of the renewal of worlds and reincarnation, were doubtless elaborated after the separation, in the human mind, of Spirit from matter, but before mankind had lost the power to reason abstractly.

Although Pythagoras understood and believed these doctrines, he did not, as is well known, receive them from his degenerate countrymen, but, on the contrary, imbibed them from private sources among the orientals, where fragments of their remarkable learning were still extant. He said that religion consists in knowing the truth and doing good, and his ideas show the grandeur and beauty of the earlier conception of a Deity. He declared that there is only one God who is not, "as some are apt to imagine, seated above the world, beyond the orb of the universe," but that this great power is diffused throughout Nature. It is "the reason, the life, and the motion of all things."

Plato believed that human beings are possessed of two souls, the one mortal, which perishes with the body, the other immortal, which continues to exist either in a state of happiness or misery; that the righteous soul, freed from the limitations of matter, returns at death to the source whence it came, and that the wicked, after having been detained for a while in a place prepared for their reception, are sent back to earth to reanimate other bodies.

Aristotle held the opinion that the souls of human beings are sparks from the divine flame, while Zeno, the founder of the Stoic philosophy, taught that spirit acting upon matter produced the elements and the earth. There is plenty of evidence going to show that the early Fathers in the Christian church believed in the doctrines of reincarnation and the renewal of worlds. Neither is there any doubt but that this philosophy came from the East, where it originated. It is thought that the ancient philosophers who elaborated these doctrines were unable to account for the existence of evil without a belief in the immortality of the soul. Spirit was eternal, as was also matter.

A soul, upon leaving the body, in course of time found its way back to earth, surrounded by conditions suited to its stage of growth. Here it must reap all the consequences of its former life. It must also during its stay on earth make the conditions for its next appearance upon an earthly plane. So soon as through a succession of births and deaths it had perfected itself, it entered into a state of Nirvana. It was absorbed into the great Universal Soul. Nothing is ever lost.

> "Many a house of life
> Hath held me–seeking ever Him who wrought
> These prisons of the senses, sorrow fraught;
> Sore was my ceaseless strife!
> But now,
> Thou builder of this tabernacle–Thou!
> I know Thee.
> Never shalt Thou build again
> These walls of pain,
> Nor raise the roof-tree of deceits, nor lay
> Fresh rafters on the clay;
> Broken Thy house is, and the ridge-pole split!
> Delusion fashioned it!
> Safe pass I thence–deliverance to obtain."
>
> --Edwin Arnold, The light of Asia.

Regarding the opinions of the ancients on the subject of the eternity of matter, Higgins, in his learned work on Celtic Druids, says:

"The eternity of matter is a well known tenet of the Pythagoreans, and whether right or wrong there can be no doubt that it was the doctrine of the oriental school, whence Pythagoras drew his learning. It was a principle taken or mistaken from, or found amongst, the debris of that mighty mass of learning and science of a former period, of which, on looking back as far as human ken can reach, the most learned men have thought that they could see a faint glimmering. Indeed, I think I may say something more than a faint glimmering. For all the really valuable moral and philosophical doctrines we possess, Dutens has shown to have existed there."

From what is known relative to the speculations of an ancient race, the fact is observed that creation was but a reformation of matter. Wisdom, or Minerva, formed the earth and the planets; she did not create the heavens and the earth, as did the later Jewish God.

Of the seven principles of the universe, matter was the first, and of the seven principles of man, the physical body was the earliest. Through evolutionary processes, or through cyclic periods involving millions of years, mind was developed, and in course of time spirit was finally manifested.

Mai, the Mother of Gotama Buddha, was simply matter, or illusion, from which its higher manifestation, mind or spirit, was emerging. She was also the mother of Mercury. A clearer knowledge of the philosophical doctrines which were elaborated at a time when Nature-worship was beginning to decay, reveals the fact that the god-idea comprehended a profound knowledge of Nature and her laws; that while this people did not pretend to account for the existence of matter, they recognized a force operating through it whose laws were unchanged and unchanging.

With these facts relative to the intelligence of an older race before us, the question naturally arises: What was the degree of civilization attained at a time when the Deity worshipped was an abstract principle involving the actual creative processes throughout Nature? and, notwithstanding our prejudices, we are constrained to acknowledge that these earlier conceptions are scarcely compatible with the barbarism which we have been taught to regard as the condition of all the peoples which existed prior to the first Greek Olympiad. On the contrary, the origin of the philosophical opinions entertained by the most ancient oriental philosophers, and which must have arisen out of a profound knowledge or appreciation of Nature and her operations, point to a race far superior to any of those peoples which appear in early historic times. Regarding these opinions, Godfrey Higgins remarks:

"From their philosophical truth and universal reception I am strongly inclined to refer them to the authors of the Neros, or to that enlightened race, supposed by Bailly to have formerly existed, and to have been saved from a great catastrophe on the Himalaya Mountains. This is confirmed by an observation which the reader will make in the sequel, that these doctrines have been, like all the other doctrines of antiquity, gradually corrupted–incarnated, if I may be permitted to compose a word for the occasion."

Of this cycle, Bailly says: "No person could have invented the Neros who had not arrived at much greater perfection in astronomy than we know was the state of the most ancient Assyrians, Egyptians, and Greeks."

Toward the close of the eighteenth century the celebrated astronomer, Bailly, published a work entitled The History of Ancient Astronomy, in which he endeavored to prove that a nation possessed of profound wisdom and great genius, and of an antiquity far superior to the Hindoos or Egyptians, "inhabited the country to the north of India, or about fifty degrees north latitude." This writer has shown that "the most celebrated astronomical observations and inventions, from their peculiar character, could have taken place only in these latitudes, and that arts and improvements gradually travelled thence to the equator."

A colony of Brahmins settled near the Imans, and in Northern Thibet, where in ancient times they established celebrated colleges, particularly at Nagraent and Cashmere. In these institutions the treasures of Sanskrit literature were supposed to be deposited. The Rev. Mr. Maurice was informed that an immemorial tradition prevailed at Benares that all the learning of India came from a country situated in forty degrees of northern latitude. Other writers are of the opinion that civilization proceeded from Arabia; that the old Cushite race carried commerce, letters, and laws to all the nations of the East. Which of these theories is true, if either, may not with certainty be proved at present; yet that in the far distant past a race of people existed whose achievements exceeded those of any of the historic nations may not be doubted.

That the length of the year was calculated with greater exactness by an ancient and forgotten people than it was by early historic nations is proved by the cycle of the Neros. This cycle, which was formed of 7.421 lunar revolutions of 29 days, 12 hours, 44 minutes, and 3 seconds, or 219,146 days and a half, was equal to 600 solar years of 365 days, 5 hours, 51 minutes, and 36 seconds, which time varies less than three minutes from the present observations of the year's length. The length of the year as calculated by the Egyptians and other early historic nations was 360 days, which fact would seem to indicate that a science of astronomy had been developed in an earlier age which by the most ancient peoples of whom we have any historic records has been lost or forgotten. It has been said that if this cycle of the Neros "were correct to the second, if on the first of January at noon a new moon took place, it would take place again in exactly 600 years at the same moment of the day, and under all the same circumstances."[60]

The Varaha Calpa has the famous cycle of 4,320,000,000 years for its duration. This system makes the Cali Yug begin 3098 years B.C. A dodecan consisted of 5 days, and 72 dodecans formed a natural year of 360 days. According to the earlier calculations, 360 solar diurnal revolutions constituted a natural year. The doctrine of the ancients concerning these cycles is thus set forth by Godfrey Higgins:

"The sun, or rather that higher principle of which the sun was the emblem or the shekinah, was considered to be incarnated every six hundred years. Whilst the sun was in Taurus, the different incarnations, under whatever names they might go, were all considered but as incarnations of Buddha or Taurus. When he got into Aries, they were in like manner considered but as incarnations of Cristna or Aries, and even Buddha and Cristna were originally considered the same, and had a thousand names in common, constantly repeated in their litanies–a striking proof of identity of origin. Of these Zodiacal divisions the Hindoos formed another period, which consisted of ten ages or Calpas or Yugs, which they considered the duration of the world, at the end of which a general renovation of all things would take place. They also reckoned ten Neroses to form a period, each of them keeping a certain relative location to the other, and together to form a cycle. To effect this they doubled the precessional period for one sign– viz: 2160 years–thus making 4320, which was a tenth of 43,200, a year of the sun, analogous to the 360 natural days, and produced in the same manner, by multiplying the day of

---

[60] Godfrey Higgins, Celtic Druids, ch. ii., sec. 14.

600 by the dodecans 72 = 43,200. They then formed another great year of 432,000 by again multiplying it by 10, which they called a Cali Yug, which was measurable both by the number 2160, the years the equinox preceded in a sign, and by the number 600. They then had the following scheme:

A Cali Yug, or 600 (or a Neros)	432,000
A Dwapar, or Duo-par Age	864,000
A Treta, or tree-par Age	1,296,000
A Satya, or Satis Age	1,728,000
	4,320,000

altogether 10 Ages, making a Maha Yug or Great Age. These were all equimultiples of the Cycle of the Neros 600, and of 2160, the twelfth part of the equinoctial precessional Cycle, and in all formed ten ages of 432,000 years each."[61]

The two great religious festivals of the ancients occurred the one in the spring, at Easter, when all Nature was renewed, the other in the autumn, after the earth had yielded her bounties and the fruits were garnered in. It was at these gatherings that the Great Mother Earth received the devout adoration of all her children.

It is supposed that the Neros, or cycle of 600, is closely connected with this worship, and that it was invented to regulate the season for these festivals. In process of time it was discovered that this cycle no longer answered, that the festival which had originally fallen on the first of May now occurred on the first of April. This, we are told,

"led ultimately to the discovery that the equinox preceded about 2160 years in each sign or 25,920 years in the 12 signs, and this induced them to try if they could not form a cycle of the two. On examination, they found that

---

[61] *Anacalypsis*, vol. i., p. 232.

the 600 would not commensurate the 2160 years in a sign, or any number of sums of 2160 less than ten, but that it would with ten, or that in ten times 2160, or in 21,600 years, the two cycles would agree; yet this artificial cycle would not be enough to include the cycle of 25,920. They, therefore, took two of the periods of 21,600, or 43,200; and, multiplying both by ten—viz: 600 X 10 = 6000, and 43,200 X 10 = 432,000—they formed a period with which the 600-year period and the 6000-year period would terminate and form a cycle. Every 432,000 years the three periods would commence anew; thus the three formed a year or cycle, 72 times 6000 making 432,000, and 720 times 600 making 432,000."[62]

To form a great year, which would include all the cyclical motions of the sun and moon, and perhaps of the planets, they multiplied 432,000 by ten; thus they had ten periods answering to ten signs. Concerning these cycles Godfrey Higgins observes:

"Persons of narrow minds will be astonished at such monstrous cycles; but it is very certain that no period could properly be called the great year unless it embraced in its cycle every periodical movement or apparent aberration. But their vulgar wonder will perhaps cease when they are told that La Place has proved that, if the periodical aberrations of the moon be correctly calculated, the great year must be extended to a greater length even than 4,320,000 years of the Maha Yug of the Hindoos, and certainly no period can be called a year of our planetary system which does not take in all the periodical motions of the planetary bodies."

It is thought that as soon as these ancient astronomers perceived that the equinoxes preceded, they would at once attempt to determine the rate of precession in a given time; the precession, however, in one year was so small that they

---

[62] Higgins, Anacalypsis, p. 235.

were obliged to extend their observations over immense periods. Jones informs us that the Hindoos first supposed that the precession took place at the rate of 60 years in a degree, or 1800 in a Zodiacal sign, and of 21,600 in a revolution of the entire circle. They afterwards came to think that the precession was at the rate of 60 years and a fraction of a year, and thus that the precession for a sign was in 1824 years, and for the circle in 21,888 years. Subsequently they discovered, or thought they had discovered, the Soli-Lunar period of 608 years, hence they attempted to make the two go together. Both, however, proved to be erroneous.

In referring to the fact that among the ancient Romans existed the story of the twelve vultures and the twelve ages of 120 years each, Higgins remarks:

"This arose from the following cause: They came from the East before the supposition that the precession took place a degree in about 60 years, and 1824 years in a sign had been discovered to be erroneous; and as they supposed the Neros made a correct cycle in 608 years, and believed the precessional cycle to be completed in 21,888, they of course made their ages into twelve. As both numbers were erroneous, they would not long answer their intended purpose, and their meaning was soon lost, though the sacred periods of twelve ages and of 608 remained."

According to Hipparchus and Ptolemy, the equinoxes preceded at the rate of a degree in 100 years, or 36,000 hundred years in 360 degrees. This constituted a great year, at the end of which the regeneration of all things takes place. This is thought to be a remnant of the most ancient Hindoo speculations, and not the result of observation among the Greeks. Some time after the arrival of the sun in Aries,

"at the vernal equinox, the Indians probably discovered their mistake, in giving about 60 years to a degree; that they ought to give 50" to a year, about 72 years to a degree, and about 2160 years to a sign; and that the Luni-Solar cycle, called the Neros, did not require 608 years, but 600 years only, to complete its period. Hence arose the more perfect Neros."

It is thought by various writers that the knowledge of the ancient Hindoos regarding the movements of the sun and moon in their cycles of nineteen and six hundred years–the Metonic cycle, and the Neros–proves that long before the birth of Hipparchus the length of the year was known with a degree of exactitude which that astronomer had not the means of determining. It is positively asserted by astronomers that at least twelve hundred years were required, "during which time the observations must have been taken with the greatest care and regularly recorded," to arrive at the knowledge necessary for the invention of the Neros, and that such observations would have been impossible without the aid of the telescope.

On the subject of the great learning of an ancient race, Sir W. Drummond says:

"The fact, however, is certain, that at some remote period there were mathematicians and astronomers who knew that the sun is in the centre of the planetary system, and that the earth, itself a planet, revolves round the central fire;–who calculated, or like ourselves attempted to calculate, the return of comets, and who knew that these bodies move in elliptic orbits, immensely elongated, having the sun in one of their foci;–who indicated the number of the solar years contained in the great cycle, by multiplying a period (variously called in the Zend, the Sanscrit, and the Chinese ven, van, and phen) of 180 years by another period of 144 years;–who reckoned the sun's distance from the earth at 800,000,000 of Olympic stadia; and who must, therefore, have taken the parallax of that luminary by a method, not only much more perfect than that said to be invented by Hipparchus, but little inferior in exactness to that now in use among the moderns;–who could scarcely have made a mere guess when they fixed the moon's distance from its primary planet at fifty-nine semi-diameters of the earth;—who had measured the circumference of our globe with so much exactness that their calculation only differed by a few feet from that made by our modern geometricians; —who held that the moon and the other planets were worlds like our own, and that the moon was diversified by mountains and valleys and seas;— who asserted that there was yet a planet which revolved round the sun, beyond the orbit of Saturn;—who reckoned the planets to be sixteen in number; —and who reckoned the length of the tropical year within three minutes of the true time; nor, indeed, were they wrong at all, if a tradition mentioned by Plutarch be correct."[63]

Bailly, Sir W. Jones, Higgins, and Ledwich, as well as many modern writers, agree in the conclusion that the Indians, the Egyptians, the Assyrians, and the Chinese were simply the depositaries, not the inventors, of science. The spirit of inquiry which in later times is directing attention to the almost buried past is revealing the fact that not merely the germs whence our present civilization has been developed descended to us from the dim ages of antiquity, but that a great number of the actual benefits which go to make up our present state of material progress have come to us from prehistoric times. The art of writing, of navigation (including the use of the compass), the working of metals, astronomy, the telescope, gunpowder, mathematics, democracy, building, weaving, dyeing, and many of the appliances of civilized life, have been appropriated by later ages with no acknowledgment of the source whence they were derived. When Pythagoras exhibited to the Greeks some beautiful specimens of ancient architecture which he had brought from Egypt and Babylon, they simply claimed them as their own, giving no

---

[63] Drummond, On the Zodiacs, p. 36.

credit to the people who originated them; and subsequent ages, copying their example, have refused to acknowledge that anything of value had been achieved prior to the first Greek Olympiad.

When Philip of Macedon opened the gold mines of Thrace, a country in which it will be remembered the worship of the Great Mother Cybele was indigenous, he found that they had been previously worked "at great expense and with great ingenuity by a people well versed in mechanics, of whom no monuments whatever are extant."

The decorations on the breasts of some of the oldest mummies show that the early Egyptians understood the art of making glass. It is now known that the lens as a magnifying instrument was in use among them. Attention has been drawn to the fact that the astronomical observations of the ancients would have been impossible without the aid of the telescope. Diodorus Siculus says there was an island west of the Celtae in which the Druids brought the sun and moon near them. An instrument has recently been found in the sands of the Nile, the construction of which shows plainly that 6000 years ago the Egyptians were acquainted with our modern ideas of the science of astronomy.

William Huntington, who has travelled widely in India, Borneo, the Malay Peninsula, and Egypt, says:

"I think, on the whole, the most interesting experience I ever had was in an ancient city on the Nile in Egypt. . . . When I was there a year ago, and men were digging among the ruined temples, some curious things were brought to light, and these I regard as the strangest things seen in all my wanderings. In an old tomb was found a curious iron and glass object, which on investigation proved to be a photographic camera. It was not such a camera as is used now, or has been since our photography was invented, but something analogous to it, showing that the art which we thought we had discovered was really known 6000 years ago."

The same writer states that a plow constructed on the modern plan was also found. "It was not of steel but of iron, and it had the same shape, the same form of point and bend of mold board as we have now."

It is reported that the dark continent possesses means of communication entirely unknown to Europe. Upon this subject a correspondent to the New York Tribune writes:

"When Khartoum fell in 1885 I was in Egypt, and I well remember that the Arabs settled in the neighborhood of the pyramids knew all about it, as well as about Gen. Gordon's death, days and days before the news reached Cairo by telegraph from the Soudanese frontier. Yet Khartoum is thousands of miles distant from Cairo and the telegraph wires from the frontier were monopolized by the government."

The same correspondent observes that these Arabs told him, months previously, of the defeat of the Egyptian army under Baker Pasha at Tokar–that they not only gave him the news, but several particulars concerning the matter, two full days before intelligence was received from the Red Sea coast. In answer to the suggestion that such information might have been conveyed by means of signal fires, this writer says that such fires would have attracted the attention of the English and native scouts, and that the whole country is unpropitious to such methods; besides, no system of signal fires, no matter how elaborate, could have conveyed the news so quickly and in such detail. The whole matter is summed up as follows:

"The Arabs, therefore, have, manifestly, some other means of rapid communication at their command. One is inclined to the presumption that they, like the learned Pundits of Northern India, have a knowledge of the forces of Nature that are yet hidden from our most eminent scientists."

Can it be that the Arabs are acquainted with the very recently discovered scientific principle, that it is possible to transmit telegraphic communications without wires, and simply by means of magnetic currents in earth and water?

Nor is this remarkable skill confined to the "barbarians of the Old World." A correspondent from the far West to the New York Press wrote that long before the news of the Custer massacre reached Fort Abraham Lincoln the Sioux had communicated it to their brethren. The scouts in Crook's column to the south knew of it almost immediately, as did those with Gibbon farther northwest. The same writer says that several years ago a naval lieutenant ran short of provisions. He pushed on to a settlement as rapidly as possible and upon arriving there found that the inhabitants had provided for his coming and had a bounteous store awaiting him. The people in the village were of a different tribe from those whose domain he had passed, and so far as could be learned were not in communication with them.

The earliest accounts which we have of Egypt and Chaldea reveal the fact that at a very remote period they were old and powerful civilizations, that they had a settled government, a pure and philosophical religion, and a profound knowledge of science and art; yet, notwithstanding the great antiquity of these civilizations, that of the people which created them must have been infinitely more remote.

The earliest historic nations recognized the greatness of these ancient people and the extent of their dominion. In the oldest geographical writings of the Sanskrit people, the ancient Ethiopia, or land of Cush of Greek and Hebrew antiquity, is clearly described. Stephanus of Byzantium, who is said to represent the opinions of the most ancient Greeks, says: "Ethiopia was the first established country on the earth, and the Ethiopians were the first who introduced the worship of the Gods and who established laws."[64]

Heeren in his researches says:

"From the remotest times to the present, the Ethiopians have been one of the most celebrated, and yet the most mysterious of nations. In the earliest traditions of nearly all the more civilized nations of antiquity, the name of this distant people is found. The annals of the Egyptian priests are full of them, and the nations of inner Asia, on the Euphrates and Tigris, have interwoven the fictions of the Ethiopians with their traditions of the wars and conquests of their heroes; and, at a period equally remote, they glimmer in Greek mythology. When the Greeks scarcely knew Italy and Sicily by name, the Ethiopians were celebrated in the verses of their poets, and when the faint gleam of tradition and fable gives way to the clear light of history, the lustre of the Ethiopians is not diminished."

Homer says of them that they were a "divided people dwelling at the ends of the earth toward the setting and the rising Sun." Although it is possible at the present time to discover very many of the facts bearing upon the civilization of this ancient people, it is impossible in the present condition of human knowledge to discover when civilized life began on the earth. Whether the ancient Arabians or Ethiopians who belonged to the old Cushite race, and who are believed by many to be the most ancient people of whom we have any trace, were the first colonizers, or whether they were preceded by a still older civilization, history and tradition are alike silent; yet the fact seems to be tolerably well authenticated that this enlightened race, now nearly extinct, carried civilization to Chaldea more than seven thousand years B.C., that it colonized Egypt, engrafted its own institutions in India, colonized Phoenicia, and by its maritime and commercial

---

[64] Quoted by John D. Baldwin, Prehistoric Nations, p. 62.

enterprise, introduced civilized conditions into every quarter of the globe. Even in Peru, in Mexico, in Central America, and in the United States are evidences of the old Cushite religion and enterprise.

Baldwin, commenting on the greatness of this remarkable people, says that early in the period of its colonizing enterprise, commercial greatness, and extensive empire, it established colonies in the valleys of the Nile and the Euphrates, which in later ages became Barbary, Egypt, and Chaldea. The ancient Cushite nation occupied Arabia and other extensive regions of Africa, India, and Western Asia to the Mediterranean. While remarking upon the vastness and antiquity of this old Cushite race, Rawlinson says that they founded most of the towns of Western Asia. The vast commercial system which formed a connecting link between the various countries of the globe, was created by this people, the great manufacturing skill and unrivalled maritime activity of the Phoenicians which extended down to the time of the Hellenes and the Romans having been a result of the irgenius. It was doubtless during the supremacy of the ancient Cushite race that a knowledge of astronomy was developed and that the arts of life were carried to a high degree of perfection. However, through the peculiar influences which were brought to bear upon human experience, this knowledge, which was bequeathed to their descendants or to the nations which they had created, was subsequently lost or practically obscured, only fragments of it having been preserved from the general ruin.

Within these fragments have been preserved in India certain evidences of a profound knowledge of Nature, or of the at present unknown forces in the universe, a demonstration of which, in our own time, would probably be looked upon as a miraculous interposition of supernatural agencies.

Regarding the refinements and luxuries of this ancient people, Diodorus Siculus declares that they flowed in streams of gold and silver, that "the porticoes of their temples were overlaid with gold, and that the adornments of their buildings were in some parts of silver and gold, and in others of ivory and precious stones, and other things of great value."

From various observations, it is plain that the Etrurians represented a stage of civilization far in advance of the Pelasgians who founded Rome –a race which, although superior in numbers, arms, and influence, were, when compared with this more ancient people, little better than barbarians.[65]

Nothing, perhaps, proclaims the degree of civilization attained by the ancient Etrurians more plainly than the exquisite perfection which is observed in the specimens of art found in their tumuli. Within the tombs of Etruscans buried long prior to the foundation of Rome, or the birth of the fine arts in Greece, have been found unmistakable evidence of the advanced condition of this people. The exquisite coloring and grouping of the figures on their elegant vases, one of which, on exhibition in the British Museum, portrays the birth of Minerva, or Wisdom, show the delicacy of their taste, the purity of their conceptions, and their true artistic skill.

Among their mechanical arts, a few specimens of which have been preserved, is the potter's wheel, an invention which, so far as its utility is concerned, is

---

[65] It is thought that as early as the nineteenth century B.C. the Pelasgians or Pelargians went to Aenonia, or Ionia. It was a detachment of this people which, according to Herodotus, captured a number of Athenian women on the coast of Africa, lived with them as wives, and raised families by them, but, "because they differed in manners from themselves," they murdered them, which act was attended by a "dreadful pestilence." It is the opinion of certain writers that these women were of a different religious faith from their captors, and that so intense and bitter was the feeling upon the comparative importance of the sex functions in pro-creation, that their husbands, unable to change their views, put an end to their existence.

declared to be absolutely perfect–the most complete of all the instruments of the world. "It never has been improved and admits of no improvement." In fact all that may be gathered concerning the ancient Etrurians, a people who by the most able writers upon this subject is believed to have been one of the first to leave the Asiatic hive, is in perfect accord with the facts already set forth regarding that mighty nation, perhaps of upper Asia, who carried the study of astronomy to a degree of perfection never again reached until after the discovery of the Copernican system, who invented the Neros and the Metonic Cycle, who colonized Egypt and Chaldea, and who carried civilization to the remotest ends of the earth.

The philosophy of the Etrurians corresponds with that of the most ancient Hindoo system, and displays a degree of wisdom unparalleled by any of the peoples belonging to the early historic ages. According to their cosmogony, the evolutionary or creative processes involved twelve vast periods of time. At the end of the first period appeared the planets and the earth, in the second the firmament was made, in the third the waters were brought forth, in the fourth the sun, moon, and stars were placed in the heavens, in the fifth living creatures appeared on the earth, and in the sixth man was produced. These six periods comprehended one-half the duration of the cycle. After six more periods had elapsed, or after the lapse of the entire cycle of twelve periods, all creation was dissolved or drawn to the source of all life. Subsequently a new creation was brought forth under which the same order of events will take place. The involution of life, or its return to the great source whence it sprang, did not, however, involve the destruction of matter. The seeds of returning life were preserved in an ark or boat–the female principle, within which all things are contained. This indrawing of life constituted "the night of Brahme." It was represented by Vishnu sleeping on the bottom of the sea.

From the facts adduced in relation to the Etrurians we are not surprised to find that their religion was that of the ancient Nature worshippers, and that a mother with her child stood for their god-idea. In referring to the religion of this people, and to the great antiquity of the worship of the Virgin and Child, Higgins remarks: "Amongst the Gauls, more than a hundred years before the Christian era, in the district of Chartres, a festival was celebrated in honor of the Virgin," and in the year 1747, a mithraic monument was found "on which is exhibited a female nursing an infant—the Goddess of the year nursing the God day." To which he adds: "The Protestant ought to recollect that his mode of keeping Christmas Day is only a small part of the old festival as it yet exists amongst the followers of the Romish Church. Theirs is the remnant of the old Etruscan worship of the virgin and child." As a proof of the above, Higgins cites Gorius's Tuscan Antiquities, where may be seen the figure of an old Goddess with her child in her arms, the inscription being in Etruscan characters. "No doubt the Romish Church would have claimed her for a Madonna, but most unluckily she has her name, Nurtia, in Etruscan letters, on her arm, after the Etruscan practice."

From the monuments of Etruria the fact is observed that descent and the rights of succession were traced in the female line, a condition of society which indicates the high position which must have been occupied by the women of that country.

In Oman is said to exist a fragment of the government of the old Ethiopian or Cushite race. If this is true, then we may be able to perceive at the present time something of the character of the political institutions of this ancient nation. As no people remains stationary, and as degeneracy has been the rule with surrounding countries, we may not expect to find among the people of Oman a true representation of ancient conditions, yet, as has been observed, we may still be able to note some of the facts relative to the organization of society and their governmental institutions.

In a description furnished by Palgrave, Oman is termed a kingdom, yet it is plain from the observations of this writer that the existing form of government is that of a confederacy of nations under a democratical system, identical with that developed during the later status of barbarism. This writer himself admits that Oman is less a kingdom than an aggregation of municipalities, and that each of these municipalities or towns has a separate existence and is controlled by its own local chief; but that all are joined together in one confederacy, and subjected to the leadership of a grand chief whom the writer is pleased to term "the crown," but why, as is evident from the description given, bears no resemblance to a modern monarch. The chiefs who direct the councils of the municipalities are limited in their powers by "the traditional immunities of the vassals," the decision of all criminal cases and the administration of justice being in the hands of the local judges. In the descriptions given of their governmental proceedings, it is stated that the whole course of law is considered apart from the jurisdiction of the sovereign, who has no power to either change or annul the enactments of the people.

Here, it is observed, exists almost the identical form of government which was in use among the early historic nations, before governments came to be founded on wealth, or on a territorial basis[66]; or, in other words, before the monied and aristocratic classes had drawn to themselves all the powers which had formerly belonged to the people.

We must bear in mind the fact that under these earlier democratical institutions, the term "people" included not only men but women, and as the grand chief, the local rulers, and the judges held their positions by virtue of their

---

[66] See The Evolution of Woman, p. 238.

descent from, or relationship to, some real or traditional leader of the gens, who during all the earlier ages was a woman, we may believe that the power of women to depose their political leaders so soon as their conduct became obnoxious to them was absolute and unquestioned.

Doubtless, as we have seen, the government of Oman has undergone a considerable degree of modification since the days of Cushite splendor and supremacy; that, like all other nations which have come in contact with the Aryan and Semitic races, the tendency has been toward monarchial government; nevertheless, with its practically free institutions, representing as they do, in a measure, the political system of the grandest and oldest civilizations of which we have any knowledge, it furnishes an illustration of the degree of progress possible under gentile organization, at the same time that it points to the source whence has proceeded the fierce democratic spirit observed among succeeding nations, notably the Greeks.

Modern writers agree in ascribing to the Touaricks, a people inhabiting the Desert of Sahara, a considerable degree of civilization. We are informed that in the Sahara, which, by the way, is far less a barren waste than we have been taught to suppose it, "the Touaricks have towns, cities, and an excellent condition of agriculture"; that with them fruit is cultivated with great success and skill. Their method of political organization is democratic and similar in construction and administration to the old Cushite municipalities. Baldwin, quoting from Richardson, says: "Ghat, like all the Touarick countries, is a republic; all the people govern. The woman of the Touaricks is not the woman of the Moors and Mussulmans generally. She has here great liberty, and takes an active part in the affairs and transactions of life."[67]

---

[67] Prehistoric Nations, p. 341.

One who is disposed to search for it, will find no lack of evidence going to prove that in an earlier age of the world, prior to the written records of extant history, the human race had attained to a stage of civilization equal in all and superior in many respects to that of the present time.

That this remarkable stage of progress, the actual extent of which has not yet been fully realized, was attained during a period of pure Nature-worship, or while the earth and the sun were venerated as emblems of the great creative energy throughout the universe, is a proposition which, when viewed by the light of more recently acquired facts, is perfectly reasonable, and exactly what might be expected.

That this high stage of civilization was reached while women were the recognized heads of families and of the gentes, and at a time when Perceptive Wisdom, or the female energy in the Deity, was worshipped as the supreme God, is a fact which in time will be proved beyond a doubt. Indeed, had not the judgment of man become warped by prejudice, and his reason clogged by superstition and sensuality, the fact so plainly apparent in all ancient mythologics, that in the early god-idea two principles were contained, the female being in the ascendancy, would long ere this have been acknowledged, and our present religious systems, which are but outgrowths from these mythologies, would, with the partial return of civilized conditions, have been so modified or changed as to embrace some of the fundamental truths which formed the basis of early religion.

Regarding the religion of the ancient race which we have been considering, we are told that they worshipped a dual Deity, under the appellations of Ashtaroth and Baal, and that this God "comprehended the generative or reproductive powers in human beings and in the sun, together with Wisdom or Light." In other words, they adored the great moving force throughout Nature, a force which they venerated as the Great Mother.

Before the Zend and Sanskrit branches of the Aryan race had separated, their religion was doubtless that given them by their Cushite civilizers. The worship of the sun and the planets, with which were inextricably interwoven the fructifying agencies in Nature, explains their devotion to the study of the heavenly bodies and their advanced knowledge of astronomy. The types of regeneration or reproduction which they venerated were symbols of abstract principles, and, from facts connected with their religious ceremonies as practiced by their immediate successors, and from the pure significance attached to their emblems, we are justified in the conclusion before referred to, that the sensuous element, which became so prominent in later religious developments, constituted no part of their worship.

The number of ages during which the most primitive religion, namely, that of pure Nature-worship, prevailed among the inhabitants of the earth may not be conjectured, and the exact length of time during which earth and sun adoration unalloyed by serpent and phallic faiths remained is not known. It is probable, however, that its duration is to be measured by that of the supremacy of the altruistic or mother element in human affairs, and that the gradual engrafting of the later-developed sensuous faiths upon their earlier god-idea, marks the change from female to male supremacy.

We have observed that whenever a remnant of the civilization of the ancient Cushites appears, exactly as might be expected, women hold an exalted position in human affairs, at the same time that the female principle constitutes the essential element in the Deity.

Of the ancient Persians who received their religion and their civilization from this older race Malcolm observes:

"The great respect in which the female sex was held was, no doubt, the principal cause of the progress they made in civilization. . . . It would appear that in former days the women of Persia had an assigned and honorable place in society; and we must conclude that an equal rank with the male creation, which is secured to them by the ordinances of Zoroaster, existed long before the time of that reformer, who paid too great attention to the habits and prejudices of his countrymen to have made any serious alteration in so important an usage. We are told by Quintus Curtius, that Alexander would not sit in the presence of Sisygambis, till told to do so by that matron, because it is not the custom in Persia for sons to sit in the presence of their mothers. There can be no stronger proof than this anecdote affords, of the great respect in which the female sex were held in that country, at the time of this invasion."[68]

No one I think can study the sacred books of the Persians without observing the emphasis which is there placed on purity of character and right living. Indeed, within no extant writings is the antithesis between good and evil more strongly marked, at the same time that their hatred of idolatry is clearly apparent. The same is observed in the early writings of the Hindoos. Within the Vedas, although they have been corrupted by later writers, may still be traced a purity of thought and life which is not apparent in the writings of later ages. Not long ago I was informed by a learned native of India that the original writing of the Vedas was largely the work of women.

That the early conceptions of a Deity in which women constituted the central and supreme figure were in Egypt correlated with the exercise of great temporal power, may not, in view of the facts at hand, longer be doubted. By means of records revealed on ancient monuments, we are informed that in the age of Amunoph I. a considerable degree of sovereign power in Egypt was exercised by a woman, Amesnofre-are, who had shared the throne with

---

[68] See History of Persia.

Ames. She occupied it also with Amunoph, and, notwithstanding the statement of Herodotus, that women did not serve in the capacity of priests, this Queen is represented as pouring out libations to Amon, an office which was doubtless the highest connected with the priesthood.

Less than forty years later, it is observed that another woman, Amun-nou-het, shared the throne with Thotmes I. and II. and that "she appears to have enjoyed far greater consideration than either of them." Not alone are monuments raised in her name, but she appears dressed as a man, and "alone presenting offerings to the gods." So important a personage was she that she is believed by many to be the princess who conquered the country, perhaps even Semiramis herself. Her title was the "Shining Sun."[69]

As these women doubtless belonged to the old Arabian, Ethiopian, or Cushite race, the people who had brought civilization to Egypt, we are not surprised to find them holding positions which were connected with the highest civil and religious offices. The Labyrinth, in the country of the Nile, is described by ancient writers as containing three thousand chambers. Strabo says of it that the enclosure contained as many palaces as there formerly were homes, and that there the priests and priestesses of each department were wont to congregate to discuss difficult and important questions of law.

According to the Greeks, the Egyptian God Osiris corresponds to their Jupiter; and Sate, the companion of Kneph, is identical with Juno. It is quite evident, however, that the Greeks understood little of the true significance of the gods which they had borrowed, or which they had inherited from older nations. It would seem that as a people their conceit prevented them from acknowledging the dignity even of their gods, hence, they endowed them with

---

[69] Rawlinson, History of Herodotus, app., book ii., ch. viii.

and these facts of different kinds, unite in producing the same results."

That the descendants of a once mighty nation lapsed into barbarism, forgetting the profound knowledge of the sciences possessed by their ancestors, is a fact too well attested at the present time to be doubted by those who have taken the pains to acquaint themselves with the evidence at hand.

Regarding the manner in which this ancient civilization was reached, or concerning the way in which it was achieved, history and tradition are alike silent, although it is believed that the present methods of investigation will, at least in a measure, unravel the mystery. At present we only know that, as far in the remote past as human ken can reach, evidences of a high stage of civilization exist which it must have required thousands upon thousands of years to accomplish.

Chapter VII.
Concealment of the Early Doctrines

After the decline of Nature-worship, and when through the constantly increasing power gained by the ruder elements in human society a knowledge of the scientific principles underlying ancient religion had been partially lost or forgotten, it became necessary for philosophers to conceal the original conception of the Deity and to clothe their sacred writings in allegory. Hence it is observed that every ancient form of religion has a cabala containing its secret doctrines–doctrines the inner meaning of which was known only to the few. In order that these truths might be preserved, they were inscribed on the leaves of trees in characters or symbols understood only by the initiated. The allegories beneath which these higher truths were concealed were handed down as traditions to succeeding generations–traditions in which history, astrology, and mythology are strangely combined.

After long periods, through war, conquest, and the various changes incidental to shifting environment, these traditions were in the main forgotten. Fragments of them, however, were from time to time gathered together, and, intermingled with later doctrines, were used by the priests as a means of increased self-aggrandizement and power.

It is now thought that the Iliad (Rhapsodies) of Homer is only a number of "detached songs" which perhaps for centuries were delivered orally, and that they contain the secret doctrines of the priests. Porphyry says that "we ought not to doubt that Homer has secretly represented the images of divine things under the concealment of fable." It has been said of Plato that he banished the poems of Homer from his imaginary republic for the reason that the people might not be able to distinguish what is from what is not allegorical. Hippolytus informs us that the Simonists declared that in Helen resided the principle of intelligence; "and thus, when all the powers were for claiming her for themselves, sedition and war arose, during which this chief power was manifested to nations." These songs which were gathered together by Pisistratus and revised by Aristotle for the use of Alexander, have generally been regarded merely as a bit of history recounting a severe and protracted struggle between the Greeks and Trojans.

Within the earliest historical accounts which we have of the Egyptians, we observe that their ceremonies and symbols have already become multitudinous, the true meaning of the latter being concealed. The masses of the people, who had grown too sensualized and ignorant to receive the higher divine "mysteries," and too gross to be entrusted with their true significance, had become idolaters.

Not only the Egyptian and Chaldean priests, but Moses and the Jewish doctors were well versed in religious symbolism. The fact is observed, also, that as late as medieval Christianity, the fathers in the Church, the Christian painters, sculptors, and architects, still employed signs and symbols to set forth their religious doctrines. Even at the present time, many of the emblems representing certain ideas connected with the creative principles, and which were part and parcel of the pagan worship, are still in use. The masses of the people, however, are without a knowledge of their origin or early significance.

Everywhere, throughout the early historic nations, were worshipped symbols of the attributes or functions of the dual or triune God. Each symbol represented a distinctive female or male quality. Animals, trees, the sea, plants, the moon, and the heavens were, at a certain stage of religious development, symbolized as parts of the Deity and worshipped as possessing certain female or male characteristics or attributes.

It is plain that, with the decline of female power, and the consequent stimulation of the animal instincts in man, the pure creative principles involved in Nature-worship gradually became unsuited to the sensualized capacities and tastes of the masses; but in addition to this were other reasons why the female principle in the Deity should be concealed. Women were already deposed from their former exalted position as heads of families and as leaders of consanguine communities. All their rightful prerogatives had been usurped. The highest development in Nature had become the slave of man's appetites, and motherhood, which had hitherto been accepted as the most exalted function either in heaven or on the earth, trailed in the dust.

Under these conditions it is not perhaps singular that the capacity to bring forth, and the qualities and attributes of women which are correlated with it, namely, sympathy–a desire for the welfare of others outside of self, or altruism,–should no longer have been worshipped as divine, or that in their place should have been substituted the leading characters developed in man. From the facts at hand it is plain that at a certain stage of human growth physical might and male reproductive energy, or virility, became the recognized God. With passion as the highest ideal of a Creator, the female element appeared only in a sensualized form and simply as an appendage to the god which was dependent upon her ministrations. Under the above conditions it is not in the least remarkable that by the priests it should have been deemed necessary to conceal from women the facts bound up in their nature. Woman's importance as a creative agency and as a prime and most essential factor in the universe must be concealed. "Isis must be veiled."

Through the appropriation of the titles of the original dual God by reigning monarchs, is perceived at least one of the processes by which the great universal female Deity of the ancients has been transformed into a male god. We are assured that the "redundant nomenclature of the deities of Babylon renders an interpretation of them impossible. Each divinity has many distinct names, by which he is indifferently designated." It is observed that each

Deity has as many as forty or fifty titles, each of which represents a certain attribute.

Since the invention of the cuneiform alphabet, by which pictures have been reduced to phonetic signs, the attempt has been made to arrange or classify these gods according to their proper order in the Pantheon, but thus far much obscurity and doubt seem to pervade their history.

In Assyrian, Babylonian, and Egyptian mythologies are observed much confusion and no small degree of mystery surrounding the positions occupied by certain gods. "Children not unfrequently change positions with parents," but more frequently, we are told, "women change places with men," or, more properly speaking, the titles, attributes, and qualities ascribed to the Great Universal female God are now transferred to the reigning monarch. Thus not unfrequently a deity is observed which is composed of a male triad, the central figure of which is the king or military chieftain, and to which is usually appended a straggling fourth member, a female, who, shorn of her power, and with a doubtful and mysterious title, appears as wife or mistress to his greatness, while upon her is reflected, through him, a slight hint of that dignity and honor which was originally recognized as belonging exclusively to the recognized Deity.

The Goddess Vishnu, from whose navel as she slept on the bottom of the sea sprang all creation, after her transformation into a male God, is supplemented by a wife–Lacksmir. Lacksmir means wisdom; but she has become only an appendage to her "lord," upon whom is reflected all her former glory.

So greedy did rulers become for the splendid titles belonging to the female divinities that we are told that "the name of the Great Goddess Astarte not unfrequently appears as that of a man."

Although man had usurped the titles of the female God and had denied her recognition as an active creative agency, still, as nothing could be created without her, she was permitted, as we have seen, to remain as wife or mistress to the reigning monarch, in whom had come to reside infinite wisdom and power. Her symbol was an ark, chest, boat, box, or cave. This woman, although dignified by the title "Mother of the Gods," and even by that of "Queen of Heaven," is utterly without power.

Not only is it plain that the titles and attributes of female gods have been appropriated by males, but it is also true that the more ancient deities, which are now known to have been female, have by later investigators been represented as male.

The interpretations which have hitherto been put upon the Babylonian and Assyrian deities by many of those who have attempted to unravel the mysteries of an earlier stage of religious worship, is doubtless due to the fact that since the so-called historic period began, the qualities which have been considered godlike have all been masculine; it has therefore never occurred to the minds of these writers that the ancients may have entertained quite different notions from their own regarding the attributes of a Deity; hence, whenever the sex of a god has appeared doubtful, especially if it be in the least degree powerful or important, it has at once been denominated as masculine, and this, too, notwithstanding the fact that such rendering has oftentimes involved inconsistencies, contradictions, and absurdities which it is impossible to reconcile either with established facts or with common sense.

Unless the symbols representing religious belief and worship are viewed in the light of later developed facts in mythology, archaeology, and philology, there occur many seeming absurdities and numberless facts which it is found difficult to reconcile with each other; especially is this true in regard to some of the symbols used to express the distinctive female and male qualities. The serpent, for instance, although a male symbol, in certain ages of the world's history appears as a beautiful woman.

This is accounted for by the fact that a woman and a serpent once stood for the god-idea. Together they constituted an indivisible entity–the creating power in the universe. They therefore became interchangeable terms. The woman when appearing alone represented both, as did also the serpent.

"In most ancient languages, probably all, the name for the serpent signifies Life, and the roots of these words generally also signify the male and female organs, and sometimes these conjoined. In low French the words for Phallus and life have the same sound, though, as is sometimes the case, the spelling and gender differ"; but this fact is thought to be of no material importance, as "Jove, Jehova, sun, and moon have all been male and female by turn."

No doubt many of the inconsistencies hitherto observed in the religion of the ancients will disappear so soon as we obtain a clearer knowledge of their chronology; and events which now seem contradictory will be satisfactorily explained when placed in their proper order with regard to date. Religion, like everything else, is constantly shifting its position to accommodate itself to the changed mental conditions of its adherents; hence, ideas which at any given time in the past were perfectly suited to a people, would, in the course of five hundred or one thousand years, have become changed or greatly modified.

During a certain stage in human history "all great women and mythical ladies were serpents"; but when monumentally or pictorially represented, they appeared "with the head of a woman, while the body was that of a reptile." This figure represented Wisdom and Passion, or the spiritual and material planes of human existence. The mythical woman whom Hercules met in Scythia, and who was doubtless the original eponymous leader of the Scythian people, had the head of a woman and the body of a serpent.[72] Even the Mexicans declare that "he, the serpent, is the sun, Tonakatl-Koatl, who ever accompanies their first woman." Their primitive mother, they said, was Kihua-Kohuatl, which signifies a serpent. In referring to this Mexican tradition, Forlong remarks: "So that the serpent here was represented as both Adam and Adama; and their Eden, as in Jewish story, was a garden of love and pleasure."[73]

The traditions extant among all peoples seem to connect the introduction of the serpent into religious symbolism, with a time in the history of mankind when they first began to recognize the fact, that through the abuse of the reproductive functions, evil, or human wretchedness, had gained the ascendency over the higher forces. The Deity represented by a woman and a serpent involved the idea not alone of good, but of good and evil combined. Together they prefigured not only Wisdom and generative power, but evil as well. Mythologically they represented the cold of winter and the heat of the sun's rays, both of which were necessary reproduction. From this conception sprang the Ormuzd and Ahryman of the Persians, the story of Adam, Eve, and the serpent in Genesis, and the legend of Kihua-Kohuatl and Tonakatl-Koatl in Mexico.

"The serpent remained in the memory and affections of most early people as wisdom, life, goodness, and the source of knowledge and science, under various names such as

---

[72] Herodotus, book iv., 9.
[73] Rivers of Life, vol. i., p. 143.

Toth, Hermes, Themis, the Kneph or Sophia of Egyptians and Gnostics, and Set, Shet, or Shem of the Jews."[74]

The Serpent Goddess, although embracing evil as well as good, was still the "Giver of Life" and the "Teacher of Mankind." These were the titles which in later ages began to be coveted by monarchs, and then it was that the attributes belonging to this Deity began to appear in connection with royalty.

There is no ancient divinity about which there seems to be connected so much mystery as the Assyrian Hea. When referring to the "great obscurity" which surrounds this God we are assured that there is at present "no means of determining the precise meaning of the cuneiform Hea, which is Babylonian rather than Assyrian," but that it is doubtless connected with the Arabic Hya, which is said to mean "life," or the female principle in creation. This Deity is the God of "glory" and of "giving," titles which during the earlier ages of human existence belonged to the Queen of Heaven, the Celestial Mother.

The representation of the god Amun or Amun-ra, which superseded the triune Deity, Kneph, Sate, and Anouk at Thebes, and from which in Assyria doubtless proceeded the trinity, Amun, Bel-Nimrod, and Hea, is supposed to be identical with the Greek Zeus, which means the sun. This God is represented by a female figure seated on a throne. It is crowned with two long feathers, and in the right hand is observed the cross, the emblem of life. Manetho, the celebrated Egyptian historian, declares that the name of this God signifies "concealed."

There can be little doubt that the titles of the ancient Deity–the Destroyer or Regenerator, or, in other words, those of the God of life which embraced the idea of the moving force throughout Nature, were, in course of time, appropriated by the rulers of the people. It is stated that the

---

[74] Forlong, Rivers of Life, etc., vol. i., p. 143.

name of a certain Egyptian God appears first in connection with royalty, that "his name was substituted for some earlier divinity whose hieroglyphics were chiselled out of the monuments to make place for his."

According to the testimony of Rawlinson, the God Hea is represented by the great serpent, which occupies a conspicuous position among the symbols of the gods on the black stones recording Babylonian benefactions. Now these flat black stones are themselves said to symbolize the female element in the Deity, in contradistinction to the obelisks, which prefigure the male, while the serpent, for reasons which have already been explained, appeared for ages in connection with the figure of a woman. In later inscriptions "king" is everywhere attached to the name of the God Hea, which fact shows that the titles ascribed to her were those particularly coveted by royalty. Hence we are not surprised to find that in an inscription of Sardanapalus, in the British Museum, there "occurs a remarkable phrase in which the king takes the titles of Hea."

Among the Assyrian inscriptions appear Bel-Nimrod, Hea, and Nin or Bar. In view of the facts which have come to light regarding Hea, it is altogether probable that the triad Bel-Nimrod, Hea, and Nin represent the trinity as figured by the father, mother, and child. That Nin was the son or the child of Bel-Nimrod "is constantly asserted in the inscriptions." He appears also as the son of Hea, yet the fact that Hea should be represented as a woman, or as the mother of Nin, and the central figure in the trinity, seems not to have been observed by those who thus far have been engaged in deciphering these inscriptions. By representing Hea as male, Nin is made to appear as the offspring of two fathers while he is left absolutely motherless. To obviate this difficulty an ingenious attempt has been made to account for his existence by substituting his own wife as the author of his being. Although in the numerous accounts which I had read of Hea, in my search for information concerning her, she had always been designated as male, still I was satisfied from the descriptions given that originally this Deity was female. Therefore upon receiving a copy of Forlong's Rivers of Life and Faiths of Man in All Lands, I was not surprised to find the following:

"Hoa or Hea, the Hu of our Keltic ancestors, whose symbol was the shield and the serpent, was worshipped near rivers and lakes, and if possible on the sea-shore, where were offered to her such emblems as a golden vessel, boat, coffer, or fish, and she was then named Belat Ili (the mistress of the Gods)."[75]

She was the Goddess of Water. Of this Forlong says: "Water, perhaps more than fire, has always been used as a purifier.... Christians have but imitated the ancients, in the use of Lustral water–now-a-days called Holy Water, and into which salt should be freely put."

According to Francis Vasques, the Cibola tribes of New Mexico pay no adoration to anything but water, believing it to be the chief support of all life. The Hindoo faith and the Greek Christian Church prescribe "adorations, sacrifices, and other water rites, and hence we find all orthodox clergy and devotees have much to do with rivers, seas, and wells, especially at certain annual solar periods."

The extent to which these ancient rites are still practiced as part and parcel of modern religious observances is not realized by those who have given no special attention to the subject. As spring advances, all ranks of Russians from the Czar to the humblest peasant proceed with their clergy to the Neva, where with solemn pomp the ice is broken and the water, which is held to be of virgin purity, is sprinkled upon the heads of Czar, nobles, and other dignitaries. The following is an account given of the worship of Hea not many years ago in the public press:

---

[75] Vol. ii., p. 94.

"An Imperial and Arch-episcopal procession was formed, consisting of, first, the High Priest of the empire in all his most gorgeous robes, the two masters of ceremonies walking backwards (probably because not of a holy enough order), long double files of white- and gold-robed bearers of sacred flambeaux or candles, for Fire must enter into every ceremony, whether it is the male or female energy which is being worshipped. Following these Religieux came all the sacred relics and fetishes of the Church, as Maya's holy cup for water, all holy books, crosses, banners, with sacred emblems in their order, and finally the Czar, humbly, and, like all his people, on foot, followed by courtly throngs. These all proceeded to a handsome pavilion or kiosk, erected close to the edge of the water, when the Metropolitan of the Church reverently made an incision in the ice, and took out a little water in a sacred golden cup bearing strange devices. The firing of guns accompanied these solemn acts in all their stages, and wherever the grave procession moved, it always did so with measured tread, chanting sacred verses to the old, old Deity of our race, and surrounded with all the pomp of war; whilst at intervals, peals of Christian bells and the booming of near and distant guns added to the solemnity of this water pageant. After the filling of the golden cup, which, of course, represents the earth and its fulness, and, at this season, the now expected increase, the High Priest placed a golden crucifix on the virgin water and blessed its return from wintry death, invoking the precious fluid to vernal life and productiveness, when lo! a holy child suddenly appears upon the scene, reminding us that this is everywhere the outcome of the 'wafers of life' in all animal as well as vegetable production. Boodha in the garden of Loobim through which flowed a holy stream, and Christ by the brook at Bethlehem, nay, the first pair in the garden of the four rivers, are all the same idea–fertility and creation. The high Russian Pontiff now slowly and solemnly stooped, and taking up some of the holy water, proceeded to sprinkle the vernal child–Jesus, whispered these crowds, but the ancients said Horus. The sacred fluid was then sprinkled on the clergy, the Czar, and all dignitaries, and finally on the sacred emblems, banners, guns, etc. Men and women, aye, wise as well as foolish, of every rank, now crowded forward, and on bended knee besought their Patriarch to sprinkle and to bless them. Finally, the great Czar put the cup to his lips, humbly and reverently, and then filled it to overflowing with a wealth of golden pieces, for it is the still living representative in the nineteenth century A.C. of 'the golden boat' of Hea of the nineteenth century B.C.'[76]

The symbol of Neith or Muth, Athene or Minerva, the great universal female principle of the Egyptians, Greeks, and Romans, was the shield and serpent. In Celtic Druids I find that Nath, the Egyptian Neith, the "goddess of wisdom and science whose symbol was the shield and serpent, was worshipped among the ancient Irish." The male God associated with her was Naith, and according to Higgins represented "the opposite of Neith."

In Rivers of Life is observed a reference to the Assyrian Goddess Hea by Lucian. In a note Forlong says that no doubt Hea is the same as Haiya or Haya. In other words she represents the universal hermaphrodite–the creative principle throughout Nature, which was originally worshipped as female. The actual signification of the word Haya is "life." In ancient Arabia it was applied to a group of kinsmen.

The Rev. Mr. Davis is of the opinion that Noe or Noah was the same as Deon and that both were Hu or Hea the mighty, whose chariot was drawn by solar rays. This God was in fact the same as Zeus, Bacchus, and all the rest of the sun and water Deities. It has been observed that, according to the ancient cosmogonies, within water was

---

[76] Forlong, Rivers of Life, vol. ii., p. 95.

contained the life principle, and as a woman presided over it, or was the only being or entity present, she must have been the self-existent Creator. From this woman sprang all creation. According to the account in Genesis, the Spirit of God moved on the face of the deep and creation began.

By all nations water has been employed as a symbol of regeneration, and as it contained the beginning of things it was female. The Hindoos regard it as sacred, and in one of their most solemn prayers it is thus invoked: Waters, mothers of worlds, purify us![77]

Doubtless it was from these ancient speculations regarding the beginnings of things that Thales, the Milesian philosopher, received his doctrine that water is the original principle. The ancient Egyptians and the Jewish people to this day have the custom of pouring out all the water contained in any vessel in a house where a death has taken place, because of the idea that as the living being comes from water, so does it make its exit through water. Hence "to drink or to use in any way a fluid which contains the life of human beings would be a foul offense."

The fact is noted by Inman that in all Assyrian mythology the water God Hea is associated with life and with a serpent. Although Rawlinson declares that Hea is Babylonian rather than Assyrian, may she not, in view of the facts concerning her, be not only Babylonian, but Egyptian, Indian, Phrygian, Mexican, and all the rest?

It would seem that in this Deity, who is figured in connection with a shield and serpent, as is Minerva, and who is worshipped near water– an emblem which is sacred to her,–and whose titles correspond exactly to those of Neith or Cybele, might be traced the remnants of a once universal worship–a worship in which the female energy constituted the Creator.

---

[77] Quoted by Inman from Colbrook, vol. i., p. 85.

Although it is declared that "great obscurity surrounds the God Hea," no one, I think, whose mind is free from prejudice, and who understands the significance of the early god-idea, and the true meaning of the symbols used in later ages to express it, can study the myths connected with this Deity without at once recognizing her identity with the great female God of Nature who was once worshipped by every people on the globe, but whose worship had become sensualized to satisfy the corrupted taste of a more depraved age–an age in which passion constituted the highest idea of a God.

Although the serpent Deity was originally portrayed with the head of a woman and the body of a serpent or fish, after the change of sex in the god-idea which has been noted in the foregoing pages had been completed, it is observed that this figure is represented by the head of a man and the body of a serpent. Hea, the great goddess to whom water, the original principle, is sacred, and who is suspiciously connected with Noah, the life-principle which appears at the close of a cycle, has changed her sex. This god is now the "Ruler of the Seas," "Master of the Life-Boat" (the ark), and "Lord of the Earth." The earth is his and the fulness thereof. He is the "Life Giver," the "Lord of Hosts," who subsequently becomes the maker of heaven and earth.

Minerva, who had been the first emanation from the Deity and the daughter of the Great Mother of the Gods, now has a father but no mother. Jove, who in course of time came to be represented as a male Creator, brought her forth from his head. Later, woman is produced from the side of man. The male principle, symbolized by a serpent, has become "the one only and true God." It is Passion –the "Healer of Nations"–the great "I Am."

No unprejudiced individual who carefully follows the results of later investigation, and who attempts to unravel the mysteries surrounding the ancient gods and the significance of the symbols of worship belonging to the earliest historic times, will fail to note the attempt which has been made in later ages to conceal the fact that the Deity worshipped in very ancient times was female. Neither will he fail to observe the modus operandi by which the attributes and prerogatives of this Deity have been shifted upon males–usually deified monarchs. After priestcraft and its counterpart, monarchial rule, had robbed the people of all their natural rights, kings assumed not alone the governing functions, but arrogated to themselves the symbols, titles, and attributes of the dual Deity. The reigning monarch became not only the temporal ruler and priest, but was actually God himself, the female principle being concealed under convenient symbols.

Chapter VIII.
The Original God-Idea of the Israelites

Not only were religious doctrines veiled beneath allegories and convenient symbols, but names also had a religious significance.

We are given to understand that in Chaldea and Assyria every child was named by the oracle or priest, and that no one thought of changing the appellation which had come to him through this heavenly source.[78]

Inman, in his Ancient Faiths, calls attention to the fact that in the Old Testament kings, priests, captains, and other great men have had names bestowed upon them, each of which has some religious signification; that this name was given the individual "at circumcision, or soon after birth."

In the ancient names of what are designated as the Shemitic races, children were called after the god alone, and sometimes in connection with an attribute. Especially were these names applied to royalty or to persons of distinction; for instance, names were given signifying, God the good, God the just or the merciful, God the strong, The Warrior God, etc.

As the higher conception of a Creator was forgotten, and as human beings, or perhaps I should say their power to control circumstances coupled with the ability to reproduce or create, had become god, they assumed the titles or names of the Deity; hence, it is not perhaps singular that in later times kings and heroes were invested with all the attributes of the gods.

---

[78] Inman, Ancient Faiths, vol. i., p. 3.

We have seen that according to various writers Om or Amm was the holy one whose name in India it was sacrilege to pronounce. It was the eternal sun, or the Great Mother. As this word stands also for "tribe or people," it seems to mean, too, that which binds, holds, or endures.

As Om or Amm signifies the Great Mother, so An or On means the Great Father. Concerning the word Am-mon, Inman writes as follows:

"The association of the words signifying mother and father indicates that it is to such conjunction we must refer creative power. With such an androgyne element the sun was associated by ancient mythologists. Jupiter was himself sometimes represented as being female; and the word hermaphrodite is in itself a union between Hermes and Aphrodite, the male and female creative powers. We may fairly conclude, from the existence of names like the above, that there was at one time in Western as there was in Eastern Asia a strong feud between the adorers of On and Am, the Lingacitas and the Yonijas, and that they were at length partially united under Ammon, as they were elsewhere under Nebo or the Nabhi of Vishnu."[79]

Inman relates that once when a friend of his was conversing with a very high-caste Hindoo he casually uttered this word Amm or Om, whereupon the man was so awe struck that he could scarcely speak, and, in a voice almost of terror, asked where his friend had learned the word. Of this word Inman says:

"To the Hindoos it was that incommunicable name of the Almighty, which no one ventured to pronounce except under the most religious solemnity. And here let me pause to remark that the Jews were equally reverent with the name belonging to the Most High; and that the third commandment was very literal in its signification."

---

[79] Ancient Faiths Embodied in Ancient Names, vol. i., p. 237.

The same writer remarks that in Thibet, too, where a worship very nearly identical in ceremony and doctrine with that of the Roman papists exists amongst the Lamas, the name of Om is still sacred.

The Iav of the Jews was equally revered, but in the later ages of their career they seem to have lost sight of its true meaning.

According to Inman's testimony and that of other etymological students, the true signification of the cognomen Jacob is the female principle.

It is believed by various writers that the story of Jacob and Esau as related in Genesis has an esoteric as well as an exoteric meaning–that Jacob has reference to the female creative energy throughout Nature, or, rather, to the great mass of people who in an early age of the human race believed in the superior importance of the female in the office of reproduction, and that Esau signifies the male. Attention is called to the fact that Esau is represented as a "hairy" man, rough-voiced and easily beguiled, while Jacob, on the other hand, is smooth-faced, soft-voiced, and the favorite of his mother.

There is indeed much in this myth which seems to indicate that it is an allegory beneath which are veiled certain facts connected with the struggle between two early contending sects regarding the relative importance of the sexes in reproduction. Of this Inman says:

"My own impression is that Esau, or Edom, and Jacob are mystic names for a man and a woman, and that round these, historians wove a web of fancy; that ultimately the cognomen Jacob was recognized, and that to allow the Jewish people to trace their descent from a male rather than a female, the appellation of Israel was substituted in later productions."[80]

---

[80] Ancient Faiths, vol. i., p. 607.

As most of the myths or allegories in Genesis are now traced to a source far more remote than the beginning of legitimate Jewish history, it is not unreasonable to suppose that this story, too, was copied by the Jews from the traditions of earlier races; nor, when we remember the true meaning of the cognomen Jacob, that the entire story should be regarded as an attempt to set forth certain facts connected with the great physiological or religious conflict between the sexes.

The significance of the idols worshipped by Jacob and his family is not for a certainty known, but it is believed by certain writers that the Seraphim and Teraphim were the usual images which were used to represent the male and female energies. "Then Jacob said unto his household and to all that were with him: Put away the strange gods that are among you." In referring to this passage, Inman, in a note, says:

"The critic might fairly say, looking at Genesis xxxv., 2, 'Put away the strange gods that are among you,' that there were images of God which were not strange, and that in these early times there were orthodoxy and heterodoxy in images as there are now. In ancient times the emblem of life-giving energy was an orthodox emblem; it is now a horror and its place is taken by an image of death. We infer from the context that Laban's gods were orthodox."

So, also, must have been the stone pillar set up by Jacob at Bethel (place of the sun). From a study of similar stones, examples of which are to be found in nearly every country of the globe, it is known that they represent the male energy, and from all the facts connected with the story of Laban's gods it is probable that they were emblems of this power. We may suppose then that the "strange gods," the unorthodox gods, which Jacob ordered put away, were those representing the female energy.

It seems strange that any person can study the history of the Israelitish Exodus by the light of later developments in biblical research without recognizing the fact that the "Lord" which brought the children of Israel out from the bondage of Egypt was the male power, which by a certain sect had been proclaimed the only actual creative agency, and therefore the "only one and true God."

Although, at the time at which Abraham is said to have lived, the knowledge of an abstract dual or triune God still remained, yet, during the five hundred years which elapsed until the time of Moses, the grossest idolatry had come to prevail. Notwithstanding the fact that Moses had learned much from the Egyptians, he seems not to have risen above a very gross conception of a deity. His god was by turns angry, jealous, revengeful, vacillating, and weak. He was in fact the embodiment of human passions and desires. We have seen that the third person in the ancient Trinity had, in Egypt, India, and Persia, come to be recognized in place of the three principles originally worshipped—that, as it really embodied the essence of the other two, little was heard of the Creator and Preserver. Doubtless this God was the one which Moses intended the Israelites to worship, but as they were unable to conceive of an abstract principle he invested it with a personality which, as we have seen, was burdened with the frailties and weaknesses common to themselves.

As the Regenerator or Destroyer represented the processes of Nature,—the dying away of the sun's rays at night only to reappear on the following day, and the withdrawal of its warmth in winter only to be renewed in the spring,—so this God portrayed also the beneficent Creator and Preserver of all things, at the same time that it was the Destroyer. It embodied the fundamental idea in all religions, namely, life and fertility. So also did the "Lord" of the Israelites represent reproductive energy, but as man being spirit had come to be a Creator of offspring, while woman being only matter furnished the body, this "Lord" was male. Connected with it was no hint of the female nature or principle, except the ark or chest in which it was carried about. To those who have acquainted themselves with the significance of ancient religious symbols, the fact is plain that the "Lord" of the Israelites, which in their journeyings toward Canaan they carried in an ark or chest, and which was symbolized by an upright stone, was none other than a "Life-giver" in the most practical sense. It was the emblem of virility, and from the facts at hand, at the present time, there is little doubt but that all the spirituality with which we find this "Lord" invested was an afterthought and comprehended no part of the belief of the Jews until after their contact with the Persians during the Babylonian captivity.

Doubtless the story in which their journeyings toward Canaan are set forth contains an esoteric as well as an exoteric significance for ages known only to the priests, and that within it is embodied not alone something of the true history of this people, but an account also of their struggle against an older religion. At this time the Israelites had practically commenced the elimination of the female principle from their god-idea, and had begun the worship of the male element, the female being represented by an ark, chest, or box. This ark, as the receptacle of the god, was still a holy thing.

Not only among the Israelites, but among other nations of the East, we find the devotees of the male god beginning to assume a position quite independent of the beliefs of their fathers. At this time great towers or pillars begin to be erected in honor of this deity, which is figured as the "God of Life," or as the "Lord of Hosts." Notwithstanding the fact that the story of the Exodus contains much historical truth, it is altogether probable that the priests have used it, as they did that of the flood, to conceal their religious doctrines.

At the time of the Exodus, the Israelites were ignorant tribes without laws or letters, and while in Egypt were menials of the lowest order. Hence, the laws written on the two tables of stone, and which it is claimed were elaborated during their wanderings in the wilderness of Sinai for the guidance of these unlettered slaves, show the desire of the priests of later times to invest the "chosen people" with the insignia of enlightenment.

Regarding the character of the god which they worshipped, we have ample proof in the Old Testament. It is plain that at the time of their bondage in Egypt the Jews had become the grossest phallic worshippers, adoring the emblems of generation, with no thought of their earlier significance as pure symbols of creative force in mortals.

The fact will doubtless be remembered that, among the Jews, to be barren was the greatest curse, and that the principal reward promised to the faithful was fruitfulness of body. The essence of this deity was heat or passion, and his emblem was the serpent or an upright stone. It has been observed that when this "Lord" was invested with personality he was subject to all the frailties of his followers. His chief and most emphatic characteristic, however, was jealousy of other gods, and most of the imprecations thundered against the chosen people were directed against the worship of the gods of surrounding nations, those which the Israelites had originally worshipped.

That portion of the Decalogue relating to a jealous god is seen to belong wholly to the Jews, or to the Israelites, who were descendants of Jacob. The older nations, among which was the ancient family of the Hebrews, knew nothing of a jealous god. Notwithstanding the fact that the God of the Jews appeared and talked face to face with Moses, that he exhibited portions of his body to him, and that he thundered his law to this people from Mt. Sinai, still they were constantly lapsing into the worship of Baal and Ashtaroth, which fact shows how deeply rooted was the belief in a dual or triune God. It is plain that this "Lord," the fierce anger of whom was kindled because of their digressions, was none other than the jealous male god which had but recently been elevated to the dignity of a supreme Creator.

Although the angel of the Lord when he came down from Gilgal commanded his followers to "throw down the altars of the people of Bochim," they nevertheless continued to do evil in the sight of the Lord, and

"followed other gods, of the gods of the people that were round about them, and bound themselves unto them and provoked the Lord to anger.

"And they forsook the Lord, and served Baal and Ashtaroth. And the anger of the Lord was hot against Israel."[81]

"And Samuel spake unto all the house of Israel, saying, If ye do return unto the Lord with all your hearts, then put away the strange gods and Ashtaroth from among you and prepare your hearts unto the Lord, and serve him only: and he will deliver you out of the hand of the Philistines.

"Then the children of Israel did put away Baalim and Ashtaroth and served the Lord only."[82]

The extreme hatred of the schismatic faction for the opposite worship, and the punishments which were meted out to those who should dare to rebel against the chosen faith, are indicated by the language which throughout the Old Testament is put into the mouth of their Lord–a Deity which rejoices in the title of a jealous God.

"If thy brother, the son of thy mother, or thy son, or thy daughter, or the wife of thy bosom, or thy friend, which is as thine own soul, entice thee secretly, saying, Let us go and serve other gods, which thou hast not known thou nor thy fathers:

---

[81] Judges ii., 12, 13.
[82] I Samuel vii., 3,4.

"Namely, of the gods of the people which are round about you, nigh unto thee, or far off from thee, from the one end of the earth even unto the other end of the earth;

"Thou shalt not consent unto him, nor hearken unto him; neither shall thine eye pity him, neither shalt thou spare, neither shalt thou conceal him:

"But thou shalt surely kill him; thine hand shall be first upon him to put him to death, and afterwards the hand of all the people.

"And thou shalt stone him with stones, that he die; because he hath sought to thrust thee away from the Lord thy God, which brought thee out of the land of Egypt, from the house of bondage.

"And all Israel shall hear, and fear, and shall do no more any such wickedness as this is among you."[83]

The constantly recurring faithlessness of the Jews, their restlessness and proneness to wander from their one-principled deity which had been set up by their priests for them to worship, was doubtless an unconscious effort on the part of the people to mitigate the outrage which had been committed against their Creator. It was but a reaching out for that lost or unrecognized element which comprehends the more essential force both in human beings and in the conception of a deity. In other words, it was an attempt at recognition, in the objects worshipped, of that missing female element which had always been worshipped, and without which a Creator becomes a misnomer–a meaningless, unexplained, and unexplainable monstrosity.

When the Jews first make their appearance in history, they are sun worshippers, as are all the nations by which they are surrounded. They are worshippers of Seth the Destroyer and Regenerator; but when the philosophical truths underlying the ancient universal religion were forgotten, or when through ignorance the language setting

---

[83] Deuteronomy xiii.

forth these mysteries was taken literally, Seth became identified with the Destroyer, or the Evil Principle. In the meantime man had come to believe himself the sole creator of offspring. He is spirit, which is eternal; woman is matter, which is not only destructible but altogether evil. He is heat or passion–the principle through which life is produced. She represents the absence of heat. She is the simoom of the desert and the chilly blast which destroys.

That it was no part of their plan to change their original form of worship for a spiritual conception of a Creator is apparent from their history. On the contrary, it is plain that they desired simply to eliminate from the hitherto dual conception of a deity the female principle, which, in their arrogance, and because of the change which had been wrought in the relations of the sexes, they no longer acknowledged as important in the office of reproduction.

It is quite true they would worship only one god–the "Lord,"–but that lord was, as we have seen, a deity of physical strength and virile might, a "Lord of Hosts," a god which was to be worshipped under the symbol of an upright stone–an object which by every nation of the globe down to a comparatively recent time has typified male pro-creative energy. That the masses of the people, even as late as the time of Jeremiah, had no higher conception of a God than that indicated by an upright stone, is shown by that prophet when he accuses the entire house of Israel, "their kings, their princes, and their priests, and their prophets," of "saying to a stock, Thou art my father; and to a stone, Thou hast brought me forth."

That the people could not, or would not, be prevailed upon to renounce the Queen of Heaven, the Celestial Mother, is seen in Jer. vii., 17, 18:

"Seest thou not what they do in the cities of Judah and in the streets of Jerusalem? The children gather wood, and the fathers kindle the fire, and the women knead their dough, to make cakes to the queen of heaven and to pour out drink offerings unto other gods."

Also in Jeremiah xliv:

"Then all the men which knew that their wives had burned incense unto other gods, and all the women that stood by, a great multitude, even all the people that dwelt in the land of Egypt, in Pathros, answered Jeremiah, saying, As for the word that thou hast spoken unto us in the name of the Lord, we will not hearken unto thee.

"But we will certainly do whatsoever thing goeth forth out of our own mouth, to burn incense unto the queen of heaven and to pour out drink offerings unto her, as we have done, we and our fathers, our kings, and our princes, in the cities of Judah, and in the streets of Jerusalem: for then had we plenty of victuals, and were well, and saw no evil.

"But since we left off to burn incense to the queen of heaven and to pour out drink offerings unto her, we have wanted all things, and have been consumed by the sword and by the famine.

"And when we burned incense to the queen of heaven, and poured out drink offerings unto her, did we make her cakes to worship her and pour out drink offerings unto her without our men?"

That the above represents a quarrel in which the women of Judah openly rebelled against the worship of the "Lord," at the same time declaring their allegiance to the female Deity, the Celestial Mother, Queen of Heaven, is only too evident, the curse pronounced upon them by Jeremiah, in the name of the lord, having little effect upon them to change their purpose.

"Therefore, hear ye the word of the Lord, all Judah that dwell in the land of Egypt; Behold, I have sworn by my great name, saith the Lord, that my name shall no more be named in the mouth of any man of Judah in all the land of Egypt, saying, The Lord God liveth.

"Behold, I will watch over them for evil, and not for good: and all the men of Judah that are in the land of Egypt shall be consumed by the sword and by the famine, until there be an end of them."

Chapter IX.
The Phoenician and Hebrew God Set or Seth

The name of one of the oldest deities of which we have any record is Set (Phoenician) or Seth (Hebrew). Traces of this God are found in all oriental countries; and in the most primitive religions, whose traditions are still extant, he (or she) appears as the supreme God. After the subjection of Egypt by the stranger kings and the consequent introduction into the country of Sabianism, the dual creative force residing in the sun is represented by Seth. We are told that Seth signifies "appointed or put in the place of the murdered Abel."

That there is some deep mystery connected with this subject none who has studied it carefully can help observing.

According to the story of creation as set forth in the Jehovistic account, on Saturday night, after God had finished his work, and immediately after he had commanded Adam to "be fruitful," he presents him with a staff, which we observe is handed down to Enoch and all the patriarchs. Here the mystery deepens, for it is declared that this staff was presented so Seth, and that it was a branch of the Tree of Life.

That beneath this allegory is veiled a contest, or perhaps a compromise, between the worshippers of two distinct sects, seems altogether probable. That the handing down of this branch of the Tree of Life, first to Adam, or man, by Aleim, and its subsequent transference to Seth, the God of Nature, the Destroyer or Regenerator, seems to indicate a victory for the adherents of a purer religion. The translator of Kallimachus says: "It is well known to the learned reader that the descendants of Cain are distinguished in Scripture by the name of the sons of man or Adam; those of Seth by the name of the sons of God." Gen. vi., 2.[84] It is stated in Julius Africanus that all the righteous men and patriarchs down to the Saviour himself have sprung from Seth and have been denominated as the sons of God in contradistinction to the sons of man.

Doubtless at the time indicated by the transference of the creative agency from Aleim to Adam, the worship of an abstract principle, or of a Trinity composed of the powers of Nature, was losing its hold on the minds of the people, and the creative power, or the reproductive energy in human beings, was rapidly taking the place of the older Deity. These higher principles forgotten, Adam, or man, had become the Creator.

It is not improbable that the terms Adam, Cain, Abel, and Seth have an esoteric meaning which for ages was known only to the priests. From various facts which in later times are being brought forward regarding the ancient myths of Genesis, it is believed that these names originally stood for races of men, and that subsequently certain religious doctrines came to be attached to them. The offering of fruit by Cain, the elder brother, who was a tiller of the ground, and that of flesh by Abel, who was a keeper of sheep, indicates a quarrel which ended in the death of the latter. After the death of Abel, or after one of these principles or sects was subdued, the older religion was revived, and Seth, as the Aleim, or as the creative power within the sun, was "appointed" or again worshipped.

It would seem that Seth was appointed to represent the third person in the ancient Trinity–the Destroyer or Regenerator which had previously come to embody all the powers of the Creator and Preserver. The fact has been

---

[84] Forlong, Rivers of Life, vol. i., p. 527.

observed that the very ancient philosophers believed matter to be eternal, hence, seeming death, or destruction, was necessary to renewed life or regeneration. In other words, creation was but continuous change in the form of matter.

Of the doctrines of the Sethians extant at the beginning of Christianity, Hippolytus says that their system "is made up of tenets from natural philosophers. These tenets embrace a belief in the Eternal Logos–Darkness, Mist, and Tempest." These elements subsequently became identified with the Evil Principle, or the Devil. The cold of winter, the darkness of night, and water, were finally set forth as the Trinity. Regarding cold, darkness, and water, or darkness, mist, and tempest, Hippolytus observes:

"These the Sethian says are the three principles of our system; or when he states that three were born in paradise–Adam, Eve, the serpent; or when he speaks of three persons, namely, Cain, Abel, Seth, and again of three others, Shem, Ham, Japheth; or when he mentions three patriarchs–Abraham, Isaac, Jacob; or when he speaks of three days before the sun, etc."

The same writer says that their entire system is derived from the ancients; that, antecedent to the Eleusinian mysteries, were enacted by them the ceremonies connected with the worship of the Great Mother.[85]

We have observed that through some process not thoroughly understood at the present time, the adherents of the older faith had succeeded in reinstating their Deity. The powers of Nature had come to be represented by Typhon Seth. It was the God of Death and of Life, of Destruction and Regeneration. The simoom of the desert and the cold of winter were Seth, as were also the genial powers of Spring. We are informed by various writers that Typhon Seth was feminine. She was the early God of the Jews. In other

---

[85] Hippolytus, Refutation of all Heresies, book v., ch. 15.

words, the Jews were formerly worshippers of a female Deity. Jehovah, Iav, was originally female.

Although the secret meaning of all the allegories contained in the Old Testament is not fully understood, still the belief that Cain, Abel, and Seth represented the self-triplicated Deity at a time when the idea of man as a creator had been accepted, or when his power to reproduce was becoming the highest idea of a creative force, is consistent with what is known of the Cabala of the Jews, or of the esoteric meaning of the Jewish scriptures formerly known only to the priests. In other words, the ancient doctrines, the true meaning of which was no longer understood by them, were patched together as a basis for the later developments in Jewish religious experience.

We have seen that six hundred years after Adam appears Noah, another self-triplicated Saviour or preserver of man, with his ark or seed vessel, beneath which is veiled the female element. Afterward Abraham becomes the Great Father or Saviour, and later Moses. That, in the time of the latter, the more ancient worship of a creative force in Nature represented by the Aleim, had, by the masses of the people, been wholly lost, is evident from the Old Testament writings. The worship of the Father, the male power, in opposition to that of the Mother, or the female power, constituted the religion of Moses. In the religion of the Jews, Jehovah came to be regarded as wholly male and as spirit, while Edam (translated "downward tending"), the female principle, was matter, or woman, which finally became identified with the Devil.

The philosophical doctrine that spirit is evolved through matter, or that matter must be raised to a certain dynamical power before spirit can manifest itself through it, was no longer understood; only the husks of this doctrine – the myths and symbols of Nature-worship–remained; these were taken literally, and thus man's religion was made to conform to his lowered estate.

When man had so far gained the ascendancy over woman as to assert that he is the sole Creator of their joint offspring, he was no longer of the earth earthy, but at once became the child of heaven. He was, however, bound to earth through his association with matter, or with woman, from whom he was unable to free himself. The "sons of God" were united "to the daughters of man." Jahvah, the "God of hosts," who was revengeful, weak, jealous, and cruel, was worshipped in the place of Aleim the great dual force throughout Nature. The ethereal, spiritual male essence resided somewhere in the heavens and created from afar, while the earth (female) furnished only the body or material substance.

In the history of the god Seth is to be found a clue to the way in which the sublime and philosophical doctrines of the ancients, after their true meaning was forgotten, were finally changed so as to conform to the enforced humiliation and degradation of women.

Seth or Typhon was for ages worshipped throughout Egypt, and as she comprehended the powers of Nature, or the creative energy residing in the sun and earth, little is heard of any other god. Strange it is, however, that Seth is worshipped more in her capacity as Destroyer than as Regenerator. So soon as we understand the origin and character of the Devil, and so soon as we divest ourselves of the false ideas which under a state of ignorance and gross sensuality came to prevail relative to the "powers of darkness," we shall perceive that his (or her) Satanic majesty was once a very respectable personage and a powerful Divinity–a Divinity which was worshipped by a people whose superior intelligence can scarcely be questioned. Regarding this subject Higgins remarks:

"Persons who have not given much consideration to these subjects will be apt to wonder that any people should be found to offer adoration to the evil principle; but they do not consider that, in all these recondite systems, the evil principle, or the Destroyer, or Lord of Death, was at the same time the Regenerator. He could not destroy but to reproduce, and it was probably not till this principle began to be forgotten, that the evil being, per se, arose; for in some nations this effect seems to have taken place. Thus Baal-Zebub is, in Iberno Celtic, Baal Lord, and Zab Death, Lord of Death; but he is also called Aleim, the same as the God of the Israelites; and this is right, because he was one of the Trimurti or Trinity.

"If I be correct respecting the word Aleim being feminine, we here see the Lord of Death of the feminine gender; but the Goddess Ashtaroth or Astarte, the Eoster of the Germans, was also called Aleim. Here again Aleim is feminine, which shows that I am right in making Aleim the plural feminine. Thus we have distinctly found Aleim the Creator (Gen. i., 1), Aleim the Preserver, and Aleim the Destroyer, and this not by inference, but literally expressed."[86]

At one period of their history the Hebrews worshipped Ashtaroth and Baal, they together representing the great Aleim, the indivisible God, but after the Israelites had chosen the worship of the male principle as an independent deity, or as the only important agency in the creative processes, as Baal might not be represented aside from his counterpart Ashtaroth, he was no longer adored but came to stand for something "approaching the Devil." Forlong has observed the fact that, although in Hebrew Baal is masculine, in the Greek translations he is feminine both in the Old and New Testaments.[87]

Jehovah was originally female, so, also, was Netpe the Holy Spirit of the Egyptian Tree of Life. We are given to understand that Netpe was the same as Rhea, the partner of Sev or Saturn, and that her hieroglyphic name was "Abyss

---

[86] Anacalypsis, ch. ii., p. 66.
[87] Forlong, Rivers of Life, p. 223.

of Heaven." Osiris was the son of this goddess who was really a Mai or Mary, the Celestial Mother, he being the only God of the Egyptians who was born upon this earth and lived among men. Of this Forlong remarks: "His birthplace was Mount Sinai; called by the Egyptians Nysa, hence his Greek name Dionysos."

As the Palm was the first offering of Mother Earth to her children, so Osiris was the first offspring of the Egyptian Celestial Virgin to mankind. He was the new sun which through the winter months had been "buried," but which in process of time arose to gladden all the earth. He was also the new Sun of Righteousness which was to renew the world, or redeem mankind from sin.

The female principle for the time being cast out of the Deity, Osiris, the male element, now outwardly assumes the position of supreme God. It was, however, reserved for a later and more sensuous age to permanently adopt an absurdity so opposed to all established ideas relative to a creative force in Nature and in man. Seth, the Destroyer, had been deposed, but, so deeply rooted in the human mind had become the idea of a female Creator, that Isis, the Queen of Heaven, a somewhat lower conception of Muth, or of universal womanhood, soon assumed the place of Seth beside Osiris. Later in the history of Egypt, when the gods have become greatly multiplied, and the original significance of the deity obscured, Horus, the child and the third member in the later Egyptian triad, not unfrequently appears in her place as one of the eight great gods.

The fact is observed that the history of Osiris is not alone the "history of the circle of the year, or of the sun dying away and resuscitating itself again, but that it is also the history of the cycle of 600." It has been said that of the component elements of his hieroglyphical name, Isis is the first, and that the name Osiris really signifies the "Eye of Isis."

According to Plutarch, Isis and Muth are identical, but from the evidence at hand it is plain that Muth comprehends divine womanhood, or the female principle as it was regarded at an earlier stage of human growth. Muth is not only the parent of the sun, or the force which produces the sun, but she is also Wisdom, the first emanation from the Deity, at the same time that she comprehends all the possibilities of Nature. Isis seems to represent the Deity at a time when the higher truths known to a more ancient people were beginning to lose their hold upon the race.

Renouf informs us that the word Maat, or Muth, means Law, "not in that forensic sense of command issued either by a human sovereign authority, or by a divine legislator, like the laws of the Hebrews, but in the sense of that unerring order which governs the universe, whether in its physical or its moral aspect."[88] The same writer observes further that Maat "is called mistress of Heaven, ruler of earth, and president of the nether world," and in a further description of the conception embodied in this Deity, refers to the fact that while she is the mother of the sun she is also the first emanation from God.

Although Typhon Seth was long worshipped as the sole Deity in Egypt, in later ages the god-idea came to be represented by Seth and Osiris. Toward the close of Typhon Seth's reign, Horus, the child, the young sun, was represented "as rising from his hiding-place, attracting beneficent vapors to return them back as dews, which the Egyptians called the tears of Isis."

Seth and Osiris represent a division of the Deity. Osiris, as the sun, represents heat; as man, or as god, he stands for desire. Seth or Typhon stands for the cold of winter, the simoom of the desert, or the "wind that blasts." Seth, Osiris, and Horus constitute a Trinity of which Muth is the Great

---

[88] The Religion of Ancient Egypt, p. 126.

Mother. Finally, with the gradual ascendancy of male influence and power, it is observed that Seth appears as the brother of Osiris.

It is the opinion of Bunsen that the fundamental idea of Osiris and Set was "not merely the glorification of the sun, but was also the worship of the primitive creative power."[89] But, as in Egypt the creative agency was regarded as both female and male, the former being in the ascendancy, this fact of itself would seem to determine the sex and position of Seth.

In the ideas concerning Seth and Osiris may be observed something of the manner in which the fructifying agencies of the sun and the reproductive power in human beings were blended and together worshipped as the Deity; while through the history of these gods are to be traced some of the processes by which the idea of the Creator was changed from female to male.

In all countries, at a certain stage in the history of religion, the transference of female deified power to mortal man may be observed. In the attempt to change Seth or Typhon into a male God may be noted perhaps the first effort in Egypt to dethrone, or lessen the female power in the god-idea.

The fact seems plain that the Great Typhon Seth, or Set, who conferred on the sovereigns of the eighteenth and nineteenth dynasties of Egypt "the symbols of life and power," was none other than the primitive Regenerator or Destroyer, who was for ages worshipped as the God of Nature the Aleim, or the life-giving energy throughout the universe.

We have observed that when the profound principles underlying the most ancient doctrines had been lost or forgotten, and when through the decay of philosophy, and through the stimulation of the sensual in human nature,

---

[89] History of Egypt, vol. iv., p. 319.

mankind had lost the power to reason abstractly, Destruction, which was symbolized by darkness or the absence of the sun's rays, finally became the evil principle, or the Devil. Darkness and cold, which had formerly been worshipped as the powers which brought forth the sun, or as mother of the sun, in process of time became the agency which is ever warring with good and which is constantly destroying that which the latter brings forth.

We are informed by Forlong that "some derive our term Devil from Niphl or Nevil, the wind that blasts or obstructs the growth of corn; and it used sometimes to be written th' evil, which is D'evil or Devil."

It was "this Dualistic heresy which separated the Zend or Persian branch of the Aryans from their Vedic brethren, and compelled them to emigrate to the westward."[90]

The ancient philosophical truth that matter is eternal, and that the destruction of vegetable life through the agency of cold was one of the necessary processes of regeneration, or the renewal of life, had evidently been lost sight of at the time when Seth was dethroned in Egypt. Wilkinson informs us that "both Seth and Osiris were adored until a change took place respecting Seth, brought about apparently by foreign influence." Sethi or Sethos, a ruler whose reign represents the Augustan age of Egyptian splendor, received his name from this Deity. It is said that during the twentieth dynasty Seth is suddenly portrayed as the principle of evil "with which is associated sin." Consequently all the effigies of this great Goddess were destroyed and all her names and inscriptions "which could be reached" were effaced.

Bunsen tells us that Schelling, who has made a study of Egyptian mythology, although totally ignorant of the later historical facts which by means of hieroglyphical monuments have been obtained, had arrived at the

---

[90] See Rawlinson, Notes on the Early History of Babylon.

conclusion that Seth had occupied an important position in the Deity down to the fourteenth century B.C. "Schelling had on mere speculative grounds been brought to lay down as a postulate that Typhon, at some early period, had been considered by the Egyptians as a beneficent and powerful God."

Wilkinson says that the character given to Seth, who was called Baal-Seth and the God of the Gentiles, "is explained by his being the cause of evil." We are assured that formerly "Sin the great serpent, or Apophis the giant, was distinct from Seth who was a deity and a part of the divine system. But after the recondite principles underlying sun-worship were lost or forgotten; when cold and darkness, or the sinking away of the sun's rays, which are necessary to the reappearance of light and warmth, came to be regarded as the destructive element, or the evil principle, woman became identified with this principle. She was the producer of evil, and came to be represented in connection with a serpent as the cause of all earthly or material things. She is Destruction, but not Regeneration. She is in fact matter. The cold of winter and the darkness of night, which are necessary to the return of the sun's warmth and which were formerly set forth as a beneficent mother who brings forth the sun, became only the evil principle–that which obscures the light. In fact Darkness or absence of the sun's heat has become the Devil. It is the "cause of evil in the world."

With woman blinded by superstition, with every instinct of the female nature outraged, and with her position as the central figure in the Deity and in the family usurped, her temples were soon profaned, her images defiled, and the titles representing her former greatness transferred to males.

There is no doubt but this doctrine was the legitimate outcome of the decay of female influence. Through the further stimulation of the lower nature of man its absurdity gradually increased, until under the system calling itself Christian it finally reached its height. This subject will be referred to later in these pages.

When we remember that the original representation of the Deity among the nations of the earth consisted of a female figure embracing a child, and when we observe that subsequently in the development of the god-idea woman appears associated with a serpent as the cause of evil in the world, the history of the God Seth, who, as we have seen, represented the processes of Nature, namely Destruction and Regeneration, seems quite significant as indicating some of the actual processes involved in this change.

There can be little doubt that the facts relating to this Deity indicate the source whence has sprung the great theological dogma underlying Christianity, that woman is the cause of evil in the world.

Chapter X.
Ancient Speculations Concerning Creation

"Daughters of Jove, All hail! but O inspire
The lovely song! the sacred race proclaim
Of ever-living gods; who sprang from Earth,
From the starred Heaven, and from the gloomy Night,
And whom the salt Deep nourished into life.
Declare how first the gods and Earth became;
The rivers and th' immeasurable sea
High-raging in its foam; the glittering stars,
The wide impending Heaven; and who from these
Of deities arose, dispensing good;
Say how their treasures, how their honors each
Allotted shar'd: how first they held abode
On many-caved Olympus:–this declare,
Ye Muses! dwellers of the heavenly mount
From the beginning; say, who first arose?
First Chaos was: next ample-bosomed Earth,
Of deathless gods, who still the Olympian heights
Snow-topt inhabit. . . .
Her first-born Earth produced
Of like immensity, the starry Heaven:
That he might sheltering compass her around
On every side, and be forevermore
To the blest gods a mansion unremoved."

--Hesiod, The Theogony.

So long as human beings worshipped the abstract principle of creation, the manifestations of which proceed from the earth and sun, they doubtless reasoned little on the nature of its hitherto inseparable parts. They had not at that early period begun to look outside of Nature for their god-idea, but when through the peculiar course of development which had been entered upon, the simple conception of a creative agency originally entertained became obscured, mankind began to speculate on the nature and attributes of the two principles by which everything is produced, and to dispute over their relative importance in the office of reproduction. Much light has been thrown upon these speculations by the Kosmogonies which have come down to us from the Phoenicians, Babylonians, and other peoples of past ages. In the Phoenician Kosmogony, according to the Mokh doctrine as recorded by Philo, out of the kosmic egg Toleeleth (female) "sprang all the impregnation of creation and the beginning of the universe." In this exposition of the beginnings of things, it is distinctly stated that the spirit which in after ages came to be regarded as something outside or above Nature, "had no consciousness of its own creation." Commenting on the above, Bunsen is constrained to admit that it is usually understood as being "decidedly pantheistic." He suggests, however, that the writer may HAVE INTENDED TO SAY (the italics are mine) that "the spirit who was heretofore the Creator was the unconscious spirit."

Berosus, the scholar of Babylon, who, until a comparatively recent time has furnished all the information extant concerning Babylonian antiquities, in his account of the creation of man and of the universe, says that in the beginning all was water and darkness; that in the water were the beginnings of life; but as yet there was no order. Men were there with the wings of birds and even with the feet of beasts. There were also quadrupeds and men with fishes' tails, all of which had been produced by a twofold principle. Over this incongruous mass a woman presided. This woman is called Omoroka by the Babylonians and by the Chaldeans Thalatth. The latter name, signifies, "bearing" or "egg producing."

In the Babylonian Kosmogony, according to Endemus, the pupil of Aristotle, the beginning of the universe was called Tauthe, which being interpreted means "Mother of the Gods." Associated with her sometimes appears the male principle–Apason. In the history of Berosus, there is given an account of Oaunes–a mythical teacher of Babylon, who appeared with the head of a human being and the body of a fish or serpent. This personage brought to the Babylonians all the knowledge which they possessed. Oaunes wrote "concerning the generation of mankind, of their different ways of life, and of their civil polity." He it was who gave the above account of creation. He says that finally Omoroka, or Thalatth, the woman who existed before the creation, was divided, one half of her forming the heavens, "the other half the earth." "All this," Berosus declares, "was an allegorical description of Nature."[91]

In the following legend will be observed the groundwork for the story of the flood. Xisuthrus was a king of Chaldea. To him the deity, Kronos, appeared in a vision and warned him that upon the fifteenth day of the month Daesius there would be a flood, by which mankind would be destroyed. He therefore enjoined him to write a history of the beginning, progress, and conclusion of all things down to the present time, and to bury it in Sippara, the City of the Sun. He was commanded also to build a vessel, and take with him into it his friends and relations, and to convey on board everything necessary to sustain life, together with all the different animals, both birds and quadrupeds, and trust himself fearlessly to the deep. Having asked the deity whither he was to sail, he was answered: "To the gods"; upon which he offered up a prayer for the good of mankind. He then obeyed the divine admonition,

---

[91] Prof. Smith, Chaldean Account of Genesis, pp. 34, 35.

and built a vessel five stadia in length and two in breadth. Into this he put everything which he had prepared, and last of all conveyed into it his wife, his children, and his friends.

"After the flood had been upon the earth, and was in time abated, Xisuthrus sent out birds from the vessel, which not finding any food, nor any place whereupon they might rest their feet, returned to him again. After an interval of some days, he sent them forth a second time; and they now returned with their feet tinged with mud. He made a trial a third time with these birds; but they returned to him no more: from which he judged that the surface of the earth had appeared above the waters. He therefore made an opening in the vessel, end upon looking out found that it was stranded upon the side of some mountain, upon which he immediately quitted it with his wife, his daughter, and the pilot. Xisuthrus then paid his adoration to the earth: and, having constructed an altar, offered sacrifices to the gods, and, with those who had come out of the vessel with him, disappeared. Him they saw no more, but they could distinguish his voice in the air, and could hear him admonish them to pay due regard to the gods. He informed them that it was on account of his piety that he had been taken away to live with the gods, and that his wife and daughter had obtained the same honor."

It is more than likely that this story, which as we have seen has extended to the remotest corners of the earth, has an esoteric meaning, and that it embodies the doctrines of the ancients relative to re- incarnation and the renewal of worlds. Doubtless it portrays not only the end of a cycle, but that by it is prefigured the fortunes of a human soul, which in its ascent, is from time to time forced into a human body.

All the early Kosmogonies are intermingled with the history of a great flood, from the ravages of which an ark which contained a man was saved. The Gothic story of creation indicates that the Scythians belonged to the same race as the Chaldeans. At the beginning of time when nothing had been formed, and before the earth, the sea, or the heavens appeared, Muspelsheim existed. A breath of heat passing over the vapors, melted them into water, and from this water was formed a cow named Aedumla, who was the progenitor of Odin, Vile, and Ve, the Trinity of the Gothic nation.

There is also another tradition, probably a later, which asserts that from the drops of water produced by the primeval breath of heat, a man, Ymer, was brought forth. The son of Ymer was preserved in a storm-tossed bark, his father being dragged into the middle of the abyss, where, from his body the earth was produced. The sea was made of his blood, the mountains of his bones, and the rocks of his teeth. As three of his descendants were walking on the shore one day, they found two pieces of wood which had been washed up by the waves. Of these they made a man and a woman. The man they named Aske and the woman Emla. From this pair has descended the human race.

The marked resemblance between the characters of the Gothic Ymer and the Chaldean Omoroka, from each of whose bodies the universe is created, has been observed by various writers. After referring to Mallet's conclusions upon this subject, Faber remarks:

"They are indeed evidently the same person, not only in point of character, but, if I mistake not, in appellation: for Ymer or Umer is Omer-Oca expressed in a more simple form. The difference of sex does by no means invalidate this opinion, which rests upon the perfect identity of their characters: for the Great Mother, like the Great Father, was an hermaphrodite; or, rather, that person from whom all things were supposed to be produced, was the Great Father and the Great Mother united together in one compound being. Ymer and Omoroca are each the same as that hermaphrodite Jupiter of the Orphic theology."

We have observed, however, that in all the older traditions this hermaphrodite conception is accounted as female, it is the Great Mother within whom is contained the male; in later ages, however, it is represented as male, the female being concealed beneath convenient symbols.

The Trinity of the Goths was male; yet as Odin could not create independently of the female energy he is provided with a wife, Frigga, to whom "all fair things belonged, and who had priestesses among the early German tribes." Frigga when worshipped alone was both female and male. According to one German tradition, Tiw (Zeus), which in its earliest conception was female, was the parent of the first man. This man begat three sons who became the fathers of the three Deutsch tribes. Ish (or Ash) was the parent of the Franks and Allemans; Ing was the progenitor of the Swedes, Angles, and Saxons; and Er, or Erman, was the eponymous leader of the tribes called by the Romans Hermiones.

The Kosmogony of the Chinese is similar in all respects to that of other countries. The first man, Puoncu, was born from an egg.

The Chinese say that this egg-born Puoncu, who is identical with Brahm, Noah, and Adam, is not the great Creator or God, but only the first man. Their great God or Tien is a Unity which comprehends three, and their human triad–a triplicated being who is the parent of the human race–is a lower expression of the same power, and to him has finally been ascribed the office of Creator.

The Kosmogony of the Japanese begins with the opening of the sacred egg from which all things were produced. This egg is identical with the ark, and from it the diluvian patriarch was born. He was "Baal-Peor or the lord of opening; and, from an idea that the Ark was an universal mother, he was considered as the masculine principle of generation, and was adored by his apostate descendants with all the abominations of phallic worship."

In the Theogony of Hesiod, Uranus is represented as being the parent of three sons, and the same legend repeated in the story of Cronus portrays him also as a triplicated deity. According to the Peruvian Kosmogony all things sprang from Viracocha who is said to be identical with the Greek Aphrodite. Besides this superior God they venerated a triad which was closely connected with the sun. These gods were called Chuquilla, Catuilla, and Intyllapa. They say that as their ancestors journeyed from a remote country to the Northwest they bore the image of their god in a coifer or box made of reeds. To the four priests who had charge of this box or ark he communicated his oracles and directions. He not only gave them laws but taught them the ceremonies and sacrifices which they were to observe. "And even as the pillar of cloud and fire conducted the Israelites in their passage through the wilderness, so this Spanish devil gave them notice when to advance forward, and when to stay."[92]

According to Marsden, the New Zealanders believe that three gods created the first man, and that the first woman was made from one of his ribs.

Among the Otaheitans and various tribes of Indians, the belief prevails that all created things have proceeded from a triplicated deity who was saved from the ravages of a flood in an ark or ship.

The fact is observed that the Theogonies and Kosmogonies of all peoples have reference to a flood or to the renewal of life after the destruction of the world, and that the Great Father who is preserved, and who comes forth from an ark or ship with the seeds of a former world, represents the beginning of a new era. Adam with his three sons, Cain, Abel, and Seth, Noah with his triad, Shem, Ham, and Japheth, Menu and his triple offspring, and so on, all

---

[92] Faber, Pagan Idolatry, book i., ch. v.

mean exactly the same thing, namely, the renewal of life at the close of a cycle, or manwantara.

From the traditions extant in nearly every quarter of the globe, it would seem that, prior to the so-called flood in the time of Noah, man, as a Creator, had not to any extent been worshipped, but, on the contrary, that the great universal dual principle which pervades Nature and which is back of matter and force, for instance Tien among the Chinese, Iav among the Hebrews, and Aum among the Hindoos, had been the Deity adored; but with the decline of virtue and knowledge, this God was gradually abandoned for a lesser one, a deity better suited to the comprehension of "fallen" man.

In the Elohistic narrative of creation which appears in the first chapter of Genesis, a dual or triune God, female and male, says, Let us make man in our own image, and accordingly a male and a female are created. In the Jehovistic account, however, in the second chapter of the same book, a document of much later date, man is made first and afterward woman. In fact, in the latter narrative she appears as an afterthought and is created simply for his use; she is taken from his side and is wholly dependent upon him for existence. This fact is recognized by Bishop Colenso in the following words:

"Thus in the second account of creation, the man is APPARENTLY created first, and the woman is CERTAINLY created the last, of all living creatures; whereas, in the older story the man and woman are created last of all, as the crowning work of Elohim, and are created together–'and Elohim created man in His own image, in the image of Elohim created He him; male and female created He them.' This ancient Elohistic narrative, then, the Jehovist had before him; and he enlarged and enlivened it by introducing a number of passages recording additional incidents in the lives of the patriarchs before and after the flood, and especially by inserting the second account of the creation, ii., 4-25."

Colenso observes that verse four of chapter second belongs to the Elohist, and that it was removed from its original position at the beginning of Gen. i., in order to form the commencement of the Jehovistic account of the creation.[93]

Quoting from Bishop Browne in the New Bible Commentary, the same writer remarks that in the Elohistic account of the creation "we have that which was probably the ancient primeval record of the formation of the world."[94]

The oldest or Elohistic portion of Genesis is, at the present time, seen to conceal great wisdom and a knowledge of Nature far surpassing that of later times.

According to Higgins, the first verse of the first chapter of Genesis, if properly translated, would not declare that in the beginning God created the heavens and the earth, but that Wisdom "formed" the earth and the planets. In none of the ancient Kosmogonies can there be a word found regarding the creation of matter. From the facts which have come down to us respecting the speculations of the ancients, it is plain that the original conception was, that within the primeval beginnings described in their Kosmogonies, in chaos or unorganized matter, was contained primeval force; no attempt, however, was made by them to account for the creation of either motion or matter.

As soon as human beings began to speculate on the attributes of their Deity; when the two principles composing it began to separate, and the idea was gaining ground that the male was the only important factor in reproduction, the sun became male, the earth and sea

---

[93] Lectures on the Pentateuch, p. 32.
[94] Ibid. p. 16.

female. Still, even then the doctrine seems not to have been questioned, that the creative agency had proceeded from matter, or that it was developed in and through it. The belief that something can be made from nothing was reserved for a later age.

In the oldest Semitic Kosmogonies, we are assured that the self-conscious God who is manifested in the order of the universe, proceeded out of the great abyss, and out of unorganized, dark, primeval matter. During the earlier historic period, however, by both Jew and Gentile, the belief was entertained that spirit is material. It is the essence of fire–a substance akin to the galvanic or electric fluid. This masculine element, the manifestation of which is desire, or heat, and which was finally set up as an eternal, self-existent, creative force, or God, was originally regarded as a manifestation of matter, and as having no independent existence. In an earlier age, this so-called creative agency is associated with a force far superior to itself, namely, Light or Wisdom. Minerva, who is the first emanation from the Deity, "formed" all things. She it is who discriminates all things and gives laws to the universe. "She represented to the Greeks that spiritual element which lifts knowledge into wisdom, and talent into genius."[95] But with the importance which began to be assumed by man when he began to regard himself as a creator, and when through ignorance and sensuality the principles of a more enlightened race were forgotten, desire, or heat, was separated from matter and came to be regarded as an independent entity, which itself had created matter out of nothing. Thus is noticed the extent to which the god-idea has been developed in accordance with the relative positions of the sexes.

According to the Grecian mythology, much of which was a comparatively late development, mortal woman was

---

[95] L. T. Ives, Art Words.

the handiwork of Vulcan the Firegod, who, being commissioned by Jove to execute "a snare for gods and man," moulded the beauteous form of woman. This is a worthy example of the contempt and scorn shown by the Greeks for women during the later period of their career as a nation. That such contempt was a later development is shown in the fact that woman was originally the gift of Pallas Athene, or Wisdom. When she first appeared on the scene she was crowned by the gods, in fact she was the first object honored with a crown. Concerning the conceptions regarding women as held at an earlier age, and those which came to prevail after she had become "the cause of evil in the world," we have the following from Tertullian:

"If there was a Pandora, whom Hesiod mentions as the first woman, hers was the first head the Graces crowned, for she received gifts from all the gods, whence she got her name Pandora. But Moses, a prophet, not a poet-shepherd, shows us the first woman Eve having her loins more naturally girt about with leaves than her temples with flowers. Pandora then is a myth."[96]

Woman, who was originally the gift of Wisdom, or Minerva, and who when created was garlanded with flowers as the crown of creation, became, in course of time, an accursed and wicked thing who must henceforth cover herself with leaves to hide her shame. Tertullian, who, with the rest of the early fathers in the Christian church, had imbibed the latter doctrine concerning her, could not believe the tradition set forth by Hesiod; therefore Pandora was a myth, while the corrupted fable, that of Eve as the tempter, was accepted as a natural representation of womanhood.

When woman was created, "all the gods conferred a gifted grace."

---

[96] Tertullian, vol. i., p. 341.

"Round her fair brow the lovely-tressed Hours
A garland twined of Spring's purpureal flowers:
The whole attire Minerva's graceful art
Disposed, adjusted, form'd to every part."
                              --Hesiod, Works and Days.

Later, however, Pandora herself becomes the pourer forth of ills on the head of defenceless man.

Chapter XI.
Fire and Phallic Worship

"Know, first a spirit with an active flame
Fills, feeds, and animates the mighty frame;
Runs through the watery worlds and fields of air,
The ponderous Earth and depths of Heav'n and there
Burns in the Sun and Moon, and every brilliant Star
Thus mingling in the mass, the general soul

Lives in its parts and agitates the whole." Although earth, air, water, and the sun were long venerated as objects of worship, as containing the life principle, in process of time it is observed that fire attracted the highest regard of human beings, and on their altars the sacred flame, said to have been kindled from heaven, was kept burning uninterruptedly from year to year, and from age to age, by bends of priests "whose special duty it was to see that the sacred flame was never extinguished." The office of the vestal virgins in Rome was to preserve the holy fire. The Egyptians, and in fact all the earlier civilized nations, knew that force proceeds from the sun, hence the frequent appearance of this orb among their symbols of life. Indeed there is not a country on the globe in which, at some time, divine honors have not been paid to fire and to light.

The Hindoos, "believing fire to be the essence of all active power in Nature, kept perpetual lamps burning in the innermost recesses of their pagodas and temples, and in the sacred edifices of the Greeks and Barbarians fires were preserved for the same reason."

The festival of lamps, which was once universal throughout Egypt, still prevails in China. On the evening of the fifteenth day of the first month in the year, every person is compelled to place before his door a lantern or light, such lights differing in size and expense according to the degree of wealth or poverty of those to whom they belong. Light was the symbol of Muth (Perceptive Wisdom). Among the Persians, the Egyptians, the Mexicans, the Jews, the Etruscans, the Greeks, and the Romans, fire was venerated as the essence of the Deity; and, at the present time, in Thibet, in China, in Japan, and in portions of Africa, it still forms an important part of worship. The Hebrew writings show conclusively that not only the Jews but all the surrounding nations were fire-worshippers, and that their sacrifices were not infrequently to the God of Fire. Of this Forlong says:

"When Rome was rearing temples to the fame and worship of Fire, we find the prophets of Israel occasionally denouncing the wickedness of its worship by their own and the nations around them; nevertheless, even to Christ's time Molok always had his offerings of children."[97]

It is believed that Abraham introduced fire-worship among the Jews from Ur in Mesopotamia, a land in which lights are still venerated, and fire altars are worshipped as containing the Deity.

The real essence of fire which was identical with the life-principle was holy. The "Lord" of the Israelites was in the fire which descended on Mt. Sinai, Exodus xix., 18. "The bush burned with fire and the bush was not consumed," Exodus iii., 2. Whether the signification of "bush" is the same as "grove," I know not, but Josephus assures us that the bush was holy before the flame appeared

---

[97] Rivers of Life and Faiths of Man in an Lands, vol. i., p. 325.

in it. Because of its sacred character, it became the receptacle for the burning "Lord" of the Jews. The ark, the religious emblem which Moses bore aloft, was simply a fire altar on which the fire must continually burn. The fact will doubtless be observed that although the ark and the bush (female emblems) were invested with a certain degree of sanctity, they were nevertheless only receptacles for the substance within them.

At the same time that the Jews kept sacred or holy fires continually burning on their altars, they carried about a serpent on a pole representing it to be the "healer of nations." They also kept a phallic emblem in a box, chest, or ark which they worshipped as the "God of Hosts," the "Life Giver," etc. It has been observed that although the Jews frequently lost their ark, they were never without their serpent-pole. At a certain stage in the religious development of mankind all the temples in Africa and Western Asia were dedicated to Vulcan the fire god or the "Lord of Fire," to whom all furnaces were sacred. The principal festivals in honor of this Deity took place in the spring, at the Easter season, and on the 23d of August, when it is said that the licentiousness practiced in the temples compared with those of the "Harvest Homes" of Europe when the sun was in Libra and the harvest had been garnered in. Vulcan was the "God of fornication" or of passion.

These excesses, which remained unchecked down to the fourth century before Christ, are said to have somewhat abated after the rise of the Stoic philosophy.

Various philosophers of early historic times as well as many of the early fathers in the Christian church believed that God was a corporeal substance which in some way is manifested through fire.

In Egypt, during the early ages of Christianity, "a great dispute took place among the monks on the question, whether God is corporeal." Tertullian declared that "God is fire"; Origen, that "he is a subtle fire"; and various others that "he is body."

There is little doubt that in early historic ages the Persians, who had undertaken to purify their religion, were the strongest and purest sect of this cult; they were in fact the genuine worshippers of the pure creative principles which they believed resided in fire.

We have observed that force or spirit was originally regarded as a part of Nature, or in other words that it was a manifestation of, or an outflowing from matter, but so soon as it began to be considered as something apart from Nature, there at once arose a desire for some corporeal object to represent this unseen and occult principle.

During many of the ages of fire-worship, holy fire, although a material substance, seems to have been too subtle to clearly represent the god-idea, hence everywhere the worship of the serpent is found to be interwoven with it. In fact, so closely are serpent, fire, pillar, and other phallic faiths intermingled that it is impossible to separate them.

The Persians are by some writers said to have been the earliest fire-worshippers: by others the truth of this statement is denied, while many claim, and indeed the Maji themselves declared, that they never worshipped fire at all in any other manner than as an emblem of the divine principle which they believed resided within it. It is probable, however, from the evidence at hand, that they, like all the other nations of the globe, prior to the reformation led by Zarathustra and his daughter, had lost or nearly forgotten the profound ideas connected with the worship of Nature.

Passion, symbolized by fire, is declared by various writers to have been the first idol, but later research has proved the falsity of this assumption. It is true that at an early age of human experience the creative processes were worshipped, but such worship involved scientific and, I might say, spiritualized conceptions of the operations of

Nature which in time were altogether lost sight of. Gross phallicism is clearly the result of degeneration, and of a lapse into sensuality and superstition.

I think no one can study the facts connected with fire and light as the Deity in the various countries in which this worship prevailed, without perceiving the change it gradually underwent during later ages, and the grossness of the ideas which became connected with it as compared with an earlier age when mankind "had no temples, but worshipped in the open air, on the tops of mountains."

In another portion of this work we have observed that in the rites connected with the worship of Cybele (Light or Wisdom), although phallic symbols were in use, the ceremonies were absolutely pure, and that throughout all the earlier ages her worship remained free from the abominations which characterized the worship of later times.

At what time in the history of the human race the organs of generation first began to appear as emblems of the Deity is not known. Within the earliest cave temples, those hewn from the solid rock, sculptured representations of these objects are still to be observed. Although until a comparatively recent period their true significance has been unknown, there is little doubt at the present time that they were originally used as symbols of fertility, or as emblems typifying the processes of Nature, and that at some remote period of the world's history they were worshipped as the Creator, or, at least, as representations of the creative agencies in the universe.

Concerning the origin and character of the people who executed them there is scarcely a trace in written history. Through the unravelling of extinct tongues, however, the monumental records of the ancient nations of the globe have been deciphered, and the system of religious symbolism in use among them is now understood.

A small volume by various writers, printed in London some years ago, entitled A Comparative View of the Ancient Monuments of India, says:

"Those who have penetrated into the abstruseness of Indian mythology, find that in these temples was practiced a worship similar to that practiced by all the several nations of the world, in their earliest as well as their most enlightened periods. It was paid to the Phallus by the Asiatics, to Priapus by the Egyptians, Greeks, and Romans, to Baal-Peor by the Canaanites and idolatrous Jews. The figure is seen on the fascia which runs round the circus of Nismes, and over the portal of the Cathedral of Toulouse, and several churches of Bordeaux."

Of the Lingham and Yoni and their universal acceptance as religious emblems, Barlow remarks that it was a "worship which would appear to have made the tour of the globe and to have left traces of its existence where we might least expect to find it." In referring to the "sculptured indecencies" connected with religious rites, which, being wrought in imperishable stone, have been preserved in India and other parts of the East, Forlong says that when occurring in the temples or other sacred places they are at the present time evidently very puzzling to the pious Indians, and in their attempts to explain them they say they are placed there "in fulfilment of vows," or that they have been wrought there "as punishments for sins of a sexual nature, committed by those who executed or paid for them." It is, however, the opinion of Forlong that they are simply connected with an older and purer worship–a worship which involved the union of the sex principles as the foundation of their god-idea.

Regarding the cause for the "indecent" sculptures of the Orissa temples, the same writer quotes the following from Baboo Ragendralala Mitra, in his work on the Antiquities of Orissa.

"A vitiated taste aided by general prevalence of immorality might at first sight appear to be the most likely one; but I can not believe that libidiousness, however depraved, would ever think of selecting fanes dedicated to the worship of God, as the most appropriate for its manifestations; for it is worthy of remark that they occur almost exclusively on temples and their attached porches, and never on enclosing walls, gateways, and other non-religious structures. Our ideas of propriety, according to Voltaire, lead us to suppose that a ceremony (like the worship of Priapus) which appears to us infamous, could only be invented by licentiousness; but it is impossible to believe that depravity of manners would ever have led among any people to the establishment of religious ceremonies. It is probable, on the contrary, that this custom was first introduced in times of simplicity–that the first thought was to honor the Deity in the symbol of life which it has given us; such a ceremony may have excited licentiousness among youths, and have appeared ridiculous to men of education in more refined, more corrupt, and more enlightened times, but it never had its origin in such feelings. . . . It is out of the question therefore to suppose that a general prevalence of vice would of itself, without the authority of priests and scriptures, suffice to lead to the defilement of holy temples."[98]

Originally the Ionians, as their name indicates, were Yoni worshippers, i. e., they belonged to the sect which was driven out of India because of their stubborn refusal to worship the male energy as the Creator. During the later ages of their history, at a time when their religion had degenerated into a licensed system of vice and corruption, and after their temples had become brothels in which, in the name of religion, were practiced the most debasing

---

[98] Rivers of Life, vol. i., p. 275.

ceremonies, the Greeks became ashamed of their ancient worship, and, like the Jews, ashamed also of their name.

It is believed that the Greeks received from Egypt, or the East, their first theological conceptions of God and religion. These ideas

"were veiled in symbols, significant of a primitive monotheism; these, at a later period, being translated into symbolical or allegorical language, were by the poets transformed into epic or narrative myths, in which the original subject symbolized was almost effaced, whilst the allegorical expressions were received generally in a literal sense. Hence, to the many, the meaning of the ancient doctrine was lost, and was communicated only to the few, under the strictest secrecy in the mysteries of Eleusis and Samothrace. Thus there was a popular theology to suit the people, and a rational theology reserved for the educated, the symbolical language in both being the same, but the meaning of it being taken differently. In course of time, as knowledge makes its way among the people, and religious enlightenment with it, much of what had been received literally will relapse into its original figurative or symbolical meaning. Reason will resume her supremacy, and stereotyped dogmas will fall like pagan idols before advancing truth."[99]

Although, during the later ages of the human career, the higher truths taught by an earlier race were lost, still a slight hint of the beauty and purity of the more ancient worship may be traced through most of the ages of the history of religion. Even among the profligate Greeks, the mysteries of Eleusis, celebrated in the temple of Ceres, were always respected. Care should be taken, however, not to confound these remnants of pure Nature- worship with that of the courtesan Venus, whose adoration, during the

---

[99] Barlow, Essays on Symbolism, p. 121.

degenerate days of Greece, represented only the lowest and most corrupt conception of the female energy.

Down to a late date in the annals of Athens there was celebrated a religious festival called Thesmophoria. The name of this festival is derived from one of the cognomens of Ceres–the goddess "who first gave laws and made life orderly." Ceres was the divinity adored by the Amazons, and is essentially the same as the Egyptian Isis. She represents universal female Nature. The Thesmophorian rites, which are believed by most writers to have been introduced into Greece directly from Thrace, were performed by "virgins distinguished for probity in life, who carried about in procession sacred books upon their heads."

Inman, in his Ancient Faiths, quotes an oracle of Apollo, from Spencer, to the effect that "Rhea the Mother of the Blessed, and the Queen of the Gods, loved assemblages of women." As this festival is in honor of Female Nature, the various female attributes are adored as deities, Demeter being the first named by the worshippers. After a long season of fasting, and "after solemn reflection on the mysteries of life, women splendidly attired in white garments assemble and scatter flowers in honor of the Great Mother."

The food partaken of by the devotees at these festivals was cakes, very similar in shape to those which were offered to the Queen of Heaven by the women of Judah in the days of Jeremiah, an offering which it will be remembered so displeased that prophet that a curse was pronounced upon the entire people.

As the strictest secrecy prevailed among the initiated respecting these rites, the exact nature of the symbols employed at the Thesmophorian festivals is not known; it is believed, however, that it was the female emblem of generation, and that this festival was held in honor of that event which from the earliest times had been prophesied by those who believed in the superior importance of the female, namely, that unaided by the male power, a woman would bring forth, and that this manifestation of female sufficiency would forever settle the question of the ascendancy of the female principle. Through a return of the ancient ideas of purity and peace, mankind would be redeemed from the wretchedness and misery which had been the result of the decline of female power. The dual idea entertained in the Thesmophorian worship is observed in the fact that although Ceres, the Great Mother, was the principal Deity honored, Proserpine, the child, was also comprehended, and with its Mother worshipped as part of the Creator. Thus we observe that down to a late date in the history of Grecian mythology the idea of a Holy Mother with her child had not altogether disappeared as a representation of the god-idea.

To prove the worthiness of the ideas connected with the Eleusinian mysteries it is stated that "there is not an instance on record that the honor of initiation was ever obtained by a very bad man."

In Rome these mysteries took another name and were called "the rites of Bona Dea," which was but another name for Ceres. As evidence of their purity we have the following:

"All the distinguished Roman authors speak of these rites and in terms of profound respect. Horace denounces the wretch who should attempt to reveal the secrets of these rites; Virgil mentions these mysteries with great respect; and Cicero alludes to them with a greater reverence than either of the poets we have named. Both the Greeks and the Romans punished any insult offered to these mysteries with the most persevering vindictiveness. Alcibiades was charged with insulting these religious rites, and although the proof of his offense was quite doubtful, yet he suffered for it for years in exile and misery, and it must be allowed that he was the most popular man of his age."[100]

In Greece, the celebration of the Eleusinian mysteries was in the hands of the Emolpidae, one of the oldest and most respected families of antiquity. At Carthage, there were celebrated the Phiditia, religious solemnities similar to those already described in Greece. During the two or three days upon which these festivals were celebrated, public feasts were prepared at which the youth were instructed by their elders in the state concerning the principles which were to govern their conduct in after life; truth, inward purity, and virtue being set forth as essentials to true manhood. In later times, after these festivals had found their way to Rome, they gradually succumbed to the immorality which prevailed, and at last, when their former exalted significance had been forgotten, they were finally sunk into "the licentiousness of enjoyment, and the innocence of mirth was superseded by the uproar of riot and vice! Such were the Saturnalia."

From the facts connected with the mysteries of Eleusis and the Thesmophorian rites, it is evident that in its earlier stages Nature-worship was absolutely free from the impurities which came to be associated with it in later times. As the organs of generation had not originally been wholly disgraced and outraged, it is not unlikely that when the so-called "sculptured indecencies" appeared on the walls of the temples they were regarded as no more an offense against propriety and decency than was the reappearance of the cross, the emblem of life, in later times, among orthodox Christians.

Neither is it probable, in an age in which nothing that is natural was considered indecent, and before the reproductive energies had become degraded, that these

---

[100] Chambers's Edinburgh Journal.

symbols were any more suggestive of impurity than are the Easter offerings upon our church altars at the present time. Whatever may now be the significance of these offerings to those who present them, sure it is that they once, together with other devices connected with Nature-worship, were simply emblems of fertility–symbols of a risen and fructifying sun which by its gladdening rays re-creates and makes all things new again.

If we carefully study the religion of past ages we will discover something more than a hint of an age when the generative functions were regarded as a sacred expression of creative power, and when the reproductive organs had not through over-stimulation and abuse been tabooed as objects altogether impure and unholy, and as things too disgraceful to be mentioned above a whisper. Indeed there is much evidence going to show that in an earlier age of the world's history the degradation of mankind, through the abuse of the creative functions, had not been accomplished, and the ills of life resulting from such abuse were unknown.

We may reasonably believe that those instincts in the female which are correlated with maternal affection and which were acquired by her as a protection to the germ, or, in other words, those characters which Nature has developed in the female to insure the safety and well-being of offspring, and which in a purer and more natural stage of human existence acted as cheeks upon the energies of the male, were not easily or quickly subdued; but when through subjection to the animal nature of man these instincts or characters had been denied their natural expression, and woman had become simply the instrument of man's pleasure, the comparatively pure worship of the organs of generation as symbols of creative power began to give place to the deification of these members simply as emblems of desire, or as instruments for the stimulation of passion.

We are assured that on the banks of the Ganges, the very cradle of religion, are still to be found various remnants of the most ancient form of Nature-worship–that there are still to be observed "certain high places sacred to more primitive ideas than those represented by Vedic gods."

Here devout worshippers believe that the androgynous God of fertility, or Nature, still manifests itself to the faithful. Close beside these more ancient shrines are others representing a somewhat later development of religious faith–shrines, by means of which are indicated some of the processes involved in the earlier growth of the god-idea. Not far removed from these are to be found, also, numerous temples or places of worship belonging to a still later faith– a faith in which are revealed the "awakening and stimulation of every sensuous feeling, and which has drowned in infamy every noble impulse developed in human nature."

Of the depravity of the Jews and the immorality practiced in their religious rites, Forlong says:

"No one can study their history, liberated from the blindness which our Christian up-bringing and associations cast over us, without seeing that the Jews were probably the grossest worshippers among all those Ophi–Phallo–Solar devotees who then covered every land and sea, from the sources of the Nile and Euphrates to all over the Mediterranean coasts and isles. These impure faiths seem to have been very strictly maintained by Jews up to Hezekiah's days, and by none more so than by dissolute Solomon and his cruel, lascivious bandit-father, the brazen-faced adulterer and murderer, who broke his freely volunteered oath, and sacrificed six innocent sons of his king to his Javah."

Of Solomon he says that he devoted his energies and some little wealth "to rearing phallic and Solophallic shrines over all the high places around him, and especially in front of Jerusalem, and on and around the Mount of Olives." On each side of the entrance to his celebrated temple, under the great phallic spire which formed the portico, were two handsome columns over fifty feet high, by the side of which were the sun God Belus and his chariots.

In a description of this temple it is represented as being one hundred and twenty feet long and forty feet broad, while the porch, a phallic emblem, "was a huge tower, forty feet long, twenty feet broad, and two hundred and forty feet high." We are assured by Forlong that Solomon's temple was like hundreds observed in the East, except that its walls were a little higher than those usually seen, and the phallic spire out of proportion to the size of the structure. "The Jewish porch is but the obelisk which the Egyptian placed beside his temple; the Boodhist pillars which stood all around their Dagobas; the pillars of Hercules, which stood near the Phoenician temple; and the spire which stands beside the Christian Church."[101]

The rites and ceremonies observed in the worship of Baal-Peor are not of a character to be described in these pages: it is perhaps sufficient to state that by them the fact is clearly established that profligacy, regulated and controlled by the priestly order as part and parcel of religion, was not confined to the Gentiles; but, on the contrary, that the religious observances of the Jews prior to the Babylonian captivity were even more gross than were those of the Assyrians or the Hindoos.

These impure faiths arose at a time when man as the sole creator of offspring became god, when the natural instincts of woman were subdued, and when passion as the highest expression of the divine force came to be worshipped as the most important attribute of humanity.

---

[101] Forlong, Rivers of Life, vol. i., p. 219.

The extent to which these faiths have influenced later religious belief and observances is scarcely realized by those who have not given special attention to this subject.

It has been stated that in the time of Solon, law-giver of Athens, there were twenty temples in the various cities of Greece dedicated to Venus the courtesan, within which were practiced, in the name of religion, the most infamous rites and the most shameless self-abandonment; and that throughout Europe, down to a late period in the history of the race, religious festivals were celebrated at certain seasons of the year, at which the ceremonies performed in honor of the god of fornication were of the grossest nature, and at which the Bacchanalian orgies were only equalled by those practiced in the religious temples of Babylon.

It is impossible longer to conceal the fact that passion, symbolized by a serpent, an upright stone, and by the male and female organs of generation, the male appearing as the "giver of life," the female as a necessary appendage to it, constituted the god-idea of mankind for at least four thousand years; and, instead of being confined to the earlier ages of that period, we shall presently see that phallic worship had not disappeared, under Christianity, as late and even later than the sixteenth century.

Such has been the result of the ascendancy gained by the grosser elements in human nature: the highest idea of the Infinite passion symbolized by the organs of generation, while the principal rites connected with its worship are scenes of debauchery and self-abasement.

At the present time it is by no means difficult to trace the growth of the god-idea. First, as we have seen, a system of pure Nature-worship appeared under the symbol of a Mother and child. In process of time this particular form of worship was supplanted by a religion under which the male principle is seen to be in the ascendancy over the female. Later a more complicated system of Nature-worship is observed in which the underlying principles are concealed, or are understood only by the initiated. Lastly, these philosophical and recondite principles are forgotten and the symbols themselves receive the adoration which once belonged to the Creator. The change which the ideas concerning womanhood underwent from the time when the natural feminine characters and qualities were worshipped as God, to the days of Solon the Grecian law-giver, when women had become merely tools or slaves for the use and pleasure of men, is forcibly shown by a comparison of the character ascribed to the female deities at the two epochs mentioned. Athene who in an earlier age had represented Wisdom had in the age of Solon degenerated into a patroness of heroes; but even as a Goddess of war her patronage was as nought compared with that of the courtesan Venus, at whose shrine "every man in Greece worshipped."

The extent to which women, in the name of religion, have been degraded, and the part which in the past they have been compelled to assume in the worship of passion may not at the present time be disguised, as facts concerning this subject are well authenticated. In a former work,[102] attention has been directed to the religious rites of Babylon, the city in which it will be remembered the Tower of Belus was situated. Here women of all conditions and ranks were obliged, once in their life, to prostitute themselves in the temple for hire to any stranger who might demand such service, which revenue was appropriated by the priests to be applied to sacred uses. This act it will be remembered was a religious obligation imposed by religious teachers and enforced by priestly rule. It was a sacrifice to the god of passion. A similar custom prevailed in Cyprus.

---

[102] See Evolution of Woman, p. 228.

Most of the temples of the later Hindoos had bands of consecrated women called the "Women of the Idol." These victims of the priests were selected in their infancy by Brahmins for the beauty of their persons, and were trained to every elegant accomplishment that could render them attractive and which would insure success in the profession which they exercised at once for the pleasure and profit of the priesthood. They were never allowed to desert the temple; and the offspring of their promiscuous embraces were, if males, consecrated to the service of the Deity in the ceremonies of this worship, and, if females, educated in the profession of their mothers.[103]

That prostitution was a religious observance, which was practiced in Eastern temples, cannot in the face of accessible facts be doubted. Regarding this subject, Inman says:

"To us it is inconceivable, that the indulgence of passion could be associated with religion, but so it was. The words expressive of 'sanctuary,' 'consecrated,' and 'sodomites' are in the Hebrew essentially the same. It is amongst the Hindoos of to-day as it was in the Greece and Italy of classic times; and we find that 'holy woman' is a title given to those who devote their bodies to be used for hire, which goes to the service of the temple."

The extent to which ages of corruption have vitiated the purer instincts of human nature, and the degree to which centuries of sensuality and superstition have degraded the nature of man, may be noticed at the present time in the admissions which are frequently made by male writers regarding the change which during the history of the race has taken place in the god-idea. None of the attributes of women, not even that holy instinct–maternal love, can by many of them be contemplated apart from the ideas of grossness which have attended the sex-functions

---

[103] Maurice, Indian Antiquities, vol. i.

during the ages since women first became enslaved. As an illustration of this we have the following from an eminent philologist of recent times, a writer whose able efforts in unravelling religious myths bear testimony to his mental strength and literary ability.

"The Chaldees believed in a celestial virgin who had purity of body, loveliness of person, and tenderness of affection, and she was one to whom the erring sinner could appeal with more chance of success than to a stern father. She was portrayed as a mother with a child in her arms, and every attribute ascribed to her showing that she was supposed to be as fond as any earthly female ever was."[104]

After thus describing the early Chaldean Deity, who, although a pure and spotless virgin, was nevertheless worshipped as a mother, or as the embodiment of the altruistic principles developed in mankind, this writer goes on to say: "The worship of the woman by man naturally led to developments which our COMPARATIVELY SENSITIVE NATURES [the italics are mine] shun as being opposed to all religious feeling," which sentiment clearly reveals the inability of this writer to estimate womanhood, or even motherhood, apart from the sensualized ideas which during the ages in which passion has been the recognized god have gathered about it.

The purity of life and the high stage of civilization reached by an ancient people, and the fact that these conditions were reached under pure Nature-worship, or when the natural attributes of the female were regarded as the highest expression of the divine in the human, prove that it was neither the appreciation nor the deification of womanhood which "led to developments which sensitive natures shun as being opposed to all religious feeling," but, on the contrary, that it was the lack of such appreciation which stimulated the lower nature of man and encouraged

---

[104] Inman, Ancient Faiths, vol. i., p. 59.

every form of sensuality and superstition. In other words, it was the subjection of the natural female instincts and the deification of brute passion during the later ages of human history which have degraded religion and corrupted human nature.

Although at the present time it is quite impossible for scholars to veil the fact that the god-idea was originally worshipped as female, still, most modern writers who deal with this subject seem unable to understand the state of human society which must have existed when the instincts, qualities, and characters peculiar to the female constitution were worshipped as divine. So corrupt has human nature become through over-stimulation and indulgence of the lower propensities, that it seems impossible for those who have thus far dealt with this subject to perceive in the earlier conceptions of a Deity any higher idea than that conveyed to their minds at the present time by the sexual attributes and physical functions of females–namely, their capacity to bring forth, coupled with the power to gratify the animal instincts of males, functions which women share with the lower orders of life.

The fact that by an ancient race woman was regarded as the head or crown of creation, that she was the first emanation from the Deity, or, more properly speaking, that she represented Perceptive Wisdom, seems at the present time not to be comprehended, or at least not acknowledged. The more recently developed idea, that she was designed as an appendage to man, and created specially for his use and pleasure,–a conception which is the direct result of the supremacy of the lower instincts over the higher faculties,– has for ages been taught as a religious doctrine which to doubt involves the rankest heresy.

The androgynous Venus of the earlier ages, a deity which although female was figured with a beard to denote that within her were embraced the masculine powers, embodied a conception of universal womanhood and the

Deity widely different from that entertained in the later ages of Greece, at a time when Venus the courtesan represented all the powers and capacities of woman considered worthy of deification.

To such an extent, in later ages, have all our ideas of the Infinite become masculinized that in extant history little except occasional hints is to be found of the fact that during numberless ages of human existence the Supreme Creator was worshipped as female.

One has only to study the Greek character to anticipate the manner in which any subject pertaining to women would be treated by that arrogant and conceited race; and, as until recently most of our information concerning the past has come through Greek sources, the distorted and one-sided view taken of human events, and the contempt with which the feminine half of society has been regarded, are in no wise surprising. We must bear in mind the fact, however, that the Greeks were but the degenerate descendants of the highly civilized peoples whom they were pleased to term "barbarians," and that they knew less of the origin and character of the gods which they worshipped, and which they had borrowed from other countries, than is known of them at the present time.

About 600 years B.C., we may believe that mankind had sunk to the lowest depth of human degradation, since which time humanity has been slowly retracting its course; not, however, with any degree of continuity or regularity, nor without lapses, during which for hundreds of years the current seemed to roll backward. Indeed when we review the history of the intervening ages, and note the extent to which passion, prejudice, and superstition have been in the ascendancy over reason and judgment, we may truly say: "The fathers have eaten sour grapes and the children's teeth have been set on edge."

Chapter XII.
An Attempt to Purify the Sensualized Faiths

It has been said of the Persians that in their zeal to purify the sensualized faiths which everywhere prevailed they manifested a decided "repugnance to the worship of images, beasts, or symbols, while they sought to establish the worship of the only true creative force, or God–Holy Fire."

From the facts to be gleaned concerning this people during the seventh and eighth centuries B.C., it is quite probable that they still had a faint knowledge of a former age of intellectual and moral greatness, and that it was their object, at that time, to return to the purer principles which characterized it. That their efforts were subsequently copied by surrounding nations is shown in the facts connected with their history.

Soon leading Syrians and Jews began to learn from their Eastern neighbor that the worship of images could scarcely be acceptable to a god which they were beginning to invest with a certain degree of spirituality. There is little doubt, at the present time, that the attempt to spiritualize the religion of the Jews was due to the influence of the Persians. However, the length of time required to effect any appreciable improvement in an established form of worship is shown by the fact that, two hundred years later, little change for the better was observed in the temples, in which licentiousness had become a recognized religious rite. Even at the present time, it is reported that in many places of worship in the East there still reside "holy women –god's women," who, like those in Babylon, described by various writers, are devoted to the "god of fire."

In a comparison made between the religion of Persia and the doctrines said to have been taught by Moses, Inman remarks:

"The religion of Persia as reformed by Zoroaster so closely resembles the Mosaic, that it would be almost impossible to decide which has the precedence of the other, unless we knew how ancient was the teaching of Zoroaster, and how very recent was that said to be from Moses. Be this as it may, we find the ancient Persians resemble the Jews in sacrificing upon high places, in paying divine honor to fire, in keeping up a sacred flame, in certain ceremonial cleansings, in possessing an hereditary priesthood who alone were allowed to offer sacrifices, and in making their summum bonum the possession of a numerous offspring."[105]

It is quite plain that by both these nations the wisdom of an earlier race was nearly forgotten. Seven hundred years B.C. the Persians had doubtless already adopted the worship of "One God" who was the Regenerator or Destroyer, a Deity which, as we have seen, originally comprehended the powers of Nature–namely the sun's heat and the cold of winter. That at this time, however, they had lost the higher truths involved in the conception of this Deity, is evident. They had become worshippers of fire, or of that subtle igneous fluid residing in fire which they believed to be creative force. Although the Persiaus like all the other nations of the globe had lost or forgotten the higher truths enunciated by an older race, there is no evidence going to show that they ever became gross phallic worshippers like the Jews; that they were not such is shown in the fact that down to the time of Alexander the women of Persia still held a high and honorable position, and that the

---

[105] Ancient Faiths, vol. ii., p. 64.

female attributes had not become wholly subject to male power.

Had we no other evidence of the comparatively exalted character of the religion of the Persians than the history of the lives of such men as Darius, Cyrus, Artaxerxes, and others, we should conclude, notwithstanding the similarity in the ceremonials of these two religions, that some influence had been at work to preserve them from the cruelty and licentiousness which prevailed among the Jews. It is related of Cyrus that he used to wish that he might live long enough to repay all the kindness which he had received. It is also stated that on account of the justice and equity shown in his character, a great number of persons were desirous of committing to his care and wisdom "the disposal of their property, their cities, and their own persons."

In striking contrast to the mild and humane character of Cyrus stands that of the licentious and revengeful David, a "man after God's own heart."

"As for the heads of those that compass me about, let the mischief of their own lips cover them."

"Let burning coals fall upon them: let them be cast into the fire; into deep pits, that they rise not up again."[106]

"Happy shall he be that taketh and dasheth thy little ones against the stones."[107]

No one I think can read the Avestas without being impressed by the prominence there given to the subjects of temperance and virtue. In their efforts to purify religion, and in the attempts to return to their more ancient faith, the disciples of Zoroaster, as early as eight hundred years before Christ, had adopted a highly spiritualized conception of the Deity. They had taught in various portions of Asia Minor the doctrine of one God, a dual entity by means of

---

[106] Psalms cxl.
[107] Ibid., cxxxvii.

which all things were created. They taught also the doctrine of a resurrection and that of the immortality of the soul. It was at this time that they originated, or at least propounded, the doctrine of hell and the devil, a belief exactly suited to the then weakened mental condition of mankind, and from which humanity has not yet gained sufficient intellectual and moral strength to free itself. This Persian devil, which had become identified with winter or with the absence of the sun's rays, was now Aryhman, or the "powers of darkness," and was doubtless the source whence sprang the personal devil elaborated at a later age by Laotse in China.

As the Jews had no writings prior to the time of Ezra or Jeremiah, it is now believed that many of the doctrines incorporated in their sacred books were borrowed from Persian, Indian, and Egyptian sources. Resurrection from the dead, or the resurrection of the body, was for hundreds of years prior to the birth of Christ an established article of Egyptian and Persian faith, while spiritual regeneration, symbolized by the outward typification of "being born again," was the beginning of a new life and an admission to the heavenly state.

In the Khordah Avesta we have the following concerning the doctrine of the resurrection and that of future rewards and punishments.

"I am wholly without doubt in the existence of the good Mazdaycinian faith, in the coming of the resurrection and the later body, in the stepping over the bridge Chinvat, in an invariable recompense of good deeds and their reward, and of bad deeds and their punishment."

The Zoroastrians, who led the way in the great intellectual and religious awakening which took place during the intervening years from 700 B.C. to 400 B.C., sought to purify all things by fire and water, the two principles which had come to be regarded as the original elements, from which, or by which, all things are produced.

Prior to this time, in Persia, and long afterwards by various other nations, baptism, a rite performed at puberty, was connected only with the sexual obligations of the person receiving it, but in the age which we are considering it became especially a cleansing or regenerating process, and was the means by which the pious devotee became initiated into the mysteries of holy living, or by which she or he was "born again."

As in their religious procedure every act was performed in connection with symbols, so in the matter of baptism they were not satisfied with the inner consciousness of regeneration, but must go through with certain processes which typified the new life upon which they had entered. According to Wilford, the outward symbolization of the "new birth" in the East is manifested in the following manner:

"For the purpose of regeneration it is directed to make an image of pure gold of the female power of nature, either in the shape of a woman or of a cow. In this statue, the person to be regenerated is inclosed, and dragged out through the natural channel. As a statue of pure gold and of proper dimensions would be too expensive, it is sufficient to make an image of the sacred Yoni, through which the person to be regenerated is to pass."

Thus at the time Nicodemus is said to have queried concerning the mysteries of the new birth, it is observed that the outward forms of regeneration had long been in use among the pagans. In passing themselves through these apertures, the applicant for regeneration was supposed to represent the condition of one "issuing from the womb to a new scope of life."

According to the testimony of various writers upon this subject, there are still extant, not alone in oriental countries, but in Ireland and Scotland as well, numerous excavations or apertures in the rocks which by an early race were used for the same purpose. Through the misconception, bigotry, and ignorance of the Roman Catholic missionaries in Ireland, these openings were designated as the "Devil's Yonies." Although these emblems typified the original conception of one of their most sacred beliefs, namely, the "new birth," still they were "heathen abominations" with which the devotees of the new (?) faith must not become defiled.

The people who executed these imperishable designs, and who have left in the British Isles innumerable evidences of their religious beliefs, are supposed by some writers to belong to a colony which, having been expelled from Persia on account of their peculiar religious beliefs, settled in the "White Island," the "Island of the Blessed." This subject will, however, be referred to later in this work.

When we closely examine the facts connected with the evolution of religion, there can be little doubt that the Persians laid the foundation for that great moral and intellectual awakening which a century or two later is represented by Confucious, Gotama Buddha, and Pythagoras. From the Persians, doubtless Jew and Gentile alike received the little leaven of spirituality which in later ages crept into their gross conception of a Deity.

By the Persians, the Hindoos, and other nations of the East, it was believed that the end of each cycle of six hundred years, at which time a new sun or savior was to come, would mark a new era of religious development. At the close of each of these cycles it was devoutly expected that the "golden age" of the past would be restored, and that mankind would again be freed from the ills which had overtaken them. As many of these cycles had passed, numerous deliverers, saviors, or solar incarnations had appeared in India, Gotama Buddha having been the ninth. In the East, about six or seven hundred years before the birth of Christ, not only one savior or prophet but three or four of them appeared.

Concerning the leader of the reform in Persia there seem to be many conflicting accounts. The learned Faber concludes that there were two Zarathustras or Zoroasters, the former being identical with Menu, the law giver and triplicated deity of India, and who by various writers is recognized as the Noah of the Hebrews. According to Pliny, the former lived thousands of years before Christ. Several writers concur in placing him five thousand years before the siege of Troy. According to Sir Wm. Jones, the latter Zoroaster lived in the time of Darius Hystaspes. It is now claimed that in the Dabistan, one of the sacred books of Persia, thirteen Zoroasters appear. The name of the last great leader, together with a few of his doctrines, and various scattered fragments in the Gathas, are all that remain on record of a man whose personality stands connected with the earliest attempt to reform a degraded and sensualized religion.

That this prophet was without honor in his own country is shown by the following lamentation:

"To what country shall I go? Where shall I take refuge? What country gives shelter to the master, Zarathustra, and his companion? None of the servants pay reverence to me, nor do the wicked rulers of the country. How shall I worship thee further, living Wise One? What help did Zarathustra receive when he proclaimed the truths? What did he obtain through the good mind? . . . Why has the truthful one so few adherents, while all the mighty, who are unbelievers, follow the liar in great numbers?"[108]

Although the prophet Zarathustra and his companion were first rejected, the fact seems plain that the monotheistic doctrines which they set forth were subsequently accepted as the groundwork of the religion of Persia.

---

[108] Quoted by Viscount Amberley from Haug's Translations.

In the opening verses of the 5th Gatha appears the following:

"It is reported that Zarathustra Spitama possessed the best good, for Ahura Mazda granted him all that may be obtained by means of a sincere worship, forever, all that promotes the good life, and he gives the same to all who keep the words and perform the actions enjoined by the good religion. . . .

"Pourutschista, the Hetchataspadin, the most holy one, the most distinguished of the daughters of Zarathustra, formed this doctrine, as a reflection of the good mind, the true and wise one."

The fact will doubtless be observed that Pourutschista was not merely a disciple of Zarathustra, but that she FORMED the doctrine which was accepted as a "reflection of the good mind."

In the 5th Gatha it is stated that among those who "know the right paths, the law which Ahura gave to the Profitable," is Pourutschista the "Holy worthy of adoration among the daughters of Zarathustra. . . . wise female worker of Wisdom."[109]

Ormuzd, or Ahura Mazda, which was the essence of heat or light, was the principle adored by the followers of the reformed religion in Persia. Throughout the Avesta the most desirable possession, and that which is most praised, is purity of life.

"We praise the pure man.
"The best purity praise we.
"The best wish praise we of the best purity.
The best place of purity praise we, the shining, endued with all brightness."[110]

---

[109] Spiegel's Translation.
[110] Vespered xxvi. Spiegel's Translation.

"This Earth, together with the women, we praise
Which bears us, which are the women, Ahura Mazda
Whose wishes arise from purity, these we praise–
Fullness, readiness, questioning, wisdom."[111]

Praise is offered to the "everlasting female companion, the instructing."

The following is a part of the marriage ceremony of the Persians as it is found in the Khorda-Avesta:

"Do you both accept the contract for life with honorable mind? In the name and friendship of Ormuzd be ever shining, be very enlarged. Be increasing. Be victorious. Learn purity. Be worthy of good praise. May the mind think good thoughts, the words speak good, the works do good. May all wicked thoughts hasten away, all wicked words be diminished, all wicked works be burnt up. . . . Win for thyself property by right-dealing. Speak truth with the rulers and be obedient. Be modest with friends, clever, and well wishing. Be not cruel, be not covetous. . . . Combat adversaries with right. Before an assembly speak only pure words. In no wise displease thy mother. Keep thine own body pure in justice."

Confucius, the great Chinese teacher and philosopher, who lived probably in the sixth century B.C., may be said to have been a humanitarian or moralist instead of a mystic. Although he believed in a great first principle, or cause, which he termed Heaven, we are given to understand that in his philosophizing little mention was made of it.

The system known as Confucianism was not originated by Confucius.

In referring to this subject Legge remarks:

"He said of himself (Analects, vii., I), that he was a transmitter and not a maker, one who believed in and loved the ancients; and hence it is said in the thirtieth chapter of

---

[111] Yacna xxxviii.

the doctrine of the Mean, ascribed to his grandson, that he handed down the doctrines of Yao and Shun, as if they had been his ancestors, and elegantly displayed the regulations of Wan and Wu, taking them as his models."[112]

The ancient books which Confucius interpreted or rewrote laid no claim to being sacred in the sense of being inspired; but, on the contrary, were works of wisdom put forth by historians, poets, and others "as they were moved in their own minds." The most ancient of these doctrines was the Shu, a work which since the period of the Han dynasty, 202 years B.C., has been called the Shu King.

A number of documents contained in this work date back to the twenty-fourth century B.C., and as they are regarded as historical are considered to be of greater importance than are any others of their ancient writings.

Second in antiquity and importance is the Shih or the Book of Poetry. This work contains the religious views of its writers, also an account of the manners, customs, and events of the times to which they belong. For 5000 years, in China, Tien or Ti has expressed the moving or creating force in the universe. In later ages it is observed that this name has been attached to royalty. Hwang Ti is the present title of the Emperor of China.

From some of the texts found in the Shu King, it would seem that the Chinese had in the remote past caught sight of the scientific fact that virtue is its own reward. "Heaven graciously distinguishes the virtuous. . . . Heaven punishes the guilty."[113]

The principal object of Confucius seems to have been to inculcate those doctrines of his ancestors which, taking root, would in time bring about a return to those principles of former virtue, a faint knowledge of which seems still to

---

[112] Legge, Preface to vol. iii. of Shu King.
[113] Max Muller, Sacred Books of the East, book iv.

have survived in China. The following precepts are found among his teachings:

"Knowledge, magnanimity, and energy are the virtues universally binding. Gravity, generosity of soul, sincerity, earnestness, and kindness constitute perfect virtue. Sincerity is the very way to Heaven. My doctrine is that of an all-pervading unity. The superior man is catholic and not partisan. The mean is partisan and not catholic. The superior man is affable but not adulatory, the mean is adulatory but not affable."

When asked for a word which should serve as a rule of practice for all our life he replied: "Is not Reciprocity such a word? What you do not want done to yourself, do not do to others." On one occasion the question was asked him: "What do you say concerning the principle that injury shall be recompensed with kindness?" To which he replied: "Recompense injury with justice, and recompense kindness with kindness."[114]

It is recorded by his disciples that there are four things from which the master was entirely free. "He had no foregone conclusions, no arbitrary predeterminations, no obstinacy, and no egoism." Contrary to the rule of most reformers or leaders of opinion, he always regarded himself as a learner as well as teacher. It is related of Confucius that he at one time desired a governmental position, thinking that through its occupancy he might the better disseminate the ancient doctrines of rectitude and virtue. Offers of individual advantage could not swerve him from his well-grounded principles of honor. On one occasion one of the rulers of the country proposed to confer upon him a city and its revenues, but Confucius replied: "A superior man will only receive reward for services which he has rendered. I have given advice to the duke-king, but he has

---

[114] Lun Yu, xiv., 26.

not obeyed it, and now he would endow me with this place! very far is he from understanding me."[115]

The fact seems evident that Confucius had not sufficient strength of character to attempt a change in the social conditions of his time. He had not that grandeur of soul which enabled him to strike the key-note of reform. Monarchical institutions and social distinctions he did not rebuke. The brotherhood of man and the levelling processes in human society were probably never thought of by him; certainly they were never attempted.

By certain writers Confucius has been accused of insincerity in a few minor matters; still, the wisdom contained in his religious doctrines, the philosophical value of his teachings relative to the regulation of human conduct, and, above all, his purity of purpose, justly entitles his name to be enrolled among the great reformers of the world.

The lasting influence which this man exerted upon the minds of his countrymen, and the appreciation in which his name and works are still held, are shown by the fact that his descendants constitute the only order of hereditary nobility in China.

"He lived five hundred years before Christ; and yet to this day, through all the changes and chances of time and of dynasties, the descendants of Confucius remain the only hereditary noblemen and national pensioners in the empire. Even the imperial blood becomes diluted, degraded, and absorbed into the body politic after the seventh generation; but the descendants of Confucius remain separate, through all the mutations of time and of government."[116]

Laotse, the founder of the smallest of the three sects in China, namely, Confucianism, Buddhism, and Taoism, was an old man when Confucius was in his prime. The word Taou signifies reason, but the doctrines believed by the

---

[115] Quoted by Amberley, Analysis of Religious Belief, vol. i., p. 197.
[116] Thomas Magee, in the Forum, vol. x., p. 204.

Taoists prove their system to be the most irrational of all the religions of the East. In an article on The Taouist Religion, Warren Benton says:

"The tendency in rationalism is toward the utter destruction of a belief in the existence of unseen spirits of evil. Enlightened reason dethrones devils; but Laotse created devils innumerable, and the chief concern of the Taouist sect has always been to manipulate these emissaries of evil. Modern rationalists deny the existence of devils, and relegate them to the category of myths and to personified ideas. Not so the rationalist of the Orient. He finds his greatest pleasure in contemplating the very atmosphere he breathes as filled with spirits constantly seeking his injury; and to outwit his satanic majesty is the chief end of life."[117]

At a time when a personal devil was gradually assuming shape, it would have been singular, indeed, if there had not arisen one who, by his peculiar temperament and natural disposition, was exactly suited to the task of elaborating this doctrine in all its grim seriousness. That such an one did arise in the person of Laotse is evident from what is known regarding his history and teachings.

The growth of religious faith had long tended in this direction. Typhon, "the wind that blasts," "Darkness," and the "cold of winter," constituted the foundation of a belief in a personal Devil; and, when the time was ripe for the appearance of his satanic majesty, it required only a hypochondriac– a disordered mental organization–to formulate and project this gloomy and unwholesome doctrine.

There is little known of the life and character of Laotse except that he labored assiduously through a long life-time for the establishment of certain principles or tenets which he believed to be essential to the well-being of humanity. In

---

[117] Pop. Science, Jan. 1890.

the twentieth chapter of his work are found to be some hints of his personality and of the gloomy cast of his character. He complains that while other men are joyous and gay, he alone is despondent. He is "calm like a child that does not yet smile." He is "like a stupid fellow, so confused does he feel. Ordinary men are enlightened; he is obscure and troubled in mind. Like the sea, he is forgotten and driven about like one who has no certain resting place. All other men are of use; he alone is clownish like a peasant. He alone is unlike other men, but he honors the nursing mother."

Of all the various teachers which arose during the fifth, sixth, and seventh centuries B.C., none of them were able to rise to the position of moral grandeur occupied by Gotama Buddha. The efforts put forth by this great teacher seem to have been humane rather than religious. In his time, especially in India, society had become encysted beneath a crust of seemingly impenetrable conservatism, while religion, or priestcraft, riveted the chains by which the masses of the people were enslaved.

The mission of Buddha was to burst asunder the bonds of the oppressed and to abolish all distinctions of caste. This was to be accomplished through the awakening of the divine life in each individual. The leading processes by which the lines of caste were weakened were in direct opposition to the established order of society. It was a blow at the old Brahminical social and religious code which had grown up under the reign of priest-craft.

Notwithstanding the sex prejudice which had come to prevail in India, it was directly stated by Buddha that any man or woman who became his disciple, who renounced the world and by abstinence from the lower indulgences of sense proclaimed her or his adherence to the higher principles of life, "at once lost either the privilege of a high caste or the degradation of a low one." Earthly distinctions were of no consequence. Rank depended not on the outward circumstance of birth, but on the ability of the individual to resist evil, or, upon his capacity to receive the higher truths enunciated by the new sun or savior–Buddha.

In one of the canonical books he is represented as saying:

"Since the doctrine which I teach is completely pure, it makes no distinction between noble and common, between rich and poor. It is, for example, like water, which washes both noblemen and common people, both rich and poor, both good and bad, and purifies all without distinction. It may, to take another illustration, be compared to fire, which consumes mountains, rocks, and all great and small objects between heaven and earth. Again, my doctrine is like heaven, inasmuch as there is room within it without exception, for whomsoever it may be; for men and women, for boys and girls, for rich and poor."[118]

There is little doubt that the religion of Buddha was an attempt to return to the almost forgotten principles of a past age of spiritual and moral greatness. According to this ancient wisdom, man is an immortal soul struggling for perfection. The growth of the real man is a natural unfolding of the divine principle within, such process of evolution being accomplished through the power of the will. As every individual must work out his own salvation, this will-force must ever be directed toward the complete mastery of the body, or the lower self. In other words, the development of the higher life depends upon the power of the individual to overcome or conquer evil. The effect of every thought, word, and deed is woven into the soul, and no one can evade the consequences of his own acts. All sin is the result of selfishness, so that only when one renounces self and begins to live for others does the soul-life begin. No one who has arrived at a state of soul-consciousness will lead a selfish or impure life. On the contrary, every

---

[118] Viscount Amberley, Analysis of Religious Belief, vol. i., p. 216.

impulse of the devout Buddhist goes out toward humanity and God, of whom he is a conscious part.

Gotama Buddha was not a "savior" in the sense of bloody sacrifice for the sins of the people. On the contrary, he was an example to mankind–a man who through moral purification and a life of self- abnegation had prepared himself for this holy office. Mythologically, or astrologically, he was the new sun born at the close of the cycle. He was the great Light which revealed the way to eternal repose– Nirvana. The mythical Buddha was the prototype of the mythical Christ. His mother was Mai or Mary, Queen of Heaven, or the Vernal Spring. He was a new incarnation of the Sun–the Savior of the world. In process of time his many miracles were offered as proof of his divine character. Although he taught the existence of a great and universal Power, he made no attempt to explain the unknowable. The Infinite is to be contemplated only through its manifestations. Nirvana is not annihilation, as has been erroneously taught by Christian missionaries. As explained by Buddhists themselves, it comprehends a state of absolute rest from human strife and wretchedness. It is the absorption or relapsing into the great First Principle, whence all life is derived–a state so pure that the human is lost in the divine.

"Lamp of the law!

I take my refuge in thy name and Thee!
I take my refuge in thy Law of Good!
I take my refuge in thy Order! Om!
The dew is on the Lotus!–rise, Great Sun!
And lift my leaf and mix me with the wave.
Om Mani Padme Hum, the Sunrise comes!
The Dewdrop slips into the shining Sea!"

--Arnold, Light of Asia.

From the Buddhist colleges at Nolanda went forth teachers who, inspired with enthusiasm in the cause of human justice and individual liberty, endeavored to abolish the abominations which had grown up under Brahminical rule. The masses of the people, however, were too deeply sunken in infamy, wretchedness, and ignorance to accept, or even understand, the pure doctrines of the great teacher, and, as might have been anticipated, priest- craft soon assumed its wonted arrogance, and eventually the whole paraphernalia of antiquated dogmas were tacked upon the new system.

Through the various efforts put forth for the elevation of mankind during the six or seven hundred years which preceded the advent of Christianity, sufficient strength had been given to the moral impetus of humanity to create in many portions of the world a strong desire for a return to purer principles, and to make the appearance of a spiritual teacher like Christ possible. The effects, however, of ages of moral and intellectual degradation, in which the lowest faculties have been stimulated to the highest degree, are not wiped out in a few centuries of struggle by the few among the people who desire reform. As true reform means growth, those who have reached a higher stage of development can only point the way to others–they are powerless to effect changes for which the masses are unprepared.

Although through a partial revival of the ideas entertained by an ancient people the attempt was made by Zoroaster, Confucius, Gotama Buddha, Pythagoras, the Stoics, and other schools of philosophy, to elevate the masses of the people, and, although the unadulterated teachings of the man called Christ were doubtless an outgrowth of this movement, yet the human mind had not, even as late as the appearance of this last-named reformer, sufficiently recovered from its thraldom to enable the masses to grasp those higher truths which had been entertained by an earlier civilized people.

While there are doubtless many points of similarity between the religious system elaborated by Gotama Buddha and that enunciated by Christ, there is little likeness between the teachings of the former and those set forth by the Romish Church, or by Paul. Seven hundred years B.C., the Persians had grasped the idea that virtue is its own reward, and that every soul is responsible for its own growth. The fundamental doctrine of the Christian Church to-day is that of a vicarious atonement–a belief which takes away man's responsibility for his own misdeeds.

Chapter XIII.
Christianity a Continuation of Paganism

By comparing the sacred writings of the Persians with the history of the events connected with the conception and birth of the mythical Christ as recorded in the New Testament, the fact is observed that the latter appears to be closely connected with the central figure of Persian mythology. It has been found that the visit of the Magi, who, following a star, were guided to the spot where the young child lay, was the fulfilment of a Persian prophecy, which is to be found in the life of Zarathustra as recorded in the Zendavesta, while the subsequent history of the same personage is seen to be almost identical with that of the Hindoo Sun-god Chrishna.

According to the sacred books of the Persians, three sons of the great Zarathustra were to appear at three successive periods of time. These sons were to be incarnations of the sun, and the result of immaculate conceptions.

"The first is named Oschederbami. He will appear in the last millennium of the world. He will stop the sun for ten days and ten nights, and the second part of the human race will embrace the law, of which he will bring the 22d portion.

"The second posthumous son of Zoroaster is Oschedermah. He will appear four hundred years after Oschederbami. He will stop the sun twenty days and twenty nights, and he will bring the 23d part of the law, and the third part of the world will be converted.

"The third is named Sosiosch. He will be born at the end of the ages. He will bring the 24th part of the law; he will stay the sun thirty days and thirty nights, and the whole earth will embrace the law of Zoroaster. After him will be the resurrection."[119] This last named son was to be born of a pure and spotless virgin, whereupon a star would appear blazing even at noonday with undiminished lustre.

"You, my sons," exclaimed the seer, "will perceive its rising before any other nation. As soon, therefore, as you shall behold the star, follow it, withersoever it shall lead you; and adore that mysterious child, offering your gifts to him, with profound humility. He is the Almighty Word, which created the heavens."[120]

Waite notices the conclusion of Faber that this prediction was long before the birth of Christ, and states that one of the reasons for such a conclusion was, that in the old Irish history a similar prophecy appears–a prophecy which was delivered by a "Druid of Bokhara." The identity of this Irish prophecy with the one in the East ascribed to Zarathustra or Zoroaster, is so singular that Faber thinks it can be accounted for only on the hypothesis "of an ancient emigration from Persia to Ireland by the northwest passage, which carried the legend with it."

By those who have investigated the origin of the early gospels, it is stated that the story of the Magi and the star appeared in the Gospel of the Infancy early in the second century, and was subsequently incorporated into the preparatory chapters of Luke and Matthew. According to Waite, there was a sect of Christians called Prodiceans whose leader, Prodicus, about A.D. 120, boasted that they had the sacred books of Zoroaster. From an extant fragment of the Chronography of Africanus is the following:

---

[119] Quoted by Waite, History of the Christian Religion, p. 168.
[120] Ibid., 169.

"Christ first of all became known from Persia. For nothing escapes the learned jurists of that country, who investigated all things with the utmost care. The facts, therefore, which are inscribed upon the golden plates, and laid up in the royal temples, I shall record; for it is from the temples there, and the priests connected with them, that the name of Christ has been heard of. Now, there is a temple there to Juno, surpassing the royal palace, which temple Cyrus, that prince instructed in all piety, built, and in which he dedicated, in honor of the gods, golden and silver statues, and adorned them with precious stones. . . . Now about that time [as the records on the plates testify], the king having entered the temple, with the view of getting an interpretation of certain dreams, was addressed by the priest Prupupius thus: 'I congratulate thee, master: Juno has conceived.' 'And the king, smiling, said to him: 'Has she who is dead conceived?' And he said: 'Yes, she who was dead has come to life again, and begets life.' And the king said: 'What is this? explain it to me.' And he replied: 'In truth, master, the time for these things is at hand. For during the whole night the images, both of gods and goddesses, continued beating the ground, saying to each other, Come, let us congratulate Juno. And they say to me, Prophet, come forward, congratulate Juno, for she has been embraced. And I said, How can she be embraced who no longer exists? To which they reply, She has come to life again, and is no longer called Juno, but Urama. For the mighty Sol has embraced her.' "[121]

There is a tradition which asserts that during the early part of the second century, St. Thomas went as a missionary to Parthia; that after he had visited the various countries of the Parthian Empire, tarrying for a time at Balkh, the capital of Bactria, and the ancient residence of the Magi, he went to India. Soon after the visit of Thomas

---

[121] Hyppolytus, vol. ii., p. 196.

to Persia and India, there appeared in Palestine and the adjacent countries a gospel of Thomas, in which were set forth various stories closely resembling the legends found in the Hindoo sacred writings. After comparing various passages of the Bhagavat Purana with those of the Infancy, and after furnishing conclusive evidence that the latter must have been copied from the former, Waite says:

"The conclusion must be, that while for some of the salient points of the Gospels of the Infancy, the authors were indebted to Zoroaster, and the legends of Persia, the outline of the story was largely filled up from the history of Crishna, as sent back to Palestine, by the Apostle Thomas, from the land of the Brahmins."

Concerning the story of Herod and his order to slay all the male infants, there has been discovered in a cavern at Elephanta, in India, a sculptured representation of a huge and ferocious figure, bearing a drawn sword and surrounded by slaughtered children, while mothers appear weeping for their slain. This figure is said to be of great antiquity.

Mary, the Mother of Jesus, like Mai, the Mother of Gatama Buddha, was regarded by certain sects in the earlier ages of Christianity as an Immortal Virgin whose birth had been announced by an angel.[122] She was in fact the ancient Virgin of the Sphere–the Mother of the Gods–the Queen of Heaven.

As soon as Christ was born he conversed with Mary, as did also Crishna with his mother, informing her of his divine mission.

Crishna was cradled among shepherds, so was Christ. Cansa, fearing the loss of his kingdom, sought to destroy the life of the divine infant in the same manner as did Herod in the case of Christ. Both children are carried away by night, after which an order is issued by the ruler of the

---

[122] See Gospels of Mary and the Protovangelion.

country that all the young children throughout the kingdom be slaughtered.

When Joseph and Mary arrived in Egypt, they visited the temple of Serapis, where "all the magistrates and priests of the idols were assembled." Upon the image being interrogated concerning the "consternation and dread which had fallen upon all our country," it answered them as follows: "The unknown god has come hither, who is truly God; nor is there anyone besides him, who is worthy of divine worship; for he is truly the son of God." And at the same instant this idol fell down, and at his fall all the inhabitants of Egypt, besides others, ran together.[123] A similar story is related of Crishna. This Indian god, the same as Christ, cured a leper. A woman, after having poured a box of precious ointment on the head of Crishna, was healed; so also a woman anointed the head of Jesus. Crishna when but a lad displayed remarkable mental powers and the most profound wisdom before the tutor who was sent to instruct him. Christ astonished the schoolmaster Zaccheus with his great learning.

Crishna had a terrible encounter with the serpent Calinaga; the infant Christ had also a dreadful adventure with a serpent. Now this Calinaga which Crishna encountered was a serpent goddess who was worshipped by the sect in India which was opposed to the adoration of the male principle. The early Christians, however, being ignorant of the allegorical meaning of the legend, transferred it to Christ literally.

The mother of Crishna looked in his mouth and beheld all the nations of the earth. The same story is reported of Christ and his mother. Finally Christ, like Crishna, was crucified, and like him was buried. He descended into hell and on the third day arose and ascended into heaven.[124]

---

[123] Gospel of the Infancy, ch. iv.
[124] It will doubtless be urged that I am quoting from the Apocryphal Gospels–that the genuine books of the New Testament are silent

In the poetical myths of the ancients the sun is yearly overpowered by cold or by the destructive agencies in Nature. Astronomically, or astrologically, it wanders in darkness and desolation during the winter months; in fact dies, and descends into hell in order that he may rise at the Easter season to gladden and make all things new again. Mythologically, this new sun becomes incarnate; enters again his mother's womb, and is born into the world in the form of a man whose mission is to renew human life. Hence we have an explanation of the Eastern Buddhas and Crishnas, all of which were born of virgins at the winter solstice.

The new sun which at the close of each cycle was believed by the more ancient people of the globe to "issue forth from the womb of Nature to renew the world," now that the truths underlying Nature-worship were lost, became a redeemer or mediator between earth and heaven, or between spirit and matter. It is stated that at the time of the appearance of Christ not alone the Jews, but the Persians, the Romans, the ancient Irish, and in fact all the nations of the globe, were anxiously awaiting the event of another incarnation of the solar Deity; and that maidens of all classes and conditions were in a state of eager expectation, the more pious, or at least the more ambitious among them, being in almost constant attendance at the temples and sacred shrines, whither they went to pay homage to the male emblem of generation, thereby hoping to be honored as a Mai or Mary.

On the wall of the temple at Luxor are a series of sculptures,

---

concerning many of these Eastern legends. We must bear in mind, however, that during the earlier ages of Christianity, these finally rejected gospels were, equally with the canonical books, considered as the word of God. The Infancy is thought to be one of the earliest gospels. Justin Martyr was acquainted with it, A.D. 150 to 160. It is referred to by Irenaeus, A.D. 190.

"in which the miraculous annunciation, conception, birth, and adoration of Amunoph III., the son of the Virgin Queen Mautmes, is represented in a manner similar to what is described in St. Luke's Gospel (ch. 1 and 2) of Jesus Christ, the son of the Virgin Mary, and which is found also in the Gospel of St. Matthew (ch. 1) as an addition not met with in the earliest manuscripts,"[125] which fact has caused Sharpe, from whom the above is quoted, to suggest that both accounts may have been of Egyptian origin.

The titles "lamb," "anointed," etc., which were applied to Christ, all appear attached to former in- carnations of the sun, the first named standing for the sun in Aries. The effigies of a crucified savior found in Ireland and Scotland in connection with the figure of a lamb, a bull, or an elephant, the latter of which is not a native of those countries, shows that they do not represent Christ, but a crucified sun-god worshipped by the inhabitants of the British Islands ages before the birth of the great Judean philosopher and teacher.

It is plain that Crishna of India and the Persian Mithra furnished the copy for the Jesus of the Romish Church, all of whom mean one and the same thing–the second person in the Solar Trinity. By the Jews, who attempted to ignore the female principle, this God is called the "Lord of Hosts" and "God of Sabaoth," which astronomically means God of the stars and constellations, and astrologically the creator or producer of the multitudes. Of this God, ieue, I H S, the author of Anacalypsis says that he was the son of the celestial virgin, which she carries in her arms; the Horus, Lux, of the Egyptians, the Lux of St. John.

"It is from this infant that Jesus took his origin; or at least it is from the ceremonies and worship of this infant that this religion came to be corrupted into what we have of it. This infant is the seed of the woman who, according to

---

[125] Barlow, Symbolism, p. 127.

Genesis, was to bruise the head of the serpent, which, in return, was to bruise his foot or heel, or the foot or heel of her seed as the figure of the Hindoo Crishna proves. From the traditionary stories of this god Iao, which was figured annually to be born at the winter solstice, and to be put to death and raised to life on the third day at the vernal equinox, the Roman searchers after the evangelion or gospel made out their Jesus. The total destruction of everything at Jerusalem and in Judea–buildings, records, everything–prevented them from coming to any absolute certainty respecting this person who, they were told by tradition, had come to preach the gospel of peace, to be their savior, in fulfilment of the prophecy which their sect of Israelites found in their writings, and who had been put to death by the Jews. From all these circumstances he came to have applied to him the monogram of I H S. . . . and to him at last all the legendary stories related of the god Iao were attributed."[126]

According to Faber, Jesus was not originally called Jesus Christ, but Jescua Hammassiah–Jescua meaning Joshua, and Jesus, Savior. Ham is the Om of India, and Messiah, the anointed. Commenting on this Higgins remarks: "It will then be, The Savior Om the Anointed, precisely as Isaiah had literally foretold; or reading in the Hebrew made, The Anointed Om the Savior. This was the name of Jesus of Bethlehem."

We have observed the fact that at the time of the birth of Christ the entire world was expecting a Savior–a new incarnation of the sun. The end of a cycle had come and the entire earth was to undergo a process of renovation.

In a poem by Virgil, who was a Druid, the birth of a wonderful child is celebrated, and the prophecy of a heathen Sibyl is seen to be identical with that of Isaiah.

---

[126] Godfrey Higgins, Anacalypsis, book vi., ch. iv., p. 455.

"The last period sung by the Sibylline prophetess is now arrived; and the grand series of ages. That Series which recurs again and again in the course of our mundane revolution begins afresh. Now the Virgin Astrea returns from heaven; and the primeval reign of Saturn recommences; now a new race descends from the celestial realms of holiness. Do thou, Lucina, smile propitious on the birth of a boy who will bring to a close the present age of iron and introduce throughout the whole world, a new age of gold. Then shall the herds no longer dread the fury of the lion, nor shall the poison of the serpent any longer be formidable. Every venomous animal and every deleterious plant shell perish together. The fields shall be yellow with corn, the grape shall hang its ruddy clusters from the bramble, and honey shall distil spontaneously from the rugged oak. The universal globe shall enjoy the blessings of peace, secure under the mild sway of its new and divine sovereign."

There is no lack of evidence to prove that for several centuries great numbers of Christians regarded Christ as a solar incarnation similar to those which from time to time were born in the valleys of the Nile and the Ganges. By the fathers in the church Jesus Christ was named the New Sun, and in the early days of Christianity the Egyptians struck a coin representing O. B. or the holy Basilisk, with rays of light darting from his head, on the reverse side of which was figured "Jesus Christ as the New Solar Deity."

The similarity if not the actual identity of the religion of Christ and that of the pagans in the second century is shown by various writers. The Emperor Hadrian writing to his friend Servianus says:

"Those who worship Serapis are also Christians; even those who style themselves the Bishops of Christ are devoted to Serapis. . . . There is but one God for them all; him do the Christians, him do the Jews, him do all the Gentiles also worship."

It has been said that the head of Serapis supplied the first idea of the portrait of Christ. Before the figure of Serapis, in his temple, used to stand Isis, the Celestial Virgin, with the inscription "Immaculate is our Lady Isis." In her hand she bore a sheaf of grain.

As Serapis, or Pan, finally became Christ, so Isis, or the Queen of Heaven, became his mother, and to the latter were transferred all the titles, ceremonies, festivals, and seasons which from the earliest time had belonged to the great Goddess of Nature. Subsequently, probably about the close of the second century, Christianity began slowly to emerge from the worship of Mithras and Serapis, "changing the names but not the substance."

Upon the coinage of Constantine appears Soli Invicto Comita–"To the invincible sun my companion or guardian," and when the Greek and Roman Christians finally separated themselves from the great body of pagan worshippers they apologized for celebrating the birthday of their Savior on the 25th of December, saying that "they could better perform their rites when the heathen were busy with theirs." We are assured that the early Christians no less than the Maji acknowledged Mithras as the first emanation from Ormuzd, or the God of Light. He was the Savior which in an earlier age had represented returning life–that which follows the cold of winter. It was doubtless while they worshipped the Persian Mithras that many of the so-called Christians gathered their first ideas concerning the immortality of the soul and of future rewards and punishments.

The analogy existing between the festivals, seasons, mythoses, etc., of the various incarnations of the sun which were worshipped by the early historic nations and those belonging to Christianity is too striking to be the result of chance.

Buddha originally represented the sun in Taurus. Crishna was the sun in Aries. The laborings and sufferings of Hercules, a god who was an incarnation of the latter, portrays the history of the passage of the sun through the signs of the Zodiac.

All the principal events of Christ's life correspond to certain solar phases; or, in other words, all ecclesiastical calendars are arranged with reference to the festivals which commemorate the important events of his life from his conception and birth to his ascension and reception in heaven. Each and every one of the solar deities has been born at midnight, on the 25th of December, at the time when the sun has reached its lowest position and begins to ascend. Macrobius, a learned Roman writer, observes that the early historic nations "believed that the sun comes forth as a babe from its cradle at the winter solstice." Neith is made to say, "The sun is the fruit of my womb."

The 15th of August, assumption day, the time when Mary, the mother of Jesus, ascends to heaven is the day when the Zodiacal constellation Virgo, "the Greek Astrea, leaves the European horizon," and the "8th of September, when Virgo emerges from the sun's rays, is held sacred as the Nativity of the Queen of Heaven."

Of the mid-winter festival, Bede says: "The Pagans of these isles began their year on the eighth of the Kalends of January, which is now our Christmas Day. The night before that (24th Dec. eve) was called by them the Medre-Nak, or Night of Mothers, because of the ceremonies which were performed on that night."[127]

Among Christians as among Pagans the Christmas season was in honor of "returning light," the vernal equinox of "growing light" and St. John's day of "perfected light."

In England, among pagan Saxons, the midwinter festival lasted twelve days, during which time light, fire, the sun, huge stones and other similar manifestations of the Deity were adored. Christian and pagan alike worshipped

---

[127] Rivers of Life, vol. i., p. 430.

these objects. They called Christmas "the birthday of the god who is light." The Savior, or the New Sun, was the true light which lighteth every man who cometh into the world. According to the testimony of various writers, the festival held by Christians on Christmas eve used to resemble the Feast of Lights, celebrated in Egypt in honor of Neith. The tokens distributed among friends were cakes made of paste in the form of babies. These cakes were called yuledows. Dow means to "grow bigger," or, "to increase."

The Kalends of January at Rome were sacred to Janus and Juno to whom sacrifices were offered. The Etruscans also worshipped Janus who was the god (or goddess) of the year. Although this Deity does not appear among the twelve gods it is said to be the parent of them all. It was represented as having two faces. Upon one were the letters representing 365, and upon the other were the keys of life and death. According to Bryant this Deity was called Junonius, from the goddess Juno, whose name resolves itself into Juneh, a dove. In the Hebrew this name is identical with Yoni or Yuni–the female principle. On the coins of this god (which was subsequently regarded as male) is usually figured a boat, although a dove with an olive branch is sometimes observed.[128]

Juno is thought to be the same as Jana, which came from Jah of the Hebrews. Diana was Diva Jana or "Dea Jana who is the same as Astarte or Ashtaroth of the Sidonians."

Regarding the transference of the mid-winter festival of the pagans to the Christian calendar, Forlong says:

"The early Christians undoubtedly selected this Roman Saturnalia as an important period in the life of Christ, at first calling it the time of his conception, and later of his birth, this last best suiting the views and feelings of their Solo- Christian flocks. The Jews called the day of the

---

[128] See Faber, Pagan Idolatry.

Winter Solstice The Fast of Tebet. The previous time was one of darkness, and on the 28th began their Feast of Lights."[129]

In France the ancient name for Christmas is Noel, a term which until recently has baffled all antiquarian research. It is now thought that it is formed from Nuadh and Vile which together mean All Heal.

Although every possible effort has been put forward to give to this date (the 25th of December) the appearance of authenticity as the birth of Christ, still, so far as I am able to find, no one accredited with any degree of trustworthiness has ever been rash enough to attempt its ratification as a matter of history.

Tylor calls attention to the fact that in the religious symbolism of the material and spiritual sun Augustine and Gregory of Nyssa discourse on the "growing light and dwindling darkness that follow the nativity," and cites the instance of Leo the Great who, in a sermon, rebukes the "pestiferous persuasion, that this solemn day is to be honored not for the birth of Christ, but for the rising of the New Sun."

On the authority of this same prelate it is found that in the fifth century, the faithful, before entering the Basilica of St. Peter, were wont to turn and salute the shining orb of day.

The Roman winter solstice which was connected with the worship of Mithra, and which was named the "Birthday of the Unconquered Om," was adopted by the western churches some time during the fourth century. From the west it passed to the eastern churches, where it finally became "the solemn anniversary of the birth of Christ."

In Ireland the ceremonies attending the mid-winter festival were formerly regarded as exceedingly important. A short time before the approach of the winter solstice,

---

[129] Rivers of Life, vol. i., p. 430.

voices were heard throughout the island proclaiming: "The New Year is at hand! Gather the Mistletoe!" The mistletoe wreaths which formed the principal decorations of Venus' temple were at first proscribed by the Christian preachers, but, in process of time they not only found their way into the sanctuary, but were given a place over the altars, their final signification being "good will to men."[130]

Although the tokens of friendship which were distributed by the pagans at the season of the mid- winter festival differed somewhat from those which at the present time are exchanged among Christians at the same season of the year, still, there can be no doubt that the Christmas tree, loaded with gifts, is a remnant of that worship under which the sun was recognized as the source whence all blessings flow. Down to a late date, fire was a conspicuous element at the festival of the winter solstice. As the yule-log blazed upon the hearth, our ancestors set up huge stones and danced round them, thus worshipping the god of fertility.

On the 20th and 21st of March the sun illumines exactly half the earth. At this time the Day has conquered the Night. Light has dethroned Darkness, a complete victory has been gained over Typhon and the new god comes forth "with healing in his wings." On Lady's day, the 25th of March, the Virgin conceives. In Phoenicia numerous fetes were instituted to rejoice with Astarte in her conception. During the months preceding the birth of the young sun-god the Queen of Heaven receives marked homage.

In a former portion of this work we have observed that the festival which celebrated the return of spring was instituted by the inventors of the Neros thousands of years prior to the beginning of the Christian era, to celebrate the vernal equinox and to commemorate a return of Nature's bounties; but, after male reproductive power began to be

---

[130] Rivers of Life, vol. i., p. 81.

regarded as the creator, when passion came to be considered as the moving force in the universe, and when the operations of Nature began to be typified by a dead man on a cross who was to rise again, Easter was celebrated in commemoration of a risen savior or sun-god.

The following is an account given in Ramsay's Travels of Cyrus, concerning the vernal equinox festivals in the East. When Cyrus entered the temples he found the public clad in mourning. In a cavern lay the image of a young man (the dying savior) on a bed of flowers and odoriferous herbs Nine days were spent in fasting, prayers, and lamentations, after which the public sorrow ceased and was changed into gladness. Songs of joy succeeded weeping (for Tamuz), the whole assembly singing hymns: "Adonis is returned to life, Urania weeps no more, he has ascended to heaven, he will soon return to earth and banish hence all crimes and miseries forever." This scene, it will be remembered, was presented 500 years prior to the birth of Christ. In Rome, throughout the months preceding the winter solstice, Hilaria or Ceres, was especially honored. Apollo and Diana rose on the 7th of the Julian April and on the 10th their religious festivals began.

On Easter morn, during the earlier ages of the church, the observances of Christians were exactly the same as were those of the so called pagans, all together hurried out long before the break of day that they might behold the sun ascend, or "dance" as they called it, for on this morning he was to "make the earth laugh and sing." Pagan and Christian alike greeted each other with the salutation "The Lord is risen," and the reply was "The Lord is risen indeed." On Easter morning the peasants of Saxony and Brandenburg still climb to the hilltops "to see the sun give his three joyful leaps."

In Buckland's Land and Water it is stated that on the first of May all the choristers of Magdalene College, Oxford, still meet on the summit of their tower, 150 feet high, and sing a Latin hymn as the sun rises, during which time ten bells are rung "to welcome the gracious Apollo." Formerly, high mass was celebrated here and early mass for Sol was held in the College chapel, but, as at the time of the Reformation this service was forbidden, "it has since been performed on the top of the tower." After the hymn is sung "boys blow loud blasts to Sol through bright new tin horns."

Perhaps none of the ideas which enter into present religious rites and ceremonies proclaims its eastern origin more forcibly than do those connected with the veneration of fire. The testimony of all writers upon this subject agrees that in Europe, down to a late date in the Christian era, fire was still adored, and in some mysterious manner was connected with the Creator.

Upon the subject of the continuation of sun and fire worship to modern times, it is stated that the ancient bonfires with which the North German hills used to be ablaze mile after mile are not altogether given up by local custom. In Ireland as late as the year 1829, the ancient Canaanitish and Jewish rite of passing children through fire as a cleansing or regenerating process was still in operation. It is related that at stated seasons great fires were lighted in public places, on which occasions, fathers, taking their children in their arms, would leap and run through the flames. At the same time, two large fires were kindled a short distance from each other through which the cattle were driven. It was believed that by means of this ceremony, fecundity is imparted both to man and beast. May, the month in which all Nature revives, and in which life starts anew, is the time selected for the lighting of those sacred fires. May is the month of the fires of Baal. According to Maurice in his work on the Antiquities of India, the festival and the May-pole of Great Britain are the remnants of a religious ceremony once common in Egypt, India, and Phoenicia, which nations all worshipping the same Deity, celebrated the entrance of the sun into the sign of Taurus at the vernal equinox, but which in consequence of the precession of the equinoxes is removed far in the year from its original situation. This festival is thought to be coeval with a time when the equinox actually took place at that time. It was formerly in honor of the goddess Bhavania, who, under various names, was once worshipped in every country of the globe. "She is identical with the Dea Syria of Chaldea, and the Venus Urania of Persia."

At the present time there is direct and indisputable evidence that sacred fires once flamed over the whole of Britain. A few days prior to Bealtine season, every flame was ordered extinguished, to be relighted on the first of May by holy fire drawn directly from the sun. Of fire-worship Toland observes:

"On May-day the Druids made prodigious fires on these cairns, which being every one in sight of some other could not but afford a glorious show over a whole nation. These fires were in honor of Beal, or Bealan, Latinized by the Roman writers into Belanus, by which name the Gauls and their colonies understood the sun, and therefore, to this hour, the first of May is, by the aboriginal Irish, called la Bealtine, or the day of Belan's fires. May-day is likewise called la Bealtine by the Highlanders of Scotland, who are no contemptible part of the Celtic offspring. So it is with the Isle of Man: and in Armorica a priest is called Belee, or the servant of Bel, and the priesthood Belegieth."[131]

Down to a comparatively recent time, in the British Isles, the youth of both sexes used to arise long before daybreak on May-day, and in large companies set out for the woods, there to gather flowers, boughs, and branches, which, on returning at night, were used to decorate their homes. This festival is said to be the most ancient of any known, and during the earlier and purer ages of human

---

[131] Quoted by Godfrey Higgins, Celtic Druids, ch. v., p. 181.

faith was celebrated in honor of returning spring. In later ages, however, after passion had become the only recognized god, May-day was celebrated with "all manner of obscenity and lewdness."

Although the uneducated masses among the Gauls worshipped Apollo, Mercury, and Mars without understanding their true significance, the Druids, who are thought to be Pythagorians, invoked one great power, the animating force which pervades the universe, the essence of which they believed resides in fire.

It is related that although after the introduction of Romish Christianity, May fires still continued to be lighted on Bealtine day, the more impressive ceremonies took place on the 23d of June, on the eve of the nativity of St. John. The early preachers, wishing to defer to the prejudices and usages of the people, "yet not so as to interfere with the celebration of Easter at the vernal equinox, retained the Bealtine ceremonial, only transferring it to the saint's day." Of these fire festivals and their adoption by the Christian church Tylor says:

"The solar Christmas festival has its pendant at midsummer. The summer solstice was the great season of fire festivals throughout Europe on the heights, of dancing round and leaping through the fires, of sending blazing fire-wheels to roll down from the hills into the valleys, in sign of the sun's descending course. These ancient rites attached themselves in Christendom to St. John's Eve.

"It seems as though the same train of symbolism which had adapted the mid-winter festival to the Nativity, may have suggested the dedication of the mid-summer festival to John the Baptist, in clear allusion to his words 'He must increase but I must decrease.' "[132]

In a description recently given of the "moral, religious, and social disease" which broke out A.D. 1374, in the

---

[132] Tylor, Primitive Culture, vol. ii., p. 271.

lower Rhine region, and which was denominated as the "greatest, perhaps, of all manifestations of possession," Andrew D. White says: "The immediate origin of these manifestations seems to have been the wild revels of St. John's Day."[133]

Upon this subject Toland observes that he has seen the people of Ireland running and leaping through the St. John's fire proud of passing through it unsinged. Although ignorant of the origin of this ceremony, they nevertheless regarded it as some kind of a lustration by means of which they were to be specially blessed.

To every domestic hearth was carried the seed of Bealtine, or St. John's fire, which during the year was not permitted to go out.[134]

According to the testimony of Tylor, the festival of John the Baptist was celebrated in Germany down to a late date. This writer quoting from a low German book of the year 1859, refers to the "nod fire" which was sawed out of wood to light the St. John's bonfire "through which the people leapt and ran and drove their cattle."

With regard to the worship of Fire and Light it is related that in Jerusalem, at the present time, the Easter service is performed by the bishop of the church emerging from a tomb with lighted tapers "from which all crave lights."

On the authority of Peter Martyr, Bishop of Alexandria in the third century, we are informed that the place in Egypt where Christ was banished, which is called Maturea, a lamp is kept constantly burning in remembrance of this event. Although the story of this banishment is doubtless borrowed from the life of the Hindoo god Crishna, the fact

---

[133] Pop. Science, vol. xxxv., p. 3.

[134] Although the preservation of holy fire upon every hearth was clearly a religious observance, still, as in those days there were no matches, the material benefit to be derived from this precaution doubtless had a significance apart from that connected with worship.

is evident that those who appropriated it, and used it in furbishing the mythical history of Christ, had no scruples against fire worship–a religion which we have been taught to regard as belonging exclusively to the pagans.

In the ecclesiastical processions of the Church of Rome is frequently to be observed the figure of a dragon, in the mouth of which "holy and everlasting fire" is observed to be burning. A boy follows the procession with a lighted taper, so that in case the fire is extinguished it may be relighted. In referring to this subject the Rev. J. B. Deane says:

"The whole ceremony may be considered as a lively representation of an ophite procession as it advanced through the sinuous paralleiths of Karnak. So that no wonder the illiterate races were deceived into thinking that there was no harm in calling themselves Christians, for all their dear old faiths are here–fire, arks, poles, and fire in an ark."

Almost innumerable instances are given by various writers upon this subject, showing that the sun worship of the ancients has been continued to the present time by the so called followers of Christ, in the shrines of the East, with no change even of names to distinguish it from that of the Christian faith. By those who have spent much time in investigating the Holy Land, it is related that nearly all the spots in and about Jerusalem, sacred to Greek and Romish Christians as connected with the life and death of their risen Lord, are equally sacred to the pagans as commemorating the life and death of their Savior–the New Sun. Even Gethsemane is marked by characteristics which prove that it is no less interesting to pagans, or, more properly speaking, to the pagan followers of Christ, than it is to those of the Greek and Romish churches. Here is a holy tree, and not far distant is a cave of Mithras. There is also to be seen a trinity of stones "those of Janus (Chemosh),

Petros and Ion, all solar terms and connected with the sitting or sinking down to rest of the Kuros."

Messrs. Maundrell and Sandys, who in 1697 visited all the holy places in and around Jerusalem, state that the entire city, but especially the sites of Moriah, Zion, and suburbs were hotbeds of fire and phallic worship as usually developed still in the East.

The topography of ancient Delphi, on the site of which was built the village of Kastri, and at which place excavations are now being made under the direction of the American School of Archaeology, has ever been a place of peculiar interest to the mystic. Here are to be found all the natural features and objects which gladden the heart and stimulate the imagination of a solo-phallic worshipper. The holy Mt. Parnassus, the fountain of Kastali, the deep cave said to be Pythian, and the remnants of huge sepulchres hewn in the rocks all conspire to make of this spot a perfect abode for the god, or goddess, of fertility. Here, too, is a beautiful lake and near it a sacred fig-tree which has been struck by lightning, or, "touched by holy fire." Of this sacred place Forlong writes:

"Christianity has never neglected this so-called Pagan shrine, nor yet misunderstood it, if we may judge by the saint she has located here, for Mr. Hobhouse found in the rocky chasm dipped in the dews of Castaly, but safe in a rocky niche, a Christian shrine; and close by a hut called the church of St. John; yea verily of Ione, she who had once reigned here supreme; whilst on a green plot a few yards below the basin, in a little grove of olive trees, stood the monastery of Panhagia or Holy Virgin, so that here we still have and beside her sacred form in the cleft, men who have consecrated their manhood to the old Mother and Queen of Heaven, just as if she of Syria had never been heard of.

Doubtless they knew little of what civilized Europe calls Christianity, for I have spent many days conversing with such men, and seen little difference between them and those similarly placed in the far East–fervid Christians though Greeks and Syrians are."

Perhaps nothing shows the extent to which the religion of the pagans has been retained by Christianity more than does the worship of the serpent. It has been said that this reptile enters into every mythology extant. Ferguson is authority for the statement that "he is to be found in the wilderness of Sinai, the groves of Epidaurus, and in Samothracian huts." He constitutes a prominent factor in the religious worship of India, Assyria, Palestine, and Egypt, and, notwithstanding the fact that he is not a native of Ireland, in an earlier age representations of him appear in profusion among the symbols of that country. It has been said that there is scarcely an Egyptian sculpture known in which this reptile does not figure. The serpent whenever it appears as a religious emblem always typifies desire–creative energy–which, proceeding from the sun, is manifested in man and in animals. Whether it be a veritable snake in a box, a serpent connected with the figure of a woman, or as a carved representation on monuments or stones, or as chains or wreaths on columns, bas-reliefs or friezes, the signification is the same.

The sacred character of this reptile among the Gnostics is shown by the accounts given of their religious rites and ceremonies. By many of these sects this holy creature was kept in a box, ark, or chest, and when the eucharistic service was to be performed, he was enticed forth from his resting- place by a bit of bread. So soon as his holiness had wound himself about the offering, the sacrifice was complete and the service was concluded by "singing a hymn to Almighty God, and praying for acceptance in and through the serpent."

In later ages when the attempt was made to abolish serpent worship from the Christian church, it was declared by the leaders in the movement that Ophiolatry had been imported from Persia–that it had been brought in by ignorant devotees who were too weak to renounce their former faith.[135]

The extent to which the symbols representing Serpent, Sun, Tree, and Plant worship are still retained as part and parcel of the symbolism of Christianity is shown by the following report regarding the adoption of a seal by the Presbyterian Church which appeared in the daily press only a few years ago.

"After the assembly opened, the committee for the selection of a seal made a report recommending: That the general assembly hereby adopts as its official seal the device of a serpent suspended upon a cross, uplifted within a wilderness, in form as represented upon the official seal of the trustees of the general assembly, and displayed upon a circular field of the same proportions. In addition thereto the figure of a rising sun appearing above the margin of the wilderness, whose out-shooting beams shall occupy the centre of the field. Further, the decoration of a demi-wreath of two palm branches (in the form of the wreath upon the seal of the Westminster assembly of divines), placed around the margin of the upper hemisphere of the field; and on the lower hemisphere of the field a demi-wreath composed of a branch of oak united with an olive branch. Further, that the words of the motto, 'Christus Exaltus Salvatar,' shall be displayed in a semi-circle upon the upper part of the field, on either side of the standard of the cross, and, encompassing the whole in a bordure, the following words, in full or in proper abbreviation thereof, 'The Seal of the General Assembly of the Presbyterian Church in the United States of America.' "

The origin of the rite of Baptism as performed at the present time in Christian churches, may be traced directly to the worship of the sun, within which were supposed to reside the reproductive powers of Nature. All nations have

---

[135] Forlong, Rivers of Life.

had ceremonies corresponding to our baptism and confirmation rites, such baptism being either by fire or water. When we remember that for ages fertility, or the power to reproduce, constituted the idea of the Deity, we are not surprised to find that the original signification of the rite of baptism had, and still has, in some of the oriental countries, special reference to the child's sexual obligations.

In India, the religious rites performed upon the individual occur at birth or soon after; at betrothal, which takes place in childhood; at puberty; at marriage, and at death. The fact will be noticed that all sexual (spiritual) obligations and seasons fall within the domain of priestly supervision and surveillance. The child at baptism is dedicated to Vesta, or Hestia, the Queen of Hearths and Homes, a divinity who is supposed to assist him in securing the special evidence of divine favor, namely, fruitfulness of body.

Among Hindoos and Jews, excessive reproduction was the Lord's mark of favor. In India there has been a special hell provided for childless women, and with Jewesses no curse was equal to barrenness.

Baptism, or the ceremony connected with the naming of children in Christian countries, is seen to be identical with that performed in Mexico among the Aztecs. After the lips and bosom of the infant had been sprinkled with water, the Lord was implored to "permit the holy drops to wash away the sin that was given to it before the foundation of the world, so that the child might be born anew."

Among the petitions which are offered to the Deity is the following: "Impart to us, out of thy great mercy, thy gifts which we are not worthy to receive through our own merit." In their moral code appear these maxims: "Keep peace with all; bear injuries with humility; God who sees, will avenge you." "He who looks too curiously on a woman, commits adultery with his eyes."[136]

---

[136] Quoted by Prescott from Sahagun. Conquest of Mexico, book i., chap 3.

Chapter XIV.
Christianity a Continuation of Paganism

From the facts recorded in the foregoing pages, we have seen that true Christianity was but a continuation of that great movement which was begun in Persia seven or eight centuries before, and whose gathering strength had been emphasized by the humane doctrines set forth in the various schools of Greek philosophy.

In the first century of the Christian era may be observed among various sects, notably the Gnostics, a desire to popularize the teachings of an ancient race, and to accentuate those principles which had been taught by Buddha, Pythagoras, the Stoic philosophers, the Roman jurisconsults and others. In other words the object of the new religion was to stimulate the altruistic characters which had been developed during the evolutionary processes, and to strengthen and encourage the almost forgotten principles of justice and personal liberty upon which early society was founded, but which through ages of sensuality and selfishness had been denied expression.

When we remember the tenacity with which the human mind clings to established beliefs and forms, it is not perhaps singular that in a comparatively short time these principles were lost sight of, and that the entire system of corrupt paganism, with Christ as the New Solar Deity, was reinstated; neither is it remarkable, when we reflect upon the length of time required to bring about any appreciable change in human thought and action, that the principles which this Great Teacher enunciated are at the present time only just beginning to be understood.

To one who carefully studies the history of Christianity by the light of recently developed truths, the fact will doubtless be discovered that the fundamental difference existing between Catholic and Protestant sects is grounded in the old feud arising out of the relative importance of the sex-principles. From the days of Zoroaster to the final establishment of Christianity by Paul, the tendency–although slight–had been toward the elevation of woman, and consequently toward a greater acknowledgment of the female element in the god-idea. Considerable impetus was given to the cause of woman's advancement through the doctrines of the various schools of philosophy in Greece, and subsequently by the efforts put forth by the Roman lawyers to establish their equality with men before the law; hence, during the first hundred years of the Christian era the "new religion" seems to have contained much of the spirit of the ancient philosophy.

By several of the early Christian sects, the second person in the trinity was female, as was also the Holy Ghost.

In a "fragment of a gospel preserved by St. Jerome, and believed to have been from the original Aramaean Gospel of St. Matthew, with additions, the Holy Ghost (ruach), which in Hebrew is feminine, is called by the infant Savior, 'My Mother, the Holy Ghost.' "[137]

The mission of Christ was that of a Regenerator of mankind, an office which had been symbolized by the powers of the sun. He was to restore that which was lost. He attempted to teach to the masses of the people the long neglected principles of purity and peace. He did not condemn woman. He was baptized by John (Ion or Yon) in water, the original symbol for the female element, and while in the water; the Holy Ghost in form of a dove (female) descended upon him. To those who have given

---

[137] Barlow, Essays on Symbolism, p. 135.

attention to the symbolism of the pagan worship these facts are not without signification.

Because of the peculiar tendency of Christ's teachings women soon became active factors in their promulgation. If there were no other evidence to show that they publicly taught the new doctrines, the injunction of St. Paul, "I suffer not a woman to teach," would seem to imply that they were not silent.

The doctrines of the Gnostics were particularly favorable to women. Marcellina, who belonged to this order, was the founder of a sect called Marcelliens. Of her works Waite observes: "It would scarcely be expected that the heretical writings of a woman would be preserved amid such wholesale slaughter of the obnoxious works of the opposite sex. The writings of Marcellina have perished."[138] Not only did women teach publicly, and write, but according to Bunsen they claimed the privilege of baptizing their own sex. The reason for this is evident. Before baptism it was customary for the newly-made converts to strip and be anointed with oil. After the establishment of Paul's doctrines, however, "the bishops and presbyters did not care to be relieved from the pleasant duty of baptizing the female converts."[139]

Although the utmost care has been exercised to conceal the fact that women equally with men, performed the offices connected with the early church, yet by those who have paid attention to the true history of this movement, there can be no doubt about the matter. Notwithstanding the early tendencies of the "new religion" toward the recognition of women, and toward the restoration of the female principle in the Deity, the policy to be pursued by the church was soon apparent, for Paul, the real founder of the system calling itself Christian, and a

---

[138] History of the Christian Religion, p. 405.
[139] Ibid., p. 23.

man imbued with Asiatic prejudices concerning women, arrogantly declared that "man is the head of woman as Christ is the head of the Church." Women were commanded to be under obedience. Neither was the man created for the woman, but the woman for the man; thus was re-established and emphasized the absurd doctrine of the Lingaites, that the male is an independent entity, that he is spirit and superior to the female which is matter. After this indication of the policy to be pursued under the new regime, it would scarcely be expected that theefforts put forth by the various sects among the Gnostics toreinstate the female element either on the earth or in heavenwould be successful, and as might be anticipated from the factsalready adduced, as early as the year 325, at the council of Nice, a male trinity was formally established, and soon thereafter, the Collylidians, a sect which rigorously persisted in the adoration of the female principle, were condemned. At the council of Laodicea, A.D. 365, the 11th canon forbade the ordination of women for the ministry and the 44th canon prohibited them from entering the altar.

The devotees of female worship, although for a time silenced, were evidently not convinced, and to force their understanding into conformity with the newly established order, the Nestorians, in the year 430 A. D., reopened the old dispute, and formally denied to Mary the title of Mother of God. Their efforts, however, were of little avail, for in the year 451, at the council of Ephesus, the third general council, the decision of the Nestorians was reversed and the Virgin Mother reinstated. Upon this subject Barlow remarks: "Well might those who made this symbolical doctrine what it now is, at length desire to do tardy justice to the female element, by promoting the mother to the place once occupied by the Egyptian Neith, and crowning her

Queen of Heaven."[140] The fact will doubtless be observed, however, that by the Romish Church the idea of the godmother differs widely from the Queen of Heaven–the original God of the ancients. Mary the Mother of Jesus is not a Creator, but simply a mediator between her Son and His earthly devotees–a doctrine only a trifle less masculine in texture than that of an Almighty Father and his victimized son. The worship of Mary was adopted by the so-called Christians in response to a craving in the human heart for a recognition of those characters developed in mankind which may be said to contain the germ of the divine. The masculine god of the Jews was feared not loved, and his son had already been invested with his attributes. He was all powerful, hence a mediator, a mother, was necessary to intercede in behalf of fallen man, and this, too, notwithstanding the fact that woman had become the "cause of evil in the world."

The Great Goddess of the ancients, Perceptive Wisdom, the Deity of giving, she who represented the purely altruistic characters developed in mankind, and whose worship involved a scientific knowledge of the processes of Nature, when engrafted upon the so-called Christian system, although indicating an important step toward the recognition of the genuine creative principles, was not understood. Although her effigies were brought from the East and made to do duty as representations of Mary, the Mother of Christ, a knowledge of her true significance lay hurled beneath ages of sensuality and selfishness.

By those who have made it their business to investigate this subject, it is observed that there is scarcely an old church in Italy in which there is not to be found a remnant of a black virgin and child. In very many instances these black virgins have been replaced by white ones, the older figures having been retired to some secluded niche in the

---

[140] Essays on Symbolism, p. 134.

church where they are held especially sacred by the ignorant devotees who know absolutely nothing of their original significance. We are assured that many of these images have been painted over, ostensibly in imitation of bronze, but the whites of the eyes, the teeth, and colored lips reveal the fact that they are really not intended to represent bronze, but figures of a black virgin goddess and child whose worship has been imported into Europe from the East. I had been told that one of the oldest of these images extant was to be found in Augsburg; a thorough search, however, in all the churches and cathedrals of that city failed to reveal it, but in the museum at Munich such a figure is to be seen. It is in a state of decay, one arm of the mother and a portion of the child's figure being worn away. Upon this subject Godfrey Higgins remarks:

"If the author had wished to invent a circumstance to corroborate the assertion that the Romish Christ of Europe is the Crishna of India, how could he have desired anything more striking than the fact of the black virgin and child being so common in the Romish countries of Europe? A black virgin and child among the white Germans, Swiss, French, and Italians!!!"[141]

We have observed that during an earlier age in the history of religious worship, as the female was supposed to comprehend both the female and male elements in creation, a belief in the possible creative power of the female independently of the male was everywhere entertained, and that after the schismatic faction arose which endeavored to exalt the male, the production of a son by a woman unaided by man, was among the Yonigas to be the sign which would forever settle the question of the superior importance of the female functions in the processes of reproduction, and consequently, also, her claim to the greater importance in the deity.

---

[141] Anacalypsis, book iv., ch. i., p. 175.

The sacred books of India show that from a former belief in one or the other of the two creative principles throughout Nature as God, the people had come to accept both female and male as necessary elements in reproduction, the latter being the more important. In course of time this change seems to have been universal and to have extended to all the countries of the globe.

As the male could not create independently of the female, or, as spirit was dependent on matter for its manifestations, there arose a necessity for a Savior to redeem man from the evil effects arising from his relations with woman who was regarded as matter, and who in course of time became the cause of evil.

Concerning the doctrines which prevailed in the earlier ages of Christianity relative to the ancient dual principle in creation, and regarding the offices which were performed by the two elements, male and female, in the deity, we have the following from Justinus, who is said to have been contemporary with Peter and Paul:

"When Elohim had prepared and created the world as a result from joint pleasure, He wished to ascend up to the elevated parts of heaven, and to see that not anything of what pertained to the creation laboured under deficiency. And He took His Own angels with Him, for His nature was to mount aloft, leaving Edem below; for inasmuch as she was earth, she was not disposed to follow upward her spouse. Elohim, then, coming to the highest part of heaven above and beholding a light superior to that which He himself had created, exclaimed: 'Open me the gates, that entering in I may acknowledge the Lord.' "

As he enters the Good One addresses him in the following manner: "Sit thou on my right hand." Then the soaring male principle says to the Good One "permit me Lord to overturn the world which I have made, for my spirit is bound to men." To which the Good One replies: "No evil canst thou do while thou art with me, for both thou and

Edem made the world as a result of conjugal joy. Permit Edem then, to hold possession of the world as long as she wishes; but you remain with me." While the father is drawn away from earth to Heaven, Edem, in the meantime is bringing woes innumerable upon man. Naas, who has received his evil nature from her, and who is a child of the Devil, has debauched Eve, "Henceforward vice and virtue are prevalent among men." The Father seeing these things dispatches Baruch his third angel to Moses, and through him spake to the children of Israel, that they might be converted unto the Good One. But the third angel, Naas, by the soul of which came from Edem upon Moses, as also upon all men, observed the precepts of Baruch, and caused his own peculiar injunctions to be hearkened unto.

Again, after these occurrences Baruch, the angel of the Good One, was sent to the prophets to warn them against the wiles of Edem, but in the same manner Nass, the Devil, enticed them away, they being allured by him to their own destruction. Again Elohim selected Hercules, an uncircumcised prophet, and sent him to quell the disturbance caused by Naas or Edem and to release the Father from their power.

"These are the twelve conflicts of Hercules which He underwent, in order, from first to last, viz.: Lion, and Hydra, and Boar, and the others successively. For they say that these are the names of them among the Gentiles, and they have been derived, with altered denomination, from the energy of the maternal angels. When he seemed to have vanquished his antagonists, Omphale (now she is Venus) clings to him and entices away Hercules, and divests him of his power, viz.: the commands of Baruch which Elohim issued. And in place of this power Babel, or Venus, envelops him in her own peculiar robe, that is, in the power of Edem, who is the power below; and in this way the prophecy of Hercules remained unfulfilled and his work."

As men were still bound by the power of Edem, or the Devil, in the days of Herod the king, Baruch was again dispatched by Elohim, and coming to Nazareth delivered his message to Jesus, son of Joseph and Mary. Nass, who, as we have seen, was the evil spirit in Edem, wished to entice away Jesus also. He was not, however, disposed to listen but remained faithful to Baruch. Naas, overcome by anger at not being able to seduce him, caused him to be crucified.

"He, leaving the body of Edem on the accursed tree, ascended to the Good One; saying to Edem, 'Woman, thou retainest thy Son,' that is, the natural and the earthly man. But Jesus himself commending his spirit into the hands of the Father, ascended to the Good One. Now the Good One is Priapus, and he it is who antecedently caused the production of everything that exists. On this account he is styled Priapus, because he previously fashioned all things according to his design. For this reason, he says, in every temple is preserved his statue, which is revered by every creature; and there are images of him in the highways carrying over his head ripened fruits, that is, the produce of the creation, of which he is the cause, having in the first instance formed, according to his design, the creation, when as yet it had no existence."[142]

Thus the fact is observed not only that in the time of Paul, phallic worship still existed, but by the writings of Justinus and others is shown the manner in which the doctrine that woman is the cause of evil in the world became formulated and adopted as part and parcel of the Christian belief.

Staniland Wake, director of the anthropological society of London, when commenting on the obscene myths upon which the Christian religion rests, remarks:

---

[142] Hippolytus, Refutation of All Heresies, book v., p. 188.

"The fundamental basis of Christianity is more purely phallic than that of any other religion now existing, and its emotional nature . . . shows how intimately it was related to the older faiths which had a phallic basis."

After stating that the myth of creation and that of the flood have their exact counterpart in India, the Rev. Mr. Faber remarks that "there is no rite or ceremony directed in the Pentateuch of which there is not an exact copy in the rites of the pagans."

The Christian doctrines as established by Paul, and afterwards formulated into a system by the Romish Church, were adopted by the ignorant multitude who, being incapable of understanding the higher principles involved, accepted the allegories beneath which were veiled the ancient mysteries literally, and as the highest expression of divine wisdom. Hence the comparatively recent observation that the "new religion was eventually but the gathering in of the superstitions of paganism" is a matter of little surprise to those who have carefully examined the facts connected with the growth of religious faith.

Under the new regime Christ became the New Solar Deity and round him were finally ranged all the myths of Solo-phallic worship which had prevailed under the adoration of Crishna at a time when the higher truths underlying pure Nature-worship had been forgotten.

Chapter XV.
Christianity in Ireland

According to the accounts in the New Testament, the wise men of the East, meaning Persia, had foretold the coming of Christ. The fulfilment of the ancient Persian prophecy as applied to Jesus, together with the reference to the "star" which the Maji saw, and which went before them till it came and stood over where the young child lay, furnishes a striking illustration of the manner in which Eastern legends and ancient sacred writings are interwoven with the doctrines relating to Christianity.

In the sacred books of the East it is prophesied that "after three thousand and one hundred years of the Caligula are elapsed, will appear King Saca to remove wretchedness from the world." We have seen that at the birth of Christ the time had arrived for a new solar incarnation.

Regarding the introduction of Christianity into Ireland it is claimed by certain writers that the Irish did not receive the "new religion" from Greek missionaries; but when at the close of the cycle, a new solar deity, an avatar of Vishnu or Crishna was announced, and when missionaries from the East proclaimed the glad tidings of a risen Savior, the Irish people gladly accepted their teachings, not, however, as a new system, but as the fulfilment to them of the prophecy of the most ancient seers of the East, and as part and parcel of the religion of their forefathers. Therefore when the devotees of the Romish faith, probably about the close of the fifth century of the Christian era, attempted to "convert" Ireland, they found a religion differing from their own only in the fact that it was not subject to Rome, and was free from the many corruptions and superstitions which through the extreme ignorance and misapprehension of its Western adherents had been engrafted upon it.

Concerning the form of religious worship in Great Britain, and the fact that phallic worship prevailed there, Forlong writes: "The generality of our countrymen have no conception of the overruling prevalence of this faith, and the number of its lingham gods throughout our Islands." These symbols were always in the form of an obelisk or tower, thereby indicating the worship of the male energy. Although emblems of the female element in the deity were present, they were less pronounced and of far less importance than those of the male.

These monuments were erected on knolls, at crossroads and centers of marts or villages, and were placed on platforms which were usually raised from five to seven steps. A few years ago the shires of Gloucester, Wilts, and Somerset still claimed over two hundred of these crosses, though all of them were not at that time in a perfect state of preservation.

It would seem that in Britain and Ireland the seed of the "new" doctrine, that which involved a recognition of the mother element in the god-idea, had fallen on more congenial soil, for within three centuries after the birth of Christ, the various original monuments typifying the male principle had all been ornamented with the symbols representing the female in the deity. The ancient religious structures of the Lingaites still continued as recognized faith shrines, changed only by the emblems of the new religion which had been engrafted upon them.

The earliest Greek and Roman missionaries knew full well the significance of these symbols, and we are given to understand that "a few of the more spiritual of the Christian sects made war upon them and all their ephemeral substitutes, such as Maypoles, holy-trees, real crosses, etc."

It is declared also that, as "later" Christians were unacquainted with the significance of these emblems, "they adopted them as their own, employing them as the mystic signs of their own faith."

Although the earliest Greek and Roman missionaries understood the signification of these faith shrines, the complaints against them seem soon to have ceased, and the "fierce wars" waged over them appear to have left little trace of their ravages, except that the female emblems with which these monuments had been supplied by those who had received the new faith direct from the East, were all removed. As the male monuments and symbols were all permitted to remain undisturbed, this fact of itself would seem to indicate that the "pagan abominations" against which these pious devotees of a "spiritual religion" thundered their denunciations, included only the female emblems.

The fact must be borne in mind that the Western Church, which was rapidly usurping the ecclesiastical authority of Britain and Ireland, had not itself at this time adopted the worship of the Virgin Mary.

A set of iconoclastic monks whom the Christian world is pleased to designate as St. Patrick, and who probably early in the fifth century of our era amused themselves by chiseling from the Irish monuments many of the symbols of the female power, removed also the figures of serpents which had for ages appeared in connection with the emblems of woman, and by this act won the plaudits of an admiring Christian world; chiefly, however, for the skill manifested in "banishing snakes from Ireland." In addition to this dignified amusement, we find that the same person or set of persons ordered to be burned hundreds of volumes of the choicest Irish literature, volumes which contained the annals of the ancient Irish nation, and in which, it is believed, was stored much actual information concerning the remote antiquity of the human race.

The extent to which the worship of the male emblems of generation prevailed in the Christian Church even as late as the 16th century, proves that it was not the particular symbols connected with the worship of fertility upon which the Western Christian missionaries made war, but, on the contrary, that it was the recognition by them of that detested female element against which, even before the erection of the Tower of Babel, there had been almost a constant warfare. The rites of Potin, or Photin, Bishop of Lyons, who was honored in Provence, Languedoc and the Lyonais as St. Fontin, also the rites performed in many of the Christian Churches as late as the 16th century, prove that the devotees of the Christian system were not at this time a whit behind their Pagan predecessors in their zeal for "heathen abominations." The only difference being that the Druids, a people who still retained a faint conception of ancient Nature worship, had not become entirely divested of the purer ideas which in an earlier age of the race had constituted a creative force.

That the war of the sexes was revived, and that for many centuries much strife was engendered over the exact importance which should be ascribed to the female element in the Deity may not be doubted.

An ancient homily on Trinity Sunday has the following: "At the deth of a manne, three bells should be ronge as his kuyl in worship of the Trinitie, and for a woman, who was the Second Person of the Trinitie two bells should be ronge." Upon this subject Hargrave Jennings remarks: "Here we have the source of the emblematic difficulty among the master masons who constructed the earlier cathedrals, as to the addition, and as to the precise value of the second (or feminine) tower of the Western end or Galilee of the Church."[143]

---

[143] Rosicrucians, vol. i., p. 206.

The fact that the religion of the ancient Irish, who, were phallic worshippers, was modified but not radically changed by the introduction of Christianity, is believed by at least one of the Irish historians of that country. He says:

"The church festivals themselves, in our Christian calendar, are but the direct transfers from the Tuath-de-danaans' ritual. Their very names in Irish are identically the same as those by which they were distinguished by that early race. If, therefore, surprise has heretofore been excited at the conformity observable between our church institutions and those of the East, let it in future subside at the explicit announcement that Christianity, with us, was the revival of a religion imported amongst us many ages before by the Tuath-de-danaans from the East, and not from any chimerical inundation of Greek missionaries–a revival upon which their hearts were lovingly riveted, and which Fiech, the Bishop of Sletty, unconsciously registers in the following couplet, viz.:

"The Buddhists of Irin prophesied
That new times of peace would come."
--The Round Towers of Ireland

The conditions surrounding the ancient inhabitants of the "White Island," or Ireland, a remnant of which people may be observed in the Highlanders of Scotland, furnish an example of the fact that a much higher standard of life had been preserved among them than is known to have prevailed either among the Jews or the Greeks. The comparatively advanced stage of progress which is now known to have existed in Ireland at the beginning of the present era, which even the bigotry and falsehood of Roman priestcraft have not been able wholly to conceal, is seen to have been a somewhat corrupted remnant of a civilization which followed closely on ancient Nature worship.[144]

Hence the intermingling of races and tongues among the ancient Irish. The Druids adopted, or appropriated, the religion and culture of the Tuath-de-danaans, who, it is claimed, were the real Hibernians. The Scythians changed the name of Irin to Scotia–the latter being retained until the 11th century. According to the annals of the ancient Irish, Scotland was formerly called Scotia Minor to distinguish it from Scotia Major, or Ireland.

Because of their isolated position, or for some cause at present unknown, these people do not seem to have degenerated into a nation of sensualists. It is true they had departed a long distance from the early conditions of mankind under which altruism and the abstract principle of Light or Wisdom were worshipped under the form of a Virgin Mother and her child, but they never wholly rejected the female element in their god-idea, nor never, so far as known, attempted to degrade womanhood. Women were numbered among their legislators, at the same time that they officiated as educators and priestesses. In fact wherever the Druidical order prevailed women exerted a powerful influence in all departments of human activity. Among the Germans, Valleda, a Druidess, was for ages worshipped as a deity.

It is recorded that St. Bridget planted a monastery for women at Kildare and entrusted to its inmates the keeping of the sacred fire, and that in later times the Asiatic missionaries founded there a female monkish order. After

---

[144] It is thought by certain writers that when the Tuath-de- danaans emigrated from Persia to the "White Island" they found it inhabited by the Fir-Bolgs, a colony of Celts. After conquering the island they engrafted upon it the religion, laws, learning and culture of the mother country. In a later age the Scythians, whose religion was similar to that of the Fir-Bolgs, united with them and succeeded in making themselves masters of the situation.

the establishment of Western Christianity, however, no woman was permitted to enter into the monasteries, and we are assured that this ridiculous affectation of purity was extended even to the grave. During the earlier ages of Christianity, in many portions of Ireland there were cemeteries for men and women distinct from each other. "It had been a breach of chastity for monks and nuns to be interred within the same enclosure. They should fly from temptations which they could not resist."

Although volumes have been written to prove that Christianity was carried to Britain by Paul, and although the energies of scores of Romish writers have been employed in attempting to prove that Ireland was in heathen darkness prior to its conversion by the priests of the Romish Church, yet these efforts so vigorously put forward seem only to strengthen the evidence going to show that the Christianity of the British Isles antedates that of either Paul or Rome.

According to Scripture, Claudia, the wife of the Senator Pudens of Britain, was a Christian,[145] as was also Graecina, the wife of Plautus, who was governor of Britain in the first century. The latter, it is related, was accused before the Roman senate of "practicing some foreign superstition." Although Lingard, in his History and Antiquities of the Anglo-Saxon Church, has endeavored to annul the force of the evidence which places two Christian women from Britain in Rome during the first century of our era, he is nevertheless constrained to use the following language: "We are, indeed, told that history has preserved the names of two British females, Claudia and Pomponia Graecina, both of them Christians, and both living in the first century of our era."[146]

---

[145] 2 Timothy, iv., 21.
[146] Vol. i., p. 1.

According to the Romanists, between the years 177-181 of the Christian era, a British king named Lucius sent a messenger to the authorities at Rome, with a request that he with his people be admitted into the bosom of the "Holy Catholic Church." By those not prejudiced in favor of the Romish hierarchy, this bit of amusing "evidence" shows the anxiety manifested lest the facts concerning the religious history of the British Isles become known. Regarding this embassy of King Lucius there is an extant version which is far more in accordance with reason and with the known facts concerning this people.

When we remember the advanced stage of civilization which existed in Ireland prior to the Christian era, and when we bear in mind the fact that, as in the case of Abarras mentioned by various Greek writers, the people of the British Isles were wont to send emissaries abroad for the sole purpose of gathering information relative to foreign laws, customs, usages, manners, and modes of instruction, we are not surprised to learn that the message to Rome sent by Lucius, instead of containing a request for admission to a foreign church, embodied an enquiry into the fundamental principles underlying Roman jurisprudence; and especially does this appear reasonable when we remember that the remodeling of the Roman code on principles of equity and justice had for several centuries employed the energies of the best minds in Rome.

Concerning the planting of Christianity in Ireland, we have the following from Ledwich:

"Thus Bishop Lawrence in Bede tells us Pope Gregory sent him and Austin to preach the Gospel in Britain, as if it never before had been heard, whereas the latter met seven British Bishops who nobly opposed him. In like manner Pope Adrian commissioned Henry II. to enlarge the bounds of the church, and plant the faith in Ireland, when it had already been evangelized for eight hundred years. The faith to be planted was blind submission to Rome and the annual payment of Peter's pence."[147]

Of the exact time at which Romish and Greek missionaries first went to Ireland we are not informed, but there is ample evidence going to prove that a regular hierarchy had been established in that island before the beginning of the fifth century, and that this religion which had been brought in through the efforts of missionaries from the East was, by the legendary writers of the later Christian Church, ascribed to Romish monks.

The Jealousy of the Romish priests, and the means employed by them to usurp the ecclesiastical authority of the Irish people, is shown in the history of their councils. The 5th canon of the Council of Ceale-hythe requires

"that none of Irish extraction be permitted to usurp to himself the sacred ministry in any one's diocese, nor let it be allowed such an one to touch anything which belongs to those of the holy order. . . .; neither must he administer the eucharist to the people because we are not certain how or by whom he was ordained."

After quoting the above Ledwich queries thus: If St. Patrick had been a missionary of the Romish Church, would the Anglo-Saxon clergy have abjured the spiritual children of that see? In the year 670 Theodoret, Archbishop of Canterbury, decreed that they who were consecrated by Irish or British Bishops should be confirmed anew by Catholic ones.[148]

It is observed that as early as the fourth century A.D. there were three hundred bishops in Ireland, and to account for so large a number, it is declared that ignorant legendary writers had recourse to the fable of St. Patrick.

The remarkable "conversion" of the Irish to Romish Christianity, which it is said took place in the latter part of

---

[147] Antiquities of Ireland, p. 78.
[148] Ledwich, Antiquities of Ireland, p. 81.

the fourth century or the beginning of the fifth, is to be explained by the fact that a number of Romish priests or monks which in later ages came to be designated as St. Patrick, claimed all the monasteries, bishops, and priests already there as a result of the remarkable power and pious zeal of this miracle-working saint. It is claimed that St. Patrick founded over three thousand monasteries, consecrated three hundred bishops, and ordained three thousand priests.

According to Ledwich and other writers, this St. Patrick was not heard of earlier than the ninth century A.D., and the legend concerning him "was not accepted until the twelfth century, at which time his miracles are set forth with great gusto."

Nothing, perhaps, which is recorded of this monk will go farther toward proving him a myth than the miracles ascribed to his saintship.

While yet an infant he raised the dead, brought forth fire from ice, expelled a devil from a heifer, caused a new river to appear from the earth, and changed water into honey.

"These were but the infant sports of this wonder-working saint. The miracles recorded in holy writ, even that of creation itself, are paralleled, and, if possible, surpassed by those of our spiritual hero."[149]

Concerning St. Patrick, Forlong writes:

"Various Patricks followed from Britain and Armorika, but even the Catholic priest, J. F. Shearman, writes that he is forced to give up the idea that there ever was a real St. Patrick. Thus the name must be accepted only in its Fatherly sense, and with the fall of the man Patrick all the miraculous and sudden conversions of the kings, lords, and commons of Ireland must vanish."[150]

---

[149] Ledwich, Antiquities of Ireland.
[150] Rivers of Life, vol. ii., p. 417.

The Irish Church bishoprics differed from the Romish in that they were held by hereditary succession, after the custom of ancient nations. All bishops were married.

Prior to the introduction of the Christian system in Ireland the Sabian ceremonial had been succeeded by the Druidical, upon which had been engrafted that of the Culdees, and notwithstanding the fact that the Romish Church gradually usurped the ecclesiastical functions in Ireland, the last named people who for ages had been regarded as the depositaries of the ancient faith and the ancient system of laws, were highly respected by the people for their sanctity and learning. Many of the Greek and Roman writers who have dealt with this subject agree in ascribing to the Druids a high degree of scientific knowledge and mechanical skill. The principles of justice set forth in their judicial system, their love of learning, and the standard attained in the sciences and arts, prove the early people of Ireland to have been equal if not superior to any of the early historic nations.

In referring to the number and magnitude of the monumental remains in Ireland, and while commenting on the mechanical skill of the Druids, the Rev. Smedley says:

"I was present at the erection of the Luxor Obelisk in Paris, and yet I think that I would have felt greater emotion if I had witnessed the successful performance of the old Celtic engineer who placed on its three pedestals of stone the enormous rock which constitutes the Druidical altar here at Castle May."

It is believed that this people understood the art of mining and that they were acquainted with the use of iron. The following is an extract from one of Hamilton's letters on the Antrim coast:

"About the year 1770 the miners, in pushing forward an adit toward the bed of coal, at an unexplored part of the Ballycastle cliff, unexpectedly broke through the rock into a narrow passage, so much contracted and choked up with various drippings and deposits on its sides and bottom, as rendered it impossible for any of the workmen to force through, that they might examine it farther. Two lads were, therefore, made to creep in with candles, for the purpose of exploring this subterranean avenue. They accordingly pressed forward for a considerable time, with much labor and difficulty, and at length entered into an extensive labyrinth branching off into numerous apartments, in the mazes and windings of which they were completely bewildered and lost. After various vain attempts to return, their lights were extinguished, their voices became hoarse, and, becoming wearied and spiritless, they sat down together, in utter despair of an escape from this miserable dungeon. In the meanwhile, the workmen in the adit became alarmed for their safety, fresh hands were incessantly employed, and, in the course of twenty-four hours, the passage was so open as to admit the most active among the miners . . . On examining this subterranean wonder, it was found to be a complete gallery, which had been driven forward many hundred yards to the bed of coal: that it branched off into numerous chambers, where miners had carried on their different works: that these chambers were dressed in a workmanlike manner: that pillars were left at proper intervals to support the roof. In short it was found to be an extensive mine, wrought by people at least as expert in the business as the present generation. Some remains of the tools, and even of the baskets used in the works, were discovered, but in such a decayed state that, on being touched, they immediately crumbled to pieces. From the remains which were found, there is reason to believe that the people who wrought these collieries anciently, were acquainted with the use of iron, some small pieces of which were found; it appeared as if some of their instruments had been thinly shod with that metal."

Through various means the fact has been ascertained that although in the sixth century the buildings in Ireland were mean and wholly without artistic merit or skilful design, in an earlier age they were magnificent. Of the causes which produced the decay of architecture, the extinction of the arts and sciences, and the general degradation of the people of this island the devotees of St. Paul and of the Romish Church are alike silent.

For ages after the subjection of Ireland, in open defiance of the English, the people continued to dispense justice, and to enforce the old Brehon laws of the country.

The lack of regard shown for English law in Ireland, even as late as the sixteenth century, is set forth by Baron Fingles, who wrote in the time of Henry VIII. He says:

"It is a great abuse and reproach that the laws and statutes made in this land are not observed nor kept after the making of them eight days, while diverse Irishmen cloth abuse and keep such laws and statutes which they make upon hills in this country, firm and stable, without breaking them for any favor or reward."

By a statute of Parliament enacted at Kilkenny, it was made high treason to administer or observe these old Brehon laws. The two enactments especially obnoxious to the English were Gahail Cinne, and Eiric. The former of these enactments was that which in opposition to the English law of primogeniture declared that the estate of a parent should descend in equal proportion to all members of the family. There was another law, or custom, among this people, which provided that the chief of the tribe or people should be elected by general suffrage.

We have something more than a hint of the condition of ancient Ireland and its people in a description given by the Greeks of one of its inhabitants. Abarras, who visited Greece about six hundred years before Christ, and who was called by the Greeks a Hyperborean, was a priest of the Sun, who went abroad for the purpose of study and observation, and to renew by his presence and his gifts the old friendship which had long existed between the Celts and the Greeks. Strabo remarks concerning Abarras that he was much admired by the learned men of Greece. Himerius says of him that he came

"not clad in skins like a Scythian, but with a bow in his hand, and a quiver on his shoulders and a plaid wrapped about his body, a gilded belt encircled his loins, and trousers reaching from his waist downward to the soles of his feet. He was easy in his address, agreeable in conversation, active in dispatch and secret in the management of great affairs; quick in judging of present occurrences, and ready to take his part in any sudden emergency; provident, withal, in guarding against futurity; diligent in quest of wisdom, fond of friendship; trusting very little to fortune; yet having the entire confidence of others, and trusted with everything for his prudence. He spoke Greek with so much fluency that you would have thought that he had been bred or brought up in the Lyceum and had conversed all his life with the Academy of Athens. He had frequent intercourse with Pythagoras whom he astonished by the variety and extent of his knowledge."

From the descriptions given of the native country of Abarras by the Greeks, it is evident that it could have been none other than Ireland.

Although at this time in their history, Apollo the sun-god was the Deity worshipped in Greece and in Ireland, still both nations honored Latona his mother. The same as in the mother country (Persia, or Phoenicia), the oracles, or sybils of Ireland, had prophesied a "Savior," and three hundred years before Greek emissaries visited that country, its people, through the preaching of Eastern missionaries, had substituted for the worship of Latona and Apollo that of the new solar incarnation–the third son of Zarathustra, whose appearance had been heralded by a star.

The identity of the symbols used by the early people of Ireland who were sun worshippers, and those employed in that country for ages after the Romish Church had usurped the ecclesiastical authority, has been a subject for much comment. After describing the peculiar form of the early Christian Churches and the attention paid to the placing of the windows which were to admit the sun's rays, Smedley says: "It is possible, in an age of allegory and figures, this combination and variety expressed some sacred meaning with which we are unacquainted at present."

The similarity observed in the sacred festivals and religious seasons of the ancient inhabitants of Ireland and those of the early Christians, the extent to which large stone crosses, lighted candles, the yule log and the various other symbols belonging to fertility, or sun worship, were retained by Christianity, furnish strong evidence of the fact that the latter system is but part and parcel of the former.

Chapter XVI.
Stones or Columns as the Deity

"Throughout all the world, the first object of idolatry seems to have been a plain unwrought stone, placed in the ground as an emblem of the generative or procreative powers of Nature."[151]

In the language of symbolism the upright stone prefigures either a man, reproductive energy, or a god, all of which at a certain stage in the human career had come to mean one and the same thing; namely, the Creator.

In the earlier ages of male worship, upright stones as emblems of the Deity were plain unwrought shafts, but in process of time they began to be carved into the form of a man–a man who usually represented the ruler or chief of the people, and who, as he was the source of all power and wisdom, was supposed by the ignorant masses to be an incarnation of the sun. Thus arose the spiritual power of monarchs, or the "divine right of kings."

Wherever obelisks, columns, pillars, attenuated spires, upright stones or crosses at the intersection of roads are found, they always appear as sacred monuments, or as symbols of the Lingham god.

The Chaldean Tower of which there are extant traditions in Mexico and in the South Sea Islands; the Round Towers of Ireland; the remarkable group of stones known as Stonehenge, in England; the wonderful circle at Abury through which the figure of a huge serpent was passed; the monuments which throughout the nations of the East were set up at the intersection of roads in the center of

---

[151] Celtic Druids, ch. vi., p. 209.

market-places, and the bowing stones employed as oracles in various portions of the world, have all the same signification, and proclaim the peculiar religion of the people who worshipped them.

Whether as among the Jews in Egypt, a pillar is set up as a "sign" and a "witness" to the Lord, or whether as with the Mohammedans these figures appear as minarets with egg shaped summits, or as among the Irish they stand forth as stately towers defying time and the elements, or as among the Christians they appear as the steeple which points towards heaven, the symbol remains, and the original significance is the same.

The Lord of the Israelites who was wont to manifest himself to his chosen people in a "pillar of smoke by day" and a "pillar of fire by night" is said to be none other than a reproductive emblem, as was also the "Lord" which "reposed in the ark of the covenant." Monuments set up to symbolize the religion of the Parsees or fire-worshippers after they had succumbed to the pressure brought to bear upon them by the adorers of the male principle were each and all of them, like their great prototype the tower of Babel, typical of the universal creative power which was worshipped as male.

Notwithstanding the fact that the male energy had come to be recognized as the principal factor in reproduction, it is observed that wherever these monuments or other symbols of fertility appear, there is always to be found in close connection with them certain emblems symbolical of the female power; thus showing that although the people by whom they were erected had become worshippers of the masculine principle, and although they had persuaded themselves that it was the more important element in the deity, they had not become so regardless of the truths of Nature as to attempt to construct a Creator independently of its most essential factor.

Protestant Christianity, probably the most intensely masculine of all religious schemes which have claimed the attention of man, has not wittingly retained any of the detested female emblems, yet so deeply has the older symbolism taken root, that even in the architecture of the modern Protestant church with its ark-shaped nave and its window toward the rising sun, may be detected the remnants of that early worship which the devotees of this more recently developed form of religious faith so piously ignore.

The large number of upright columns, circles of stone, cromlechs and cairns still extant in the British Isles, bears testimony to the peculiar character of the religious worship which once prevailed in them. Of these shrines perhaps none is more remarkable than that of Stonehenge, in England. Although during the numberless ages which have passed since this temple was erected many of the stones have fallen from their original places, still by the light of more recently established facts concerning religious symbolism, it has been possible, even under its present condition of decay, for scholars to unravel the hitherto mysterious significance of this remarkable structure. Stonehenge is composed of four circles of mammoth upright shafts twenty feet high, the one circle within the other, with immense stones placed across them like architraves.

In ancient symbolism the circle was the emblem of eternity, or of the eternal female principle. Mountains were also sacred to the gods. It has been said that a ring of mountains gave rise to these circular temples. Faber assures us that a circular stone temple was called the circle of the world or the circle of the ark, that it represented at once the inclosure of the Noetic Ship; the egg from which creation was produced; the earth, and the zodiacal circle of the universe in which the sun performs its annual revolutions through the signs. Stonehenge is said to be the temple of the water god Noah, who, as we have seen, was first worshipped as half woman and half fish or serpent, but who finally came to be regarded as a man serpent (or fish) Deity.

On approaching Stonehenge from the Northeast, the first object which engages the attention is a rude boulder, sixteen feet high, in a leaning posture. This stone has been named the Friar's Heel, but until recently its signification has been wholly unknown.

Regarding the upright shaft which stands sentinel over the mysterious circles of mammoth stones called Stonehenge, Forlong says that it is no Friar's Heel, but an emblem of fertility dedicated to the Friday divinity. It is represented as the "Genius of Fire," not the genius of ordinary fire, "but of the super-sensual Divinity, celestial fire."

Regarding these remarkable stones to which the Lingham god is a mere introduction, Forlong says:

"No one who has studied phallic and solar worship in the East could make any mistake as to the purport of the shrine at Stonehenge . . . yet the indelicacy of the whole subject often so shocks the ordinary reader, that, in spite of facts, he cannot grant what he thinks shows so much debasement of the religious mind; facts are facts, however, and it only remains for us to account for them. Perhaps indeed in these later times an artificial and lower phase of sensuality has taken the place of the more natural indulgence of the passions, for procreative purposes, which principally engrossed the thoughts of early worshippers."[152]

Higgins is of the opinion that Stonehenge is the work of the same era with the caves of India, the pyramids of Egypt, and the stupendous monument at Carnac—a structure which, it is claimed, must have required for its construction an amount of labor equal to that of the pyramids.

---

[152] Rivers of Life, vol. ii., p. 233.

Undoubtedly there has never been a religious shrine which has excited more curiosity than has Abury, of which, unfortunately, nothing now remains, although in the early part of the eighteenth century enough had been preserved to prove the identity of its signification with other ancient religious monuments both in the British Isles and in the countries of the East. Perhaps there is no way by which this shrine can be better understood than by quoting the exact language of those who have written upon the subject. Especially is this true concerning the testimony of those who, after personal investigation, have given to the public the results of their research.

In the History of Wiltshisre, published by Sir R. Colt Hoare, Bart., appears the following from Dr. Stukeley:

"The situation of Abury is finely chosen for the purpose it was destined to, being the more elevated part of a plain, from whence there is almost an imperceptible descent every way. But as the religious work in Abury, though great in itself, is but a part of the whole (the avenues stretching above a mile from it each way), the situation of the whole design is projected with great judgment, in a kind of large, separate plain, four or five miles in diameter. Into this you descend on all sides from higher ground. The whole Temple of Abury may be considered as a picture, and it really is so. Therefore the founders wisely contrived that a spectator have an advantageous prospect of it as he appeared within view. When I frequented this place, which I did for some years together, to take an exact account of it, staying a fortnight at a time, I found out the entire work by degrees. The second time I was here, an avenue was a new amusement; the third year another. So that at length I discovered the mystery of it, properly speaking, which was, that the whole figure represented a snake transmitted through a circle. This is an hieroglyphic or symbol of highest note and antiquity.

"In order to put this design in execution, the founders well studied their ground; and to make their representation more natural, they artfully carried it over a variety of elevations and depressions, which, with the curvature of the avenues, produces sufficiently the desired effect. To make it still more elegant and picture-like, the head of the snake is carried up the southern promontory of Hackpen Hill, toward the village of West Kennet; nay, the very name of the hill is derived from the circumstance. . . . Thus our antiquity divides itself into three great parts, which will be our rule in describing this work. The circle at Abury, the forepart of the snake leading toward Kennet, which I call Kennet Avenue; the hinder part of the snake leading toward Beckhampton, which I call Beckhampton Avenue; for they may be well looked on as avenues to the great temple at Abury, which part must be most eminently called the Temple.

"The plan on which Abury was built, is that sacred hierogram of the Egyptians and other ancient nations, the circle and snake. The whole figure is the circle, snake, and wings. By this they meant to picture out, as well as they could, the nature of the Divinity."

The temple which represents the body of the snake is formed by a circular agger of earth having its ditch withinside. As this is contrary to the mode adopted in works of defence, it is thought to prove the religious character of Abury. In a description given of this shrine by Higgins is the following:

"These ramparts inclose an area of 1400 feet in diameter, which on the edge nearest the ditch was set round with a row of rough, unhewn stones, and in the center was ornamented with two circular temples, composed of the same native stones."[153]

---

[153] Celtic Druids. Description of plates, p. xx.

The space of ground included within the vellum has been estimated at twenty-two acres, and the outward circumvallation was computed at 4800 feet. The number of stones that formed this outer circle was originally one hundred, of which, in the year 1722, there were eighteen standing, and twenty-seven thrown down.

In the village of Rudstone in Yorkshire there stands a huge stone, the significance of which, at the present time, is by scholars clearly understood. Its depth below the surface of the ground is said to be equal to its height above, which is twenty-four feet. It is five feet ten inches broad, and two feet thick, its weight being upwards of forty tons.[154]

The gigantic rocking stones found in nearly every quarter of the globe are now known to be religious monuments of remote antiquity. Not long ago I saw a description of one of these oracles in Buenos-Ayres, South America, and a few months later there appeared the following account of a similar stone found in Sullivan Co., N. Y.:

"At first sight it would scarcely attract attention, but a closer observation reveals the remarkable position which it occupies. The total weight of the immense boulder has been variously estimated at from forty to fifty tons, and its bulk at from 500 to 700 cubic feet. It is almost perfectly round, much resembling a huge orange, and so nicely balanced on a table of stone as to be easily set in motion by a single man, providing the operator exerts his strength on the north or south sides. On either of the other sides the combined strength of forty elephants would not be sufficient to cause the least oscillation. Although it is easily rocked, we are assured that as many men as could surround it would be unable to dislodge it from the pivot on which it rests."[155]

---

[154] See Rivers of Life.
[155] The St. Louis (Mo.) Republican.

The writer of the above, who was evidently ignorant of the extent to which these monuments are scattered over the earth, seemed to regard it as a singular freak of Nature with no significance other than that of a natural curiosity.

The round towers of Ireland, over the origin of which there has in the past been so much controversy, are now pretty generally admitted to be analogous in their use and design to Stonehenge, Abury, and other extant monolithic structures.

Many writers have endeavored to prove that these towers were belfries used in connection with Christian churches; others that they were purgatorial columns or penitential heights, similar in design to the pillar of St. Simeon Stylites. Others again have argued that they were used as beacons and others that they were intended simply as receptacles for the sacred fire known to have formerly been in use in the British Isles. Although numberless arguments have been brought forward to refute these theories, it is thought that the expensive architecture alone of the elegant and stately columns known as Round Towers contradicts all these "guesses," and that their grandeur and almost absolute indestructibility proclaim for them a different origin from that of the lowly and miserable huts which in a later age were erected beside them for purposes of worship by the Romish Christians. The same objection is made also against the theory that these monuments were erected in memory of the several defeats of the Danes. As an answer to the argument that they were erected by the Danes to celebrate their victories, it is declared that such is the character of the hieroglyphics upon them as to make this theory worthless. Besides, throughout the country of the Danes and Ostmen, there is nowhere to be found an example of architectural splendor such as is displayed in the construction of these columns. In the north of Scotland was one of these monuments upon which were depicted war-like scenes, horses and their riders, warriors brandishing their weapons, and troops shouting for victory, while on the other side was a sumptuous cross, beneath which were two figures, the one evidently female, the other male.

In Cordiner's Antiquities of Scotland is a description of an elaborately carved obelisk. On one side of this column appears a mammoth cross, and underneath it are figures of uncouth animals. Among these carvings are to be seen the Bulbul of Iran, the Boar of Vishnu, the elk, the fox, the lamb, and a number of dancing human figures. In fact all the configurations are not only in their nature and import essentially Eastern, but are actually the symbols of the various animal forms under which "the people of the East contemplated the properties of the Godhead."

Carnac, in upper Egypt, is a monolith of the same symbolic character. It is hewn from a solid block of black granite and is eighty feet high.

Henry O'Brien, a cultured Irishman, who when in London became, in his own line of investigation, one of the chief contributors to Fraser's Magazine while at its best, in response to a call by the Royal Irish Academy for productions relating to the origin and use of the Round Towers, declared that they were erected by a colony of Tuath-de-danaans, or Lingham worshippers from Persia, who had left their native land because of the victories gained over them by their rivals–the Pish de-danaans–a sect of Yoni worshippers; in other words, the sect which recognized the female element as the superior agency in reproduction, and who, therefore, worshipped it as divine. In the devastating wars which swept over Persia and the other countries of antiquity prior to the age of the later Zoroaster, the Pish-de danaans were victorious, and, driving from the country the Tuath-de danaans, or male worshippers, succeeded in re-establishing, and for a time maintaining, the old form of worship. O'Brien claims that the Tuath-de-danaans who were expelled from Persia emigrated to Ireland, and there continued or preserved their favorite form of worship, the Round Towers having been erected by them in conformity to their peculiar religious views. This writer assures us that the old Irish tongue bears unmistakable evidence of the relation existing between these countries. In addition to the similarity of language which is found to exist between ancient Ireland or Iren, and Persia or Iran, the same writer observes that in all their customs, religious observances, and emblems, the resemblance is preserved.

Much regret has been expressed by all the writers who have dealt with this subject that at an earlier age when Stonehenge, Abury, and various other of the ancient monumental shrines of the British Isles were in a better state of preservation, and before bigotry and religious hatred had been aroused against them, more minute observations of their character and of all the details surrounding them could not have been made; yet, notwithstanding the late date at which these investigations were begun, it is believed that a fair amount of success has crowned the efforts which have been put forth to unravel the mysteries bound up in them.

When we remember that every detail connected with the sacred monuments of the ancients was full of significance that their religious ideas were all portrayed by means of symbols which appeared in connection with their sacred edifices–the extent to which a thorough understanding of these details would assist in revealing the mysteries involved in the universal religious conceptions may in a measure be realized.

The identity of the symbols used to express religious ideas, and the extent to which the conceptions of a creative force have been connected in all portions of the globe, are set forth in the following from Barlow:

"A complete history of religious symbolism should embrace all the religions of antiquity no less than the

Christian, and it would require as thorough a knowledge of their tenets as of our own to explain satisfactorily its influence in regulating the practice of art."[156]

---

[156] Symbolism, p. 10.

Chapter XVII.
Sacrifices

Although the sun was formerly worshipped as the source of all good, at a certain stage in the human career it came to be regarded as the cause of all evil. When Typhon Seth comprehended the powers of Nature, as the Destroyer and Regenerator she was the author of all good; but later, after the truths underlying Nature worship were lost, Typhon, the hot wind of the desert, was feared rather than worshipped.

In the history of an earlier age of existence, there is not to be found the slightest trace of human sacrifice to atone for the sins of the people, or to appease the wrath of an offended God. On the contrary, throughout the traditions and monumental records of the most ancient nations, sacrifices to the Deity– the God of Nature–consisted simply in the acknowledgment of earth's benefits by means of a free-will offering of the bounties which she had brought forth.

That the sacrifice either of human beings or of animals was not offered in an earlier age of religious faith is confidently asserted and, I think, proved by various writers. Of this Higgins says: "I think a time may be perceived when it did not exist even among the Western nations." This writer states also that it was not always practiced at Delphi. Mention is made of the fact that among the Buddhists, to whom belongs the first book of Genesis, no bloody sacrifices were ever offered.

It was doubtless under the worship of Muth, Neith, or Minerva, the first emanation from the deity and the original

Buddha, that the first book of Genesis or Wisdom was written. In this book may be observed the fact that the slaughter of animals is forbidden. It is thought that with Crishna, Hercules, and the worshippers of the sun in Aries, the sacrifice of human beings and animals began. In the second book of Genesis, which is said to be a Brahmin work, animals are first used for sacrifice, and in the third book, or the book of Generations or Re-generations of the race of man or the Adam, which was written after the pure doctrines connected with the worship of Wisdom had been corrupted, they are first allowed to be eaten as food.

It is supposed that the practice of sacrificing human beings and animals took its rise in the western parts of the world after the sun entered Aries, and that it subsequently extended even to the followers of the Tauric worship, among whom it was carried to a frightful extent. It is also thought that the history of Cain and Abel is an allegory of the followers of Crishna to justify their sacrifice of the yajna or lamb "in opposition to the Buddhist offering of bread and wine, or water, made by Cain and practiced by Melchizedek."[157]

It is now positively known that all over the world, during a certain stage of religious belief, either human beings or animals were, at stated seasons, sacrificed to the Deity. Of the universality of this practice Faber says:

"Throughout the whole world we find a notion prevalent that the gods could be appeased only by bloody sacrifices. Now this idea is so thoroughly arbitrary, there being no obvious and necessary connection, in the way of cause and effect, between slaughtering a man or a beast, and recovering of the divine favor by the slaughterers, that its very universality involves the necessity of concluding

---

[157] Anacalypsis, vol. i., p. 101.

that all nations have borrowed it from some common source."[158]

Dr. Shuckford is constrained to admit that the sacrifices and ceremonies of purification practiced by Abraham and his descendants and those of surrounding peoples, were identical, with only "such trifling changes as distance of countries and length of time might be expected to produce." The substitution of a lamb in the place of Isaac would seem to indicate a change from child-slaughter to that of animals.

Sacrifices were offerings to the god of pro- creation. Certain representatives of the life which he had bestowed must be returned to him as a free-will gift. In many countries, the victims offered to the deity were captives taken in war; but, as prisoners of war and slaves were not permitted to join in the battles of their captors, their lives were of little value; hence, later, it is observed that the sacrificial victim must be a prince or an individual whose life was of great importance to the tribe.

As in all hot countries the heat of the sun is the most destructive agency against which mankind have to contend, it is not perhaps singular, at a time when superstition had usurped the functions of the reasoning powers, that the sun-god should have been invested with the attributes inspired by terror, and that so far as possible, mankind should have deemed it necessary to propitiate its wrath, and, by rendering to it suitable offerings and sacrifices, they should have hoped to avert the calamities incident to its displeasure. Neither is it remarkable when we remember the peculiar circumstances surrounding the Jews, and the fact that the offerings demanded by their god was the life which he had bestowed, that the sacrifices offered to Moloch, the fire god, should have been the members of their own household–namely, their children.

---

[158] The Origin of Pagan Idolatry, vol. i., book 2, p. 465.

We must not forget that the reward promised this people by prophet, priest, and diviner for godliness was extreme fruitfulness of body. We have seen that to obtain this mark of godly favor, or, under pretense of serving their god, the form of worship prescribed by their priests, and adopted both in their households and in their temples was pre-eminently sensual, and calculated to stimulate and encourage to the highest extent their lower or animal nature.

As the size of a man's family, or his power to reproduce, was an index to his favor with the Almighty the pleasure of the "Lord" in this matter being but the reflection of his own desires, the result as might reasonably be expected was overpopulation to such an extent that the means of subsistence within the small boundary of Judea was inadequate to supply the demands of the swarming masses of "God's children"–children which had been created for his honor and glory. Surely some plan must be devised whereby these difficulties might be adjusted, and that, too, to use a modern expression, without flying in the face of Providence. As the Lord had been honored and man blessed in the mere bringing forth of offspring, what better scheme, so soon as such blessings became too numerous, than to return a certain number of them to the giver, the god of Moloch? It is true that by this process children were born only to be delivered over to the ravages of the fire- god, but by it, was not their deity both served and appeased at the same time that population was kept within the bounds of subsistence? That great numbers were thus sacrificed is only too apparent from the accounts in the Jewish scriptures–Abraham's acts and those of Jephtha being examples of the manner in which this god was propitiated.

In Micah, vi. chap., 7th verse, occurs an interrogation which furnishes something more than a hint of the practice among the Jews of child sacrifice. "Shall I give my first born for my transgressions, the fruit of my body for the sin of my soul?"

Although there is sufficient evidence to prove the enormous extent to which the practice of child sacrifice prevailed among the Jews, it is believed that much more proof would be found, had it not, in later times, with a view to concealing the extent of this practice, been expunged from their sacred writings. Moloch was to the Jews what Siva came to be to the Hindoos, namely, the Terrible. It is plain, however, that Siva was not formerly feared in India, but next to Vishnu was the best beloved of all their gods. Siva was originally the androgyne god who was not only the Destroyer, but the beneficent Regenerator and purifier. It was the cold of winter and the heat of the sun. It was a conception which was a direct outgrowth of Nature worship or of that religious idea which was portrayed by a mother and her child.

The conception involved in sacrifice seems to be that of a payment for services rendered, or desired. The Amazulus, when going to battle, sacrifice to the manes of their ancestors, who, as older branches of the tree of life, appear to constitute their god-idea. This is done that their gods "may have no cause of complaint, because they have made amends to them and made them bright." On appearing before the enemy they say: "Can it be, since we have made amends to the Amadhlozi, that they will say we have wronged them by anything?"[159]

At a certain stage in human history the various peoples of the globe depended upon excessive numbers for their prosperity, hence the most precious offering to the god of pro-creation was that of human victims.

In India, when a new colony or city was founded, in order to insure its prosperity, large numbers of children were delivered over as a bribe or offering of reconciliation to the god of virility. The enormous extent to which human sacrifice has prevailed in India, in Egypt, in Mexico, among

---

[159] Viscount Amberley, Analysis of Religious Belief, vol. i., p. 32.

the Carthaginians, the Jews, the Druids, and even among the Greeks and Romans, is well attested.

From the records of extant history, it would seem that human sacrifice usually accompanies a certain stage of sun-worship. Among the Aztecs in Mexico, a country in which the sun was a universal object of reverence and in which one of the prescribed duties of the boys trained in the temple was that of keeping alive the sacred fires, the immolation of victims became the most prominent feature of their public worship. We are distinctly told, however, that human sacrifice was not formerly practiced in Mexico, but that finally here as elsewhere, the idea became prevalent that by sacrificing human victims to the god of Destruction, his wrath might be appeased and the people saved from his vengeance. It is stated that human sacrifices were adopted by the Aztecs early in the fourteenth century, about two hundred years before the conquest. "Rare at first, they became more frequent with the wider extent of their empire; till, at length, almost every festival was closed with this cruel abomination."

Notwithstanding these atrocities, in their conceptions of a future state of existence, and especially in their disposition of the unregenerate after death, are to be observed certain traces of human feeling and refined sensibility which are difficult to reconcile with the cruelty practiced in their religious rites, and which bear a striking contrast to the physical torture, to which after death the wicked are subjected not only in Mexico, but in countries professing a high stage of civilization and culture.

Of their religious observances, those which had doubtless been inherited from an older civilization, Prescott, quoting from Torquemada and Sahagun, says:

"Many of their ceremonies were of a light and cheerful complexion, consisting of the national songs and dances, in which both sexes joined. Processions were made of women and children crowned with garlands and bearing offerings of fruits, the ripened maize, or the sweet incense of copal and other odoriferous gums, while the altars of the deity were stained with no blood save that of animals. These were the peaceful rites derived from their Toltec predecessors."[160]

Prior to the days of Montezuma, the Aztec priests had engrafted upon these simple ceremonies not only a burdensome ceremonial, and a polytheism similar to that of Eastern nations, but, as we have seen, human sacrifices and even cannibalism had become prominent features in religious worship. Throughout the entire ceremonial and religious conceptions of the Aztecs may be observed a display of the savage and brutal elements in human nature, in close connection with unmistakable evidence of a once higher stage of culture and refinement.

In the later ages of Aztec history their most exalted deity was Huitzilopotchi, the Mexican Moses, the god of war. His temples were the most costly and magnificent among the public edifices in the country, and his image bedecked with ornaments was an universal object of adoration. At the dedication of his temple in the year 1486 more than seventy thousand captives are said to have perished.[161]

A Deity which occupied a conspicuous place in the mythology, and which was probably an inheritance from more ancient times, was Quetzalcoatl, doubtless the same as the Eastern Goddess of Nature, or Wisdom. She was the "grain goddess," and "received offerings of fruit and flowers at her two great festivals. She also took care of the growth of corn. She was doubtless the same as the Earth Mother of the Finns and Esths, she who "undertakes the task of bringing forth the fruits." She is evidently the Demeter of the Greeks, the Ceres of the Romans, etc. She is

---

[160] See Conquest of Mexico, book I, chap. iii., p. 74.
[161] Torquemada.

also the goddess of Wisdom, for she had "instructed the nations in the use of metals, in agriculture, and in the art of government." Under this Deity the

"Earth had teemed with fruits and flowers without the pains of culture. An ear of Indian corn was as much as a single man could carry. The cotton, as it grew, took, of its own accord, the rich dies of human art. The air was filled with intoxicating perfumes and the sweet melody of birds. In short, these were the halcyon days, which find a place in the mythic systems of so many nations throughout the world. It was the golden age of Anuhuac."

We are given to understand that for some cause not explained the beneficent god Quetzalcoatl was banished, that he (or she) was deposed through the influence of some deity which had become more popular, or, at least, more powerful; but that when Quetzalcoatl departed from the country "in a winged skiff made of serpent skins," it was with a promise to return to the faithful, which promise was sacredly cherished down to the time of the Spanish invasion.

The Mexican Mars, Huitzilopotchi, was born of a virgin. His mother, a devout person, while at her devotions in the temple saw floating before her a bright colored feather ball, which she seized and placed in her bosom. She soon became pregnant, her offspring being a god, who like Minerva appeared full armed with spear and helmet.

Although the exact manner in which the Mexicans sacrificed to their Deity to atone for the sins of the people differs somewhat from the modus operandi employed in the Christian vicarious atonement, still the likeness existing between them is sufficient to indicate the fact of their common origin and the similar manner of their development.

The Mexicans were wont to select a young and handsome man from their midst, whom they invested with the dignity of a god. After having surrounded him with every luxury, and when they had showered upon him every attention, crowning him with flowers and worshipping him for a year or more as a Savior, they killed him, offering him as an atonement or sacrifice, in order that the rest of the people might escape the vengeance of their great Deity, who, it was claimed, is pleased with such offerings, and who demands sacrifices of this kind at the hands of his children. Within blood was contained life, hence the offering of a bloody victim was but the returning to their god, as a free-will gift that which he had bestowed, such sacrifice being regarded as the only acceptable means of grace or reconciliation.

That the offering of a victim to the Jewish God was deemed necessary to the fulfilment of Christian doctrine is a fact which is clearly shown by numerous passages in the New Testament. "We are sanctified through the offering of the body of Jesus Christ once for all." "By one offering he hath perfected forever them that are sanctified."[162] "Christ was once offered to bear the sins of many."[163]

That the Jewish Paschal feasts and the Eucharistic rites of Christians had their counterpart among the Mexicans is observed in the fact that shortly after the death of their god, cakes which had been prepared and blessed by the priests were offered by them to the people to be eaten as the veritable body of their sacrificed lord.

The source whence the doctrine of an atonement –a bloody sacrifice which lies at the foundation of Christian theology–has proceeded is not at the present time difficult to determine, for we shall presently see that it, like all the leading doctrines contained in this later system, and which are regarded as exclusively Christian, had its origin in the religion of past ages, a religion which although originally

---

[162] Hebrews, x., 10, 14.
[163] Ibid., ix., 28.

pure, in course of time degenerated into the grossest phallicism and even into human sacrifice and cannibalism.

Although among the Mexicans as among the Jews, human sacrifices were offered to the Deity, no hint of gross and sensual rites practiced in the temples of the latter is recorded. Hence, as the Mexicans had not arrived at that stage of religious progress (?) at which sensuality inculcated as a sacred duty, and at which moral and physical debasement was encouraged both in public and private life, we may reasonably conclude that their faith represents a somewhat earlier stage of development than does that of either Jew or Greek. In point of morality, as judged by the most ancient standards, or by the more modern, the Mexicans compare favorably with either of these nationalities. Indeed when we compare the social, religious, and civil conditions of Mexico as we find them under Montezuma with those of the Jews under David or Solomon, or with those of the Greeks under Solon, or even with those of the Christians during the Spanish Inquisition when thousands upon thousands, not of captives taken in war, but of the noblest and best of the land, were yearly slaughtered for "the glory of God," there is quite as much to meet the approval of an enlightened conscience under the first named system as under that of any one of the other three.

By priests the fact has long been understood that effects may be produced through appeals to the religious or emotional nature which under other circumstances would be impossible; and as, for thousands of years, it has been the special business of this class to formulate creeds for the ignorant masses, religious belief and the ceremonies connected with "sacred" worship, during certain periods of the world's history, have assumed a grotesqueness in design unsurpassed by the most fanciful fairy tales which the imagination has ever been able to create, at the same time that they have portrayed a depth of sensual degradation capable of being reached only by that order of creation which alone has been able to develop a religion.

Chapter XVIII.
The Cross and a Dying Savior

In Egypt, the cross when unaccompanied by any other symbol signified simply creative energy both female and male, but whenever a distinctively female emblem was present it denoted the male power alone. The Ibis, which is represented with human hands and feet, bears the staff of Isis in one hand and the cross in the other. There is scarcely an obelisk or monument in Egypt upon which this figure does not appear. The symbol or monogram of Venus was a circle and a cross, that of Saturn was a cross and a ram's horn.

Plato declared that the son of God was expressed upon the universe in the form of the letter X, and that the second power of the supreme God was figured on the universe in the shape of a cross.

There is little doubt that the early Christians understood full well the true meaning of the cross, and that it was no new device. In later ages, however, every monument of antiquity marked with this symbol was claimed by the Church and by it believed to be of Christian origin.

It is related that when the temple of Serapis at Alexandria was overthrown by one of the Christian Emperors, beneath its foundation was discovered the monogram of Christ. The Christians made use of this circumstance to prove the divine origin of their religion, "thereby making many converts." The Pagans, on the contrary, were of the opinion that "it should forever silence the claim put forward by the devotees of Christianity." It is plain, however, that the Christians had the better of the argument for "the cross being uneasy under the weight of the temple overthrew it."

On the coins of Decius, the great persecutor of the Christians, is to be observed the monogram of Christ which is also the monogram of Osiris and Jupiter Ammon. On a medal proved to be Phoenician appear the cross, the rosary, and the lamb. There is another form of the same monogram which signifies DCVIII. These devices although in use hundreds of years prior to the Christian era are all said to be monograms of Christ. At the present time they may be seen in almost every church in Italy.

In the cave of Elephanta, in India, appears the cross in connection with the figure which represents male reproductive power. Inman relates that a cross with a rosary attached has been found in use among the religious emblems of the Japanese Buddhists and the lamas of Thibet, and that in one of the frescoes of Pompeii, published at Paris, 1840, is to be seen, vol. v., plate 28, the representation of a phallic cross in connection with two small figures of Hermes.[164]

The Rev. Mr. Maurice adds his testimony to that of other investigators to show the universality of this emblem. He says that the principal pagodas in India, viz., those of Bernares and Mathura, are built in the form of a cross.

In the museum of the London University is a mummy upon whose breast is a cross "exactly in the shape of a cross upon Calvary."

The true significance of this emblem, and the reason for its adoration are not, at the present time, difficult to understand; but whence comes the symbol of a dead man on a cross, and what is its true meaning?

---

[164] Inman, Ancient Faiths Embodied in Ancient Names, vol. i., p. 408.

Perhaps there is no problem connected with ancient symbolism, or with mythical religion, which is more difficult to solve, than is the representation of a dying Savior on a cross. It is stated by those who have investigated this subject, that although the sun, or the fructifying power within it, was adored by all the historic nations, no hint of a cross is to be found amongst the most ancient Nature worshippers. We must then look for a solution of this problem to those ages in which the higher truths of an older race were partially forgotten, and to a time when phallic worship had supplanted the adoration of Light or Wisdom. The cross doubtless came into use as a religious emblem at a time when the sexes in union began to stand for the god-idea, the lower end of the upright shaft being transfixed to the horizontal bar.

As soon as the male energy became god, the cross gradually grew into the figure of a man with arms extended. It became the original "life giver," it was Adam, the creator of the race. Doubtless for ages Adam represented the god-man-phallus-Tree of Life, or cross idea. He was the progenitor of the race. From this same idea sprang ancestor worship, or the deification of the past vital spark. The adoration paid to the Lares and Penates, the household gods of the Romans, on the first of May, is an example of this worship, as is also the homage paid by the Chinese to their progenitors.

Of religious emblems R. P. Knight says that one of the most remarkable among them is a cross in the form of the letter T which was used as an emblem of creation and generation before the church adopted it as a sign of salvation. To this representation of male reproductive power "was sometimes added a human head, which gives it the appearance of a crucifix, as it has on the medal of Cyzicus."

Originally the figure of a dead man on a cross typified creation and destruction or the operations of the creative forces in Nature. Everything dies only to live again. Although man dies, and although the individual man becomes but a dead branch on the tree of life, still the tree lives. Through the cross- phallus idea, or through man's power to create, existence on the earth continues. Although the sun dies in winter, in spring it revives again to quicken and enliven Nature and make all things new.

There is much evidence to show that a dying figure on a cross was no new conception at the advent of Christianity. Crishna, whose history as we have seen is almost identical with that of Christ, and Ballaji, from whom the thorn-crowned figures of Jesus have doubtless been copied, are illustrations of this mythical figure of a crucified savior in India.

It seems altogether probable from the facts at hand that the Romans worshipped a cross with a dying figure of a man upon it. Minucius Felix, a Christian father, in defense of his religion, has the following passage:

"You certainly, who worship wooden gods, are the most likely people to adore wooden crosses, as being parts with the same substance as your deities. For what else are your ensigns, flags, and standards but crosses gilt and purified? Your victorious trophies not only represent a simple cross, but a cross with a man upon it. When a pure worshipper adores the true God with hands extended, he makes the figure of a cross. Thus you see that the sign of the cross has either some foundation in Nature, or in your own religion, and therefore not to be objected against Christians."

Higgins says that it is proved as completely as it is possible to prove a fact of this kind that the Romans had a crucified object of adoration, and that this could be no other than an incarnation of the God Sol, represented in some way to have been crucified.

An ancient medal found in Cyprus has upon one of its sides the figure of a crucified man with the chaplet or rosary, the same as those now in use by Romanists. From the style of workmanship it is thought that this medal must have been anterior to the Macedonian conquest.

There is little doubt that the early fathers and the bishops in the Christian church recognized in the cross the ancient emblem of fertility, but as the idea of a spiritual life had begun to take root, it was deemed proper to conceal its real significance; hence from a symbol representing the continuity of existence on the earth the cross now prefigured eternal life or existence after death. Henceforward although man was dead in transgressions, through the cross, or through the crucified Christ, he received eternal life.

That the original signification of this symbol was understood by early Christians is apparent from the fact that the Emperor Theodosius, between the years 378 and 395, issued a decree prohibiting the sign of the cross being sculptured or painted on the pavements of churches. Tertullian also, after declaring that the devil made the sign of the cross on the foreheads of the followers of the Persian Mithra, accused the Christians of adoring the same emblem.

In 280, A. C. Porphyry, referring to crosses, asked why theologians give passions to the gods, erect Phalli and use shameful language; to which the Christian Iamblichus in the year 336 replied: "Because Phalli and crosses are signs of productive energy, and provocative to a continuance of the world."

It was not until the second century, or until after the days of Justin Martyr, that the instrument upon which Jesus was executed was called a cross. But whatever may have been its form, as soon as the myths of former religious worship began to attach themselves to his history, he became the symbolical dead man on a cross, the original sacrifice to Mahadeva. He portrayed the same idea as did Crishna, Ballaji, the dying Osiris, and all the other sun-gods. He, like each of these, represented a new sun at the beginning of a new cycle. He was a risen savior, and to him were finally transferred all the festivals, seasons, symbols, and monograms of former solar deities. That the figure of a dead man on a cross was a familiar emblem throughout Asia and various portions of Europe, and that numberless crucified gods–incarnations of the sun–have been worshipped throughout the East, is a fact which it has been the aim of the initiated among the Christian clergy to conceal, but one which no one who has examined the evidence with a mind free from prejudice attempts to deny.

In Italy, on many of the earlier pictures of Christ, may be observed the words Deo Soli, which inscription signifies either "to the only God," or "to the God Sol."

Of the various so-called Christian antiquities which cover the walls of the Vatican, we are assured by those who have acquainted themselves with the signification of pagan symbolism that "they have no more reference to Christianity than they have to the Emperor of China." The same may be said with reference to the representations on the walls of the Catacombs.

Crishna, who was the equinoctial sun in Aries, appeared 2160 years after the first Buddha, who was the equinoctial sun in Taurus. According to Plutarch they were both modern gods when compared with the deities which gave names to the planets. Buddha, or the sun in Taurus, was worshipped in the form of a bull. Crishna, or the sun in Aries, was adored under the figure of a ram with a man's head. The true significance of these figures was the fructifying sun or reproductive energy as manifested in animal life, and this meaning to those who worshipped them was identical with the carved figures on the caves of India, the Lares and Penates of the Romans, and the stone pillars or crosses in the market-places and at the intersection of roads in Brittany.

Eusebius says that at Elephanta they adored a Deity in the figure of a man in a sitting posture painted blue, having the head of a ram with the horns of a goat encircling a disk. The Deity thus described is said to be of astronomical origin, denoting the power of the sun in Aries.

This figure, which was one of the representations of the sun-god Crishna, was worshipped both in India and in Egypt. In various of the manifestations of this Deity he appears in the act of killing a serpent. He was the dead man on a cross and also the sun, which although continually dying is constantly being revived again. Various incarnations of this God have appeared as crucified saviors.

Of the avatar of Crishna known as Ballaji or Baal-Jah little is positively known. Indeed there seems to be some impenetrable mystery surrounding this figure, which makes it impossible for scholars to absolutely prove that which by means of the evidence at hand amounts almost to a certainty.

A print by Moore of this god represents him in the shape of a Romish crucifix, but although there is a nail hole in his foot he is not transfixed to a wooden cross. Instead of a crown of thorns a Parthian coronet encircles his head. As all the avatars of Crishna are represented with coronets, this fact has caused several writers to observe that the effigies of Ballaji have furnished the copies for the thorn-crowned Jesus. Through the ignorance of the early Christians who in the second century adopted the religion of Crishna, the true significance of this coronet was not understood, hence the thorns upon the head of Christ. In referring to the effigy of a crucified savior found in Ireland the author of The Round Towers says that it was not intended for our Savior for the reason that it wore the Iranian regal crown, instead of the Jewish crown of thorns.[165]

Regarding this effigy, Higgins remarks that the crucified body without the cross reminds one that "some of

---

[165] The Round Towers of Ireland, p. 298.

the ancient sects of heretics held Jesus to have been crucified in the clouds."

Moore, who has produced several prints of Ballaji, says he is unable to account for the pierced foot of a crucified figure in India. He endeavors to prove, however, that this crucifix cannot be Hindoo "because there are duplicates of it from the same model." As the mould is made of clay, he contends that only one cast may be made from it. This argument falls to the ground, however, so soon as it is found that duplicates, or copies of these brass idols which may not be distinguished from the originals, are seen in the museum at the India House, and also in that of the Asiatic Society.

The admission of Moore that "great influence was brought to bear upon him to induce him not to publish the prints of Ballaji for fear of giving offense," serves as a hint in determining the cause for the lack of information respecting this god.

It is believed that, were the development of truth upon this subject rather than its concealment the object of Christian missionaries, the temples of Ballaji would have furnished more important information to the Christian world than would those of any other of the Hindoo gods; but while numberless pilgrimages have been made to Juggernaut and other shrines devoid of interest to the student, we have heard little concerning the shrines of this deity, although at the time Moore wrote, Terputty was in the possession of the English who made a profit of L15,000 a year from the temple.

On the Brechin Tower in Ireland are two arches one within the other in relief. At the top of the arch is a crucifix, and about midway from top to bottom on either side are two figures which, according to Romanist Christians, represent the Virgin Mary and St. John. At the bottom of the outer arch are two couchant beasts, the one an elephant and the other a bull. The figure on the cross has a Parthian coronet. The appearance of a crucifix on the towers of Britain and Ireland has in the past led many writers to ascribe to these singular structures a Christian origin. To the critical observer, however, the first question which presents itself is whence comes the elephant–an animal not found within these countries?–and again why should these beasts have been placed here as Christian emblems? The facts in the case as revealed by unprejudiced investigators are, that the towers in Ireland are not Christian monuments, and that the crucifix found on them is not that of Christ but of Ballaji, or of some one of the avatars of Crishna.

The fact that the figure of Crishna as a crucified god was found in the ruins of a temple at Thebes in Egypt, is sufficient to prove his antiquity; still, as we have seen, he represents the god-idea at a much later date than did Buddha. Regarding the evidence furnished by the Rev. Mr. Maurice of the ten avatars of the Indian sun-god, Higgins observes:

"The only fact worthy of notice here is, that Buddha was universally allowed to be the first of the incarnations; that Crishna was of later date; that, at the era of the birth of Christ, eight of them had appeared on the earth, and that the other two were expected to follow before the end of the Caliyug, or of the present age."

With reference to the fact that the Hindoo God originally represented Wisdom or the Logos, the same writer says:

"Then here is DIVINE WISDOM incarnate, of whom the Bull of the Zodiac was the emblem. HERE he is the Protagonos, or first begotten, the God or Goddess Mhtis of the Greeks, being, perhaps, both male and female. Buddha, or the wise, if the word were not merely the name of a doctrine, seems to have been an appellation taken by several persons, or one person incarnate at several periods, and from this circumstance much confusion has arisen."[166]

Concerning the religion of an ancient race the following facts have been ascertained, namely:

The first of the Buddhas or Incarnations of the Deity was Minerva, and her mother, who was the sun, was the mother of all the Buddhas. She was Mhtis, Mubt or Mai, "the universal genius of Nature, who discriminated all things according to their various kinds of species."

In the earliest ages she comprehended not only matter but the moving force in the universe. She was the Deity which by a very ancient race was represented by the mother idea–Perceptive Wisdom. She was the sun and the first emanation from the sun. She was the Divine Word, the Logos, the Holy Ghost which in the time of Christ was again by various sects recognized as female. The allegory of the Greeks concerning Jupiter taking Mhtis (Wisdom) to wife and from this union with her producing Minerva from his head, is seen to be closely connected with the doctrine of Buddha (Wisdom) or of the Rasit of Genesis. According to Faber, the import of the Greek word Nous and of the Sanscrit Menu is precisely the same: each denotes mind or intelligence, and to the latter of them the Latin Mens is nearly allied. "Mens, Menu, and perhaps our English mind are fundamentally one and the same word." All these terms in an earlier age meant Buddha, Wisdom, or Minerva.

Later, with the worship of the sun in Aries, appeared a crucified savior. During the earlier ages of Crishnaism, the ideas typified by a dying savior were still those pertaining to the processes of Nature. Matter was still believed to be indestructible and seeming death but a preparation for renewed life, or for birth into another state of existence Subsequently this dying sun-god, which disappeared in winter only to return again to re-animate Nature, became a

---

[166] Anacalypsis, book v., p. 201.

veritable man—a man on a cross who must be sacrificed to Mahadeva in order that humanity might be saved. Here we have the origin of the doctrine of a Vicarious Atonement. Later, under the system called Christianity, woman, who had previously become identified with the evil principle, became the Tempter. She was the cause of sin in the world and wholly responsible for the evil results arising from desire. Indeed, according to the doctrines annunciated by the Christian Church, had woman, who was an after thought of the Almighty, never been created, man would have lived forever in a state of purity and bliss, free alike from the toils, pains, and temptations of life, and from the crafts and assaults of the Devil.

Through the over-stimulation of the animal instincts man had become wholly unable to overcome the evil in his constitution, hence the adoption of the doctrine of Original Sin and the necessity for an Atonement, or for a crucified savior, who would take upon himself the sins of poor, weak human nature. By simply believing on this crucified redeemer, man would be saved, not from sin itself, but from the penalty of sin. To bolster up the belief in original sin and the necessity for an atonement, the allegory of the fruit tree and the serpent in Genesis was taken literally.

The more the religion of the past is studied the more plainly will the fact appear, that not only have the ceremonies, symbols, festivals, and seasons adopted by Christianity been copied from India and Persia, but also that all the leading doctrines of the so-called Christian Church originated in those countries. The belief in a Trinity, the Incarnation of the Deity, a Crucified Savior, Original Sin and a Vicarious Atonement, the last three having been elaborated after the ancient natural truths underlying sun worship had been forgotten, are all to be found in the East.

The doctrine of a Trinity is supposed to have been received directly from the Platonists, who had learned it from the Persians; while that of a Crucified Savior, and also that of the seed of the woman bruising the serpent's head, belong, as we have seen, to the religion of Crishna.

Concerning Original Sin, which is the foundation of the doctrine of the "Atonement," it is plain that it was not known to the earlier followers of Christ, but that it was subsequently copied from the corrupted religion of the Hindoos.

The symbolical meaning of the serpent and the Tree of Life was doubtless understood by the earliest adherents to the Christian faith; it is not surprising, therefore, that by them there is no mention of the doctrine of Original Sin. Their theory to account for evil in the world was the same as that of an ancient and almost forgotten race. The belief that the soul of man is a spark from, or a part of the universal soul, that at the death of the body it returns to its source, and in process of time appears as the animating principle in other bodies, was believed by Pythagoras, Aspasia, Socrates, and Plato and, in fact, for thousands of years it was entertained by the best and wisest of the human race. It was a part of the early Christian doctrine and is still believed by the followers of Buddha and by the Theosophists of Europe and America.

Doubtless the doctrines of Re-incarnation and Karma were set forth by those very ancient philosophers who were the near descendants of the inventors of the Neros and the Metonic cycle–those who believed in the indestructibility of matter, and that spirit proceeds from or is evolved through it. It was an effort on their part to solve the problem of the existence of evil, and was far more satisfactory to the reasoning mind than was the literal translation of the story of the woman, the forbidden apple, and the talking serpent in Genesis.

Original sin of which woman is said to be the cause, and the necessity for a spiritual (male) savior to deliver man from the wretchedness which she had produced, are doctrines which took their rise in the grossest ignorance, and in an entire misconception of the natural truths which had previously been set forth by the figure of a dying sun-god. Original Sin and a Vicarious Atonement–doctrines by means of which man has attempted to evade moral responsibility and the legitimate results of evil-doing–have, by weakening his moral sense, and by shifting the responsibility of his deeds upon another, resulted in greatly lowering the standard of human conduct.

Science teaches that the penalty for sin is inherent in it, and that virtue is its own reward; the so-called Christian doctrines assert that although a man's sins be as scarlet, they may, simply through a certain belief, become white as wool. It has been claimed that a belief in original sin caused all the human sacrifices in ancient times and that it "converted the Jews into a nation of cannibals."

That the system which has borne the name of Christianity is an outgrowth of Sun, Serpent, and Phallic faiths is so plainly proven by the facts brought out by later research as no longer to be a matter of reasonable doubt to those who have given any considerable degree of attention to this subject. The more exalted ideas which from the time of Zoroaster to that of Jesus had been struggling for existence, and which through various means had been gradually gaining a foothold, were, by the influx of Crishnaism, soon choked out, and mythical Christianity, which was but a gathering in of the grosser forms of the prevailing Hindoo faith, mounted the throne of the Roman Empire.

During the nineteen hundred years that have elapsed since the inauguration of this system, little has been understood concerning the real philosophy of Christ–a philosophy which is seen to be simply a recognition of those higher scientific truths enunciated by an ancient race.

The fact is observed in these later times that the altruistic principles involved in these teachings contain the highest wisdom–that they form the basis of a true social science, and that a high stage of civilization will never be reached until these principles are recognized as the foundation of human conduct Unselfishness, purity of life, and the brotherhood of man will never be realized so long as man shifts the responsibility of his wrong-doing upon another.

Quite recently the fact has been proved that the progressive principle originated in the female constitution; that in sympathy, a character which has its root in maternal affection, lies the key to human progress. Conscience and the moral sense are outgrowths of sympathy; therefore, that which distinguishes man from the lower orders of life originated in and has been developed through the female organization.

When these plain scientific truths, which are so simple as scarcely to need demonstration, become popularized, doubtless our present god-idea will undergo a process of reconstruction, and the later development will probably involve conceptions more in keeping with science and human reason. Surely a scientific age will tolerate no religious conception whose principles are not founded on truth. The worship of a male god as the sole creator and sustainer of the universe is as unphilosophical as it is unreasonable and unscientific.

As in many ways at the present time, mankind seems inclined to retrace its steps, and as upon its onward march humanity is beginning to manifest a willingness to return to truer and more primitive methods of thought and action, it is not impossible that in the not distant future, Perceptive Wisdom and the altruistic principles, together with the power to give life, may again be divinely enthroned in the place so long usurped by physical force and virile might.

www.ingramcontent.com/pod-product-compliance
Lightning Source LLC
Chambersburg PA
CBHW071658160426
43195CB00012B/1504